The
TRIALS
of ISRAEL
LIPSKI

By the same author

DETENTION BEFORE TRIAL

DOUBLE JEOPARDY

COURTS AND TRIALS:
A Multi-Disciplinary Approach

ACCESS TO THE LAW

CASES AND MATERIALS ON CRIMINAL
LAW AND PROCEDURE

NATIONAL SECURITY:
The Legal Dimensions

The

TRIALS
of
ISRAEL
LIPSKI

*A True Story of a Victorian Murder
in the East End of London*

MARTIN L. FRIEDLAND

BEAUFORT BOOKS
Publishers · New York

Library of Congress Cataloging in Publication Data

Friedland, Martin L.

The trials of Israel Lipski.

1. Lipski, Israel—Trials, litigation, etc. 2. Trials
(Murder)—England—London. I. Title.
KD372.L56F74 1985   345.42'02523   84-24474
ISBN 0-8253-0278-1   344.2052523

Published in the United States by Beaufort Books Publishers, New York.

Printed in the U.S.A.   First American Edition
10 9 8 7 6 5 4 3 2 1

Contents

List of Illustrations

Sketches at the Lipski trial
(© The British Library)

Mysterious Tragedy at Whitechapel
(© The British Library)

Mr. Justice James Fitzjames Stephen
(© Metropolitan Toronto Library Board)

Harry Bodkin Poland
(© BBC Hulton Picture Library)

Batty Street and Commercial Road today

Henry Matthews, Q.C.
(© BBC Hulton Picture Library)

W. T. Stead
(© BBC Hulton Picture Library)

Rabbi Simeon Singer

Newgate Prison
(© BBC Hulton Picture Library)

Israel Lipski
(© The British Library)

Endpapers: *Stanford's London and its Suburbs*, 1886. By permission of The Guildhall Library, City of London.

The author is grateful for the permission of the respective copyright holders to reproduce these illustrations.

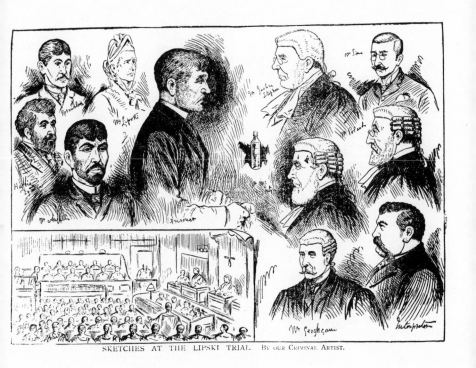

SKETCHES AT THE LIPSKI TRIAL. By our Criminal Artist.

Sketches at the Lipski trial from the *Pall Mall Gazette*, 3 August, 1887

Preface

Mr Justice James Fitzjames Stephen began his charge to the jury at the Old Bailey in the 1887 murder trial of Israel Lipksi by stating that he had 'never known a case which presented so many remarkable and singular features.' This book is the story of that trial, the conviction, and the fight for a reprieve. The case produced great controversy at the time. An East London newspaper said that 'never, perhaps, in the annals of crime have there been such efforts put forth to save a man's life as there has been in the case of the convict Lipski.' And the *New York Times* observed in a front page story that London was 'far more engrossed in the case of Israel Lipski than with the fate of the Government.'

My interest in the Lipski case arose out of my interest in the judge, Stephen, an important figure in the history of criminal law. While rather aimlessly looking through contemporary newspaper accounts of the Lipski trial I realized that this case, which has never been the subject of a major study, could serve as a good vehicle for analysing the criminal process. It also would enable me to study material on Jewish immigration from Eastern Europe, the role of the Press and the impact of a *cause célèbre* on the process of law reform. Fortunately, there was much documentary material I could draw on. I was given permission to see the Home Office records on the case, normally closed for one hundred years. This voluminous file, to my surprise, contained a transcript of the two-day trial. I also had access to the Stephen correspondence at Cambridge University, which included many letters concerning the Lipski case. There was also much information on and letters by W. T. Stead, the enigmatic editor of the *Pall Mall Gazette*, who played a key role in the story. All the facts, including conversations, set out in the manuscript have been derived from the extensive documentary, newspaper and other records available.

This story will place one trial in the context of the social, political and economic conditions of the time. A trial may in theory be an objective pursuit of truth, but in practice there are many subjective factors which influence the course of events. Justice may in theory be blind, but in practice she has altogether too human a perspective. The Lipski story is, no doubt, more dramatic, and the wealth of material richer, than in most cases; yet, by looking at this extreme example one can better understand some of the factors that may influence any criminal trial: the personality of the judge; the adequacy of counsel; the reaction of the press; the cry of popular opinion; the vulnerability of the Government, and many more.

I am grateful to many libraries and other institutions for assistance, and would particularly like to thank the following: in London, the Home Office, the Public Record Office, Bishopsgate Library, the British Library, the Law Society, the Lord Chancellor's Department, Madame Tussaud's, Middle Temple Library, the Mocatta Library, New Scotland Yard, the Royal Commission on Historical Manuscripts, and Tower Hamlets Local History Library: elsewhere in England, the University Library, Cambridge; the Bodleian Library, Oxford; Hatfield House Archives, and the Royal Archives, Windsor: in New York, the YIVO Institute for Jewish Research, and New York Public Library: in Toronto, the Beth Tzedec Library, the Great Library of Osgoode Hall, the Jewish Public Library, and Metropolitan Toronto Reference Library; and at the University of Toronto, the Centre of Criminology Library, the Faculty of Law Library, and the Robarts Library.

I was fortunate to have had the very able assistance of a number of persons. John Atkinson, a recent graduate of the Faculty of Law, University of Toronto was an excellent summer research assistant. Another recent graduate, Stephen Perry, helped track down material for me in England. Martin Maierovits, also a former student, translated the Yiddish papers for me. Paul Schabas, a student in the Faculty of Law, assisted with a number of tasks. Joyce Kawano, Patricia Kune and Kathy O'Rourke typed the manuscript. Julia Hall helped with proof-reading. The study drew on work I had been doing on the process of criminal law reform, which was funded by the Donner Canadian Foundation.

Many scholars at my own university and elsewhere provided ideas and reviewed parts of the manuscript. I am indebted to Professors John Beattie, Richard Helmstadter, Jacques Kornberg, Michael Marrus and Ann Robson of the Department of

History, Peter Richardson of the Department of Religious Studies, Jack Robson of the Department of English and Peter Russell of the Department of Political Science, all of the University of Toronto, for their valuable comments. Expert advice was also provided by Edward Greenspan, Dr Frederick Jaffe, Ian Kyer, Hartley Nathan and Rabbi Gunther Plaut, all of Toronto. I have also benefited through correspondence and discussions with Joseph Baylen, Georgia State University; William Fishman and Graham Zellick, Queen Mary College, London; Peter Glazebrook, Cambridge University; Colin Holmes and John Roach, University of Sheffield, and Vivian Lipman, London. Finally, I would like to acknowledge my indebtedness to members of my family and to my colleagues in the Faculty of Law who listened to my account of the Lipski story, read the manuscript and provided many valuable insights. To all of the above I give my sincere thanks.

Martin L. Friedland
Faculty of Law
University of Toronto

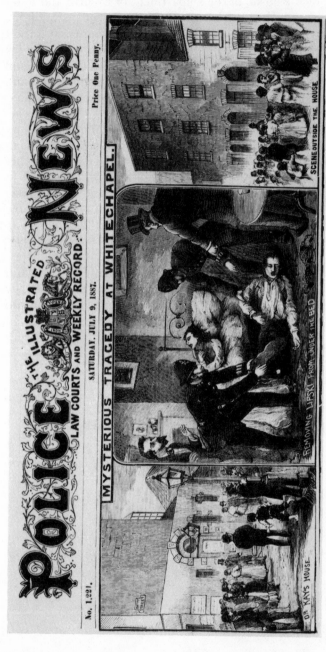

Mysterious Tragedy at Whitechapel from the *Illustrated Police News*, 9 July, 1887

Chapter One

Introduction

ON TUESDAY MORNING, 28 June 1887, in the East End of London, Miriam Angel was found dead. Nitric acid had been poured down her throat. Israel Lipski, a twenty-two-year-old Polish immigrant Jew, was charged with her murder. This is the story of Lipski's trial, conviction and the fight for his reprieve.

It was Jubilee year. Queen Victoria had completed fifty years on the throne. Jubilee week had just passed. On the Tuesday of that week, exactly seven days before Miriam Angel was killed, the Queen had made a triumphal procession – 'the most . . . triumphal . . . of all time' wrote *The Times*[1] – from Buckingham Palace to Westminster Abbey. It was a time of superlatives. *The Times* summed up the mood: 'a great Empire, a great nation, a great city, a great Sovereign, and a great occasion.'[2]

The Jewish community living in the West End of London shared this feeling of pride. 'We are Englishmen,' wrote the establishment weekly, the *Jewish Chronicle*, 'and the thoughts and feelings of Englishmen are our thoughts and feelings.'[3] Rabbi Simeon Singer, who will play an important role in our story, reminded his congregation in his Jubilee sermon of the 'unparalleled progress that had been made in the position of the Jews of England'.[4] They did not need to be reminded. They knew that Jews occupied important positions in English society. Names like Montagu, Mocatta and Montefiore conveyed a sense of substance and authority. Lord Rothschild had been on the committee that had planned the Jubilee celebrations. Baron Henry de Worms was a Parliamentary Secretary and was about to become a member of the Cabinet. Both the Rothschilds and the de Wormses had been at the State Banquet at Buckingham Palace the weekend before the murder. There were seven Jewish Members of Parliament. From 1873 to 1883 Sir George Jessel had been Master of the Rolls, one of the three most important judicial positions in

England. And, of course, former Jews had reached even higher positions: Lord Herschell had been the Lord Chancellor and Benjamin Disraeli had been the Prime Minister.

In the East End of London the Jubilee was of far less interest. The Irish dockworkers and the Jewish immigrant tailors wanted work, not pageantry. Rabbi Singer told his West End congregation that 'in no spot on the Globe and probably at no period in the world's history has there existed so glaring a contrast between riches and poverty as in this city and in this age of ours.'[5]

It had been a hard winter, with substantial unemployment in all trades in the East End. A Government survey in 1887[6] showed that over seventy per cent of the dock labourers, building craftsmen, tailors and bootmakers had been unemployed during that winter, most for more than two months. An economist has written that 'the years 1884–7 were probably the worst continuous sequence, from the point of view of unemployment,'[7] of any prior to the First World War. Radicalism was growing. In the winter of 1886 a riot had taken place – the most serious in over fifty years: all the club windows down one side of St James's Street had been broken and looting had begun in Piccadilly.[8] The Government was afraid of even greater disturbances.

There were overcrowding and unsanitary conditions in the East End. The medical journal, *The Lancet*, had earlier disclosed the unsatisfactory hygienic conditions among Jewish tailors.[9] Charles Booth started his monumental study of London in 1887 and his conclusions documented the appalling conditions in the East End.[10]

The growth in unemployment came at the same time as a rapid influx of immigrants, mainly Jewish, into England. There were then no restrictions on immigration. Between 1880 and 1886 about twenty thousand Jews came to the East End of London[11] – and, of course, many came to other parts of England. They came because of the increasingly difficult conditions in Eastern Europe.

In March 1881, Tsar Alexander II had been shot by a terrorist group, of which a young Jewish seamstress, Jessie Helfmann, was a member.[12] In the following months, and thereafter, the repercussions were felt by Jews throughout Russian-dominated Eastern Europe. On Christmas day, 1881, for example, a pogrom started in Warsaw and at the end of three days, 'forty-five hundred Jewish homes, shops, and synagogues had been devastated and looted.'[13]

Eighteen eighty-seven was the year that the first Parliamentary question was asked about restricting immigration, the year in which a public meeting was first held to discuss the issue, and the year in which the Government first gave serious consideration to the question.[14] It was also a time when there was fear that the notorious 'ritual murder', or 'blood libel', accusation (usually involving allegations of the taking of Christian blood for the Passover service) would again surface in England, as it had earlier in the decade.[15] And it was less than a year after the first discussion in the English Press about the possibility of the systematic persecution of the Jews, or, as it was called, a *Judenhetze*, taking place in England. The *Pall Mall Gazette*, about which much will be written later, printed a letter under the provocative heading *A Judenhetze Brewing in East London*, stating that 'the foreign Jews of no nationality whatever are becoming a pest and a menace to the poor native-born East-ender' and 'have a greater responsibility for the distress which prevails there probably than all other causes put together.'[16]

The murder of Miriam Angel occurred at 16 Batty Street, a small side street running off Commercial Road, a large thoroughfare cutting through the East End. The Press referred to the case under such headings as *The Whitechapel Mystery* or *The Whitechapel Tragedy*. But, as the East End local Press pointed out,[17] Batty Street is not, in fact, in Whitechapel; rather, it is in St George's-in-the-East, an even poorer area than Whitechapel, in closer proximity to the London Docks.

In 1887 Batty Street was predominantly Jewish; by the turn of the century it would be, perhaps, ninety per cent Jewish. (Today it is almost entirely Asian, with houses on only one side of the street, the other side looking as though it had been levelled by bombs during the Second World War. There is now a Ladbroke's betting shop on the corner of Batty Street and Commercial Road.) Booth's survey[18] categorised Batty Street as 'poor', meaning that an average family would earn eighteen to twenty-one shillings a week and would pay a little over six shillings a week for rent.

Number sixteen Batty Street, which was torn down in 1888 to construct somewhat larger blocks of flats, consisted of two floors plus an attic. A survey in 1871 showed that only two

17

persons occupied the small house.[19] By 1887, however, fifteen people lived there.

Israel Lipski lived alone in the attic. Isaac Angel, a boot riveter, lived with his twenty-two-year-old wife Miriam in their sparsely furnished room facing the street on the second floor. They had been in England about ten months, and had been married in a town near Warsaw two months before emigrating to England. The couple had been living in Batty Street about six weeks. Miriam was in her fifth or sixth month of pregnancy at the time she was killed. They had supplemented her husband's meagre income by occasionally repairing boots in their room. The day before the murder, Mrs Angel had had to borrow five shillings to pay the rent.

The landlady's mother and another woman, along with her child, occupied the back room on the second floor. The landlord and landlady, like Israel Lipski and the Angels, were also from Poland, and had arrived in the early 1870s. They lived with their seven children, the oldest of whom was fifteen, in the front room on the main floor. The landlord had rented the entire house from a retired tailor who, in turn, had rented it from someone else. A small kitchen was in the back room. The old Yiddish saying '*Shlof gikher, me darf di kishn*' – 'Sleep faster, we need the pillows' – certainly applied to 16 Batty Street. The landlord and landlady, coincidentally, were also named Lipski, although they were not related to Israel Lipski. Everybody living in the house was Jewish.

Shortly after six o'clock on Tuesday morning, 28 June, Isaac Angel, after saying his morning prayers, left his room in 16 Batty Street to go to work. It looked as if it was going to be another day of the glorious Jubilee weather that had marked all the events that month. His wife remained in bed. The door to the room was unlocked. It was Mrs Angel's custom to go to her mother-in-law, who lived nearby, before nine o'clock for breakfast. When she did not appear, her mother-in-law came to Batty Street to see if she was not well. In company with the landlady and one of the tenants, she went to the Angels' room. The door appeared to be locked, so they went to the stairway leading to the attic to look through a small side window. They saw Mrs Angel lying unnaturally on the bed. The door was burst open. Mrs Angel could not be roused. There was a yellow frothy substance coming from her mouth.

18

The landlady ran for the doctor, whose surgery was not far away at the corner of Batty Street and Commercial Road. He was not there, but his assistant came within a short time, realised that there was obviously foul play involved and locked the door to keep everyone out until the doctor arrived. The doctor saw immediately that Mrs Angel was dead, noting marks of corrosive poison running from her mouth and on her hands. He and others searched the room for a bottle that could have contained the poison. They pulled the bed away from the wall and discovered a body under the bed. It was Israel Lipski. He was alive, but apparently unconscious. Corrosive poison was also found in his mouth.

Israel Lipski's life up till that point was not dissimilar to those of many other poor immigrants.[20] He had been born in 1865 in Warsaw, a city which was then about forty per cent Jewish. He had three sisters and two older brothers. All had received a traditional Jewish upbringing. The family was very poor and he became apprenticed to a lathe turner. When he was sixteen the Christmas pogrom of 1881 took place in Warsaw. No doubt the possibility of leaving Poland was discussed at the time, but the family did not have the money for fares and so nothing was done. Shortly after his twentieth birthday, when it seemed likely that he would have to serve in the army, Lipski decided to leave Poland. A passport was needed to cross the border into Germany and Lipski did not have one; nor could he obtain one without the Russian authorities, who had jurisdiction over Poland, realising that he was trying to escape from military service.

The solution, which was not uncommon, was to be smuggled across the border – in his case by a miller who placed him among bags of flour. Lipski took a train to Hamburg, the principal embarkation point in Germany. He had no money, but was able to arrange passage to London by working on a cattle boat.

Lipski arrived in London in 1885, penniless. One of the many agents at the docks – many of whom preyed on immigrants – arranged for Lipski to be taken to the shop of a Mr Mark Katz, an umbrella maker. Subsequently, accomodation was arranged at the home of the Lipskis, then living at Batty Gardens. In fact, Israel Lipski's real name was Lobulsk. He changed it to Lipski after he arrived in London. It is likely that for convenience he simply adopted the name of his landlord, perhaps thinking that it was a common name. Or possibly he adopted it because he thought it was not a Jewish name: a very distinguished Polish Christian family bore the Lipski name, a family which had included among its members a cardinal and a bishop.[21]

He worked hard as a stickmaker – men made the sticks and cut the cloth and women sewed the cloth for the umbrellas in their own homes[22] – and so impressed his employer that he met and eventually became engaged to the employer's sister-in-law, Kate Lyons. Although the engagement was broken off for a period, it was later renewed. Lipski started to learn English and began to save some money.

Unfortunately, the umbrella business was very slack that spring, partly because of the very difficult economic conditions, and also because of the glorious weather that England was experiencing. There had been no rain for weeks. Lipski's future mother-in-law and others urged him to go into business for himself, manufacturing walking sticks. He withdrew the little money he had from the savings bank, pawned his watch and gold chain, borrowed additional money from his fiancée's mother and set up a workshop in his room in the attic at Batty Street. As a consequence, his rent was raised from two to five shillings a week. As in many of the sweatshops in London, it would be hard to tell the owner or 'sweater' from the employees. He bought supplies, hired an English lad, Pitman, who had worked with him at his previous job, and arranged for another fellow-worker, Simon Rosenbloom, and a workman, Isaac Schmuss, both Jewish, to work for him. The first day of work was to be Tuesday morning, the morning of the murder.

Israel Lipski, when found under the Angels' bed, was slapped by Dr Kay, revived, and taken through a large milling crowd in front of the house to the doctor's surgery at the corner, then to a nearby police station, and shortly afterwards to the large London Hospital in Whitechapel Road, the hospital where the famous Elephant Man then lived. The Jewish wards had no room and so he was placed in one of the regular wards. A police officer was stationed beside him.

His fiancée, Kate Lyons, came to the hospital as soon as she learned what had happened. She stayed with him an hour and then expressed her belief in his innocence,[23] telling the Press that he had said, 'It was not me at all. I did nothing.'[24] He asked her to get the police to come so he could make a statement and requested her to telegraph his father in Warsaw. Miss Lyons went to the police and told them that Lipski was innocent, that the murder was committed by two workmen who were working for him. Lipski, she said, was a victim, not a murderer.

Two police officers, with the unlikely names of Inspector Final and Detective Sergeant Thick, the latter known locally as 'Johnny Upright',[25] arrived that evening with an interpreter. Lipski told them, through the interpreter, the following remarkable story, alleging that the workmen, Rosenbloom and Schmuss, had committed the murder:

> At seven am a man working for me came. He asked me for work. I told him to wait. I would buy a vice for him so as he could work. I went to purchase a vice. I went to the shop but it was too soon. As I was going along I met another workman whom I knew at the corner of Backchurch Lane. I went back; the shopkeeper wanted four shillings, I offered him three shillings, he would not take it. I returned and came into the passage, and I saw the man that I met in Backchurch Lane. He asked me 'Will you give me work or not?' I said 'Go to the workshop. I am going to get my breakfast, then I will give you work.' I then told my landlady to make some coffee. I then told a man [meaning the first man] that called at seven am to fetch some brandy. I then went to the yard. I went upstairs to the first floor. I then saw both these men. I saw them open a box; they took hold of me by the throat and threw me to the ground; there on the ground opened my mouth and put in some poison, and said, 'That is the brandy.' They got my hands behind me and asked me if I had any money. 'I have got no more than the sovereign that I gave you to get the brandy with.' He then asked 'Where is your gold chain?' I said 'It is in pawn.' They said, 'If you don't give it to us you will be as dead as the woman.' They put a piece of wood in my mouth. I struggled; they put their knees against my throat. One said to the other 'Don't you think he is quite dead.' The reply was, 'He don't want any more.' They then threw me under the bed and there I lay for dead.

A coroner's inquest into the death of Miriam Angel was opened the next evening, Wednesday 29 June, by the coroner, Wynne Baxter, and a fourteen-man jury in a small room off the Vestry Hall in Cable Street in St George's-in-the-East.[26] Throughout the inquest Lipski remained in hospital. That afternoon Dr Kay had performed a post mortem examination on the body, which had been removed to the St George's mortuary. The deceased's right eye and temple showed marks of a violent blow. Dr Kay tested the poison, which turned out to be nitric acid. He traced the acid into the stomach, he told the coroner, and concluded that the deceased was on her back when the acid

21

was administered. Both sides of the heart were empty, which he said indicated that she had died by suffocation after swallowing the nitric acid. He thought she had been dead three or four hours when he saw her between 11.30 and 12.00. Dr Kay added that 'there was something in the vagina which looked like semen, but I could not say for certain if it is semen without a microscopical examination.' Isaac Angel had earlier been asked if he had recently had intercourse with his wife, and after considerable difficulty experienced by the interpreter in translating the question into Yiddish, Angel replied that he had not.

The inquest was then adjourned at the request of the coroner until Friday to permit Dr Kay to conduct further tests. On Thursday the tests were performed. The body was then taken to Mr Angel's mother's house for burial later in the day at the West Ham cemetery.[27] This was the first time Mr Angel had seen the body since his wife's murder.

When the hearing resumed – this time in the large Vestry Hall itself – Dr Kay was re-examined:

> After the last sitting of the inquest I extracted from the vagina of the deceased some matter I found there. I have put it under the microscope. There are no spermatozoa. Had there been any I could have proved it was semen. It might be semen. I agree with the remark of a textbook that the semen even of a healthy young man varies much and is scarcely ever twice alike, so that the absence of spermatozoa is no proof that the matter is not semen. There is no other test. I produce a glass bottle with some of the matter taken from the vagina, sealed and marked A. When I first saw the body of the deceased it was not exposed. The lower part of the body was covered with a feather-bed, and on the upper part there was a shirt, which was unbuttoned, but it did not expose her breasts. On turning the bed down to see if any violence had been offered to her, the legs, thighs, and the whole of her genitals, and the lower part of the abdomen were exposed, and not covered with her chemise. Her thighs were wide apart.

It is interesting to note that *The Times*, the *Pall Mall Gazette* and many other papers, including, for example, the *Illustrated Police News*, did not report these details, which were not considered proper subjects for discussion in the Press. Some papers did, however, contain more complete reports, particularly the *East London Observer*, which devoted almost half a page to many of the minute details that came out at the inquest.

The coroner heard evidence from a number of witnesses who would later give evidence at the trial, including the workman Simon Rosenbloom, who denied Lipski's statement, saying

22

that he was working in the attic all morning; a shop manager who identified Lipski in the hospital as the person who had bought nitric acid from him on the morning of the murder; and the landlady and another lodger who said that the door of the Angels' room was locked from the inside. The foreman of the jury asked Mr Angel if his wife and Lipski had known each other before coming to England and Mr Angel replied, 'As far as I am aware, they did not know each other in Poland.' Lipski was not called as a witness, Inspector Final saying, 'Lipski is in custody, and would not be produced as a witness if the inquest 'were adjourned,' which signalled that the police believed Lipski was the murderer. The coroner's jury had no difficulty in returning a verdict of 'wilful murder' against Lipski, who was committed for trial on a coroner's warrant, a procedure that no longer exists in English law.[28]

The next day, Saturday 2 July, Lipski was taken to the Thames Police Court in the custody of Inspector Final and Sergeant Thick. It was necessary to obtain formal statements from the witnesses and procure a committal for trial by a magistrate. No lawyers were present.

This was the first glimpse that the public had had of Lipski. The *East London Observer* described him as 'a slimly-built man, clean shaven, and of boyish appearance.'[29] The Yiddish weekly, *Die Tsukunft* (*The Future*), described his fair hair and dark blue eyes and observed that 'if the physical features of a person would always be a mirror which reflects the person's character, then no one who knows Israel Lipski would believe that he is the murderer.'

Inspector Final informed the magistrate that the Treasury was going to take up the case,[30] as they had the right to do in important cases. Three witnesses were called and the case was adjourned for a week. Lipski was taken to Holloway Prison (now a women's prison), to await trial. Even though he was untried, there were severe restrictions: he was locked up for twenty-two and one half out of every twenty-four hours and was permitted only one fifteen-minute visit each day by a friend.[31] 'Whilst Lipski was in Holloway,' the *Jewish World* later reported, 'we are ashamed to say no Jewish minister visited him.'[32]

A Treasury solicitor appeared as prosecutor when the hearing resumed the following week. Lipski was defended by Gerald Geoghegan, perhaps the leading Old Bailey barrister of the time. Contemporaries later reminisced about this Irish lawyer who had been called to the English bar ten years earlier: 'the most brilliant of them all';[33] 'at his best I have never known his equal';[34] 'candidate for the highest honours the Bar can bestow';[35] 'the most gifted counsel in the criminal courts at that time'.[36] In his time he was said to have defended more persons charged with murder than any other counsel.[37] He defended one of the so-called 'Dynamitards' several years earlier and later acted for the notorious murderer Dr Cream. The great Marshall Hall acted as his junior on a number of occasions.[38] Lipski was thus able to secure, through his solicitor, John Hayward, a person whom the *East London Observer* characterised as 'the very best counsel available.'[39]

Depositions of witnesses were taken that day and on two other days over the next two weeks, with Geoghegan and his junior carefully testing the Crown's case. On Friday, 22 July, when the evidence had all been taken and the accused's statement to the police read, the magistrate formally cautioned Lipski and asked if he wished to say anything. Lipski replied through the interpreter: 'I am not guilty.' Geoghegan 'reserved his defence' and Lipski was committed for trial at the next sessions of the Central Criminal Court which were to commence on the following Monday, with Mr Justice James Fitzjames Stephen presiding.

On Saturday, 23 July, Lipski was transferred from Holloway to Newgate Prison,[40] the awesome building adjoining the Old Bailey, which had been reconstructed in the late 1700s after the Gordon Riots. It was no longer a general prison and was used – and continued to be so used until torn down in 1903 to construct the present Central Criminal Courts, still known as the Old Bailey – for only two purposes: to hold prisoners then being tried at the Old Bailey, and to hold persons convicted of murder at the Old Bailey and awaiting execution.

The procedure in England then, but abolished in 1933,[41] was for a twenty-three-man grand jury[42] to consider all the cases before they were tried by a so-called petit jury, or regular twelve-man jury, at the sessions. The recorder told the grand jury in the Lipski case that it was their 'duty . . . to find a true bill, when the whole matter would be investigated.'[43] Neither the accused nor his counsel had the right to appear at this hearing. The grand jury dutifully found a 'true bill'.

Lipski was the only person to be accused of murder at the

Old Bailey that summer. Indeed, murder charges were rarer then than one might imagine. In the whole of England and Wales in 1887 there were only slightly more than one hundred and fifty suspected murders (which then included infanticides) known to the police, resulting in charges in less than half the cases, and a total of only thirty-five murder convictions.[44] Surprisingly, in every murder case at the Old Bailey over the previous three years the victim had been a woman.[45] Only two persons had so far been hanged for murder after conviction at the Old Bailey that year and only eleven in all England.[46]

On Wednesday morning Lipski was taken for the first time from Newgate Prison to the Old Bailey, along a covered corridor paved with flagstones, under which were the graves of executed murderers.

The charge was read to Lipski who, according to one Press report, pleaded not guilty 'in a firm voice'.[47] The trial did not proceed, however. Geoghegan asked the judge to put the case over until Friday to give him further time to prepare his defence. Mr Justice Stephen, after raising the suggestion, which was declined by Geoghegan, that the case might be put over until the next sessions, agreed to start the case on Friday. Lipski was taken back to his cell, again walking over the graves of the executed murderers who had gone before him.

Mr. Justice James Fitzjames Stephen from 'Spy' cartoon in *Vanity Fair*, 1885

Chapter Two

The Trial: The First Morning

THE TRIAL BEGAN on Friday morning, 29 July 1887 in the Old Court, the largest of the Old Bailey's four courts.[1] The courtroom was full; crowds waited in the corridors hoping to get seats. Lipski was brought from his cell in Newgate shortly before ten o'clock, in the company of two warders. His face pale, Lipski, followed by the warders, climbed the steps to the high glass-panelled prisoner's dock, opposite the judge's bench. Counsel often complained that it was difficult for them to communicate with their clients during the trial because of the height of the dock. The courtroom, including the public gallery above the prisoner's dock, was unusually quiet. At exactly ten o'clock, Mr Justice James Fitzjames Stephen, in his scarlet and ermine robe, and preceded by the resplendent Lord Mayor, the sheriff and other dignitaries, entered the courtroom. Everyone rose.

Stephen was, and still is, considered one of England's finest criminal lawyers.[2] His three-volume *History of the Criminal Law of England*, published in 1883, is still in print and is often cited in judicial opinions. He drafted a Criminal Code for England which, although never adopted there, was later enacted in Canada, Australia and numerous other parts of the Commonwealth.[3] Many of the most difficult criminal cases were assigned to him. Stephen had been appointed to the Bench in 1879 and was happy as a trial judge. In a letter in 1887 to his lifelong friend, Lord Lytton, regarding the possibility of his replacing Lord Blackburn in the judicial chamber of the House of Lords, Stephen stated: 'I have given up all thought of it for myself and I would take no other promotion. I do not know that I regret it much, as I like my present position exceedingly and should be sorry to give up circuit and criminal law.'[4]

Non-lawyers know of Stephen because he was part of the remarkable Stephen family.[5] His father, James Stephen, had been the Under-Secretary of State for the Colonies (sometimes,

27

because of his forceful personality, referred to as 'Mr Over-Secretary Stephen'), his brother was the man of letters, Leslie Stephen, the first editor of the *Dictionary of National Biography*, and his nieces included Virginia Woolf (five years old at the time of the Lipski trial) and Vanessa Bell.

Stephen is also known because of his book *Liberty, Equality, Fraternity*, published in 1873,[6] in which he attacked John Stuart Mill's views expressed in the essay *On Liberty*. Stephen (like Lord Devlin a century later) was *the* symbol of the enforcement of morality by the criminal law. Yet, surprisingly to the modern mind, Stephen's attitude to opium smoking was much more tolerant than his general views on morality expressed in his book. In correspondence with Lord Lytton in 1889,[7] Stephen revealed that he himself smoked opium (a practice not then illegal). 'I do still now and then smoke an opium pipe,' he wrote, 'as my nose requires one occasionally and is comforted by it.'[8] It just may be that Stephen's opium smoking clouded his judgement and his concentration in the notorious Maybrick murder case,[9] which he tried during the summer of 1889 and which is thought by many (including a later Lord Chief Justice) to have been a miscarriage of justice. Whether he was smoking opium at the time of the Lipski trial two years earlier is not known.

The judge had eight children who survived infancy, including three sons, all of whom were lawyers. As it turned out, none of his sons did particularly well at the Bar. Indeed, Stephen himself had not been a successful barrister. His private correspondence shows that in spite of his reputation he had considerable difficulty getting briefs. The correspondence also shows, in letter after letter over a number of years, an overwhelming desire to be appointed to the security and prestige of the Bench.

At the time of the Lipski trial, Stephen was fifty-eight and suffering from a number of ailments. Apart from problems with his nose, already mentioned, he had collapsed two years earlier while on Assizes and had been ordered to rest for three months. One contributing factor to Stephen's continuing ill-health was worry about his middle son, J. K. Stephen, who had suffered a severe head injury in December 1886, causing later irrational behaviour. J. K. Stephen was committed to a mental hospital several years later and died in 1892 at the age of thirty-two. An English writer, Michael Harrison, in *Clarence*, published in

1973,[10] has speculated that J. K. Stephen was, in fact, Jack the Ripper. A plausible case is built up, comparing J. K. Stephen's poems with the facts about the Ripper cases and showing from Cambridge train schedules and other evidence that Stephen, who was a Fellow of King's College, Cambridge, had the opportunity to commit the murders in 1888. I have uncovered no further evidence supporting the truth of Harrison's assertion – and as we shall see later, there are many other plausible competing claims.

The Treasury counsel were, as expected, Harry Poland and Charles Mathews. They were both formidable lawyers. Poland, the leader, often described as 'the Sleuth-Hound of the Treasury' (a name apparently first given to him by the *Pall Mall Gazette*), had been Senior Counsel to the Treasury at the Old Bailey since 1865.[11] He had been involved in some of the most important cases over the years: the Governor Eyre prosecution, the Tichborne case, the Franconia case, and the murder prosecutions of the Wainwrights, the Stauntons and the Dynamitards. The fifty-eight-year-old bachelor (it was said that he took 'his briefs to bed with him')[12] was noted for his 'untiring industry, lucidity and accuracy'.[13] He became a Queen's Counsel the year after the Lipski case and entered private practice, having been succeeded as Senior Treasury Counsel by Charles Mathews. In a very brief reference to Poland taking silk, the *Jewish Chronicle* referred to 'Mr Poland, the barrister, (who is partly Jewish by descent)', the only reference I have seen to Poland's Jewish origins.[14] Poland declined a judgeship offered by his friend Lord Halsbury, was later knighted, and died in 1928 at the age of ninety-eight.

Poland has been described as 'the greatest prosecuting counsel ever employed by the Treasury', and Charles Mathews was said to be 'only one whit behind him'.[15] Several months earlier the style of the two lawyers had been described by the *Pall Mall Gazette* in another murder case, in words no doubt also applicable to the Lipski prosecution: 'Mr Poland opened the case for the Crown in his usual dry, hard manner: slow, sure and insensible, like a file talking, though not so rasping as usual. His junior, Mr Charles Mathews, has a light speaking voice, and an insinuating manner of putting his questions which reminds you strongly of a conjurer when he asks you if you are sure you have got the card you marked and begs you to make sure that there is no deception.'[16] In the Lipski case, both counsel examined witnesses; Poland, for the most part, examining the more important ones.

To the surprise of many, a barrister unfamiliar to the regulars at the Old Bailey appeared for the defence. Geoghegan was no longer in charge. A. J. McIntyre, QC, had been retained to lead for the defence.

McIntyre was not a criminal lawyer. He was a sixty-six-year-old barrister who had been a Liberal MP from 1880 to 1885 and who had not, it seems, appeared at the Old Bailey for many years. When he died two years after the Lipski case, within a year of being appointed to the County Court Bench (a court which does not handle criminal matters), he was praised in one obituary as 'a sound commercial lawyer'.[17] Moreover, *The Times* obituary noted that he had been in failing health for four years.[18] Why was he chosen to conduct this case instead of Geoghegan?

There is nothing concrete to provide an answer. Geoghegan had handled important murder cases before this. A month earlier, in a trial before Stephen at the Old Bailey, Geoghegan had defended a seaman charged with murder on the high seas.[19] Two days preceding the Lipski case, on the day that Geoghegan had applied to put the case over until Friday, he had successfully defended, before Stephen and a jury, a man charged with the manslaughter of his wife.[20] There was no suggestion on that day that another counsel was to be brought into the case.

McIntyre was probably brought in at the last moment because Geoghegan was unable to conduct the case owing to alcohol. Contemporaries, as we have seen earlier, praised Geoghegan's brilliance; but they also commented on his drinking. 'If ever I met him,' wrote one 'it was "Come and have a drink, Fred" ';[21] another wrote that Geoghegan 'went under, owing to its influence';[22] still another commented that he drank when 'affected with the fear that he might not get his man off.'[23] His drinking eventually influenced the number of briefs he got and in 1902 he killed himself in his chambers with an overdose of an opiative sedative, probably deliberately, although the coroner's jury held that it was 'misadventure'. (Like many lawyers, Geoghegan died intestate.) Thus it is not at all unlikely that Geoghegan started drinking at the manslaughter trial on Wednesday and continued drinking during two other

30

cases he defended at the Old Bailey the following day[24] and was not in a fit condition to handle the Lipski case. The libel laws at that time gave newspapers less of a privilege to report court proceedings than today and thus it would have been unwise for them to comment, if such were the fact.[25]

Why was McIntyre brought in? Perhaps Geoghegan suggested his name to Lipski's solicitor. McIntyre and Geoghegan were members of the same Inn of Court, the Middle Temple (McIntyre had been a Bencher since 1873), and had their chambers near each other. Another possibility, although less likely, is that it was Stephen who suggested McIntyre, as McIntyre had appeared before Stephen in a number of libel cases earlier that year and had appeared before him in an election petition case earlier that month, a case which McIntyre won.

Geoghegan sat in the counsel's benches with McIntyre, but did not take an active part in the case. He examined no witnesses and did not address the court or the jury.

A jury was quickly chosen – their names were simply announced by the clerk – and they took their seats in the jury box to the left of the prisoner's dock. No objections were made to the jurors. The clerk told the accused to stand. The judge turned to the jury:

> Gentlemen of the jury, look upon the prisoner and harken to his charge. He stands indicted by the name of Israel Lipski, that Israel Lipski on or about the 28th day of June, 1887, in St George's-in-the-East, in the County of Middlesex, did unlawfully murder Miriam Angel. Upon this indictment he had been arraigned, and upon his arraignment he hath pleaded not guilty. Your charge, therefore, is to inquire whether he be guilty of the offence charged.

Harry Poland opened the case, outlining to the jury in his 'slow, sure and insensible' manner the facts he was going to prove. He then set out the theory of the Crown's case. Unfortunately, counsel's opening and closing addresses and the judge's charge to the jury are not contained in the transcript of the trial; but they were recorded in summary fashion by *The Times* reporter:[26]

> It was alleged on the part of the prosecution that the prisoner entered the deceased's room for some purpose, locked the door on the inside, and being discovered by the deceased it was suggested that he first battered her with his fist and then administered the nitric acid to her, when, finding

31

that she was dead, he took a portion himself, but the quantity he took was not sufficient to occasion his death. A *post mortem* examination was made of the deceased, and it was found that she had died from suffocation caused by the nitric acid burning her throat. Mr Poland said it was clear that the prisoner could not have gone into the deceased's room with the door locked on the inside for any proper purpose. It was not suggested that the prisoner bought the nitric acid for the purpose of administering it to the deceased, but having it in his pocket at the time he used it. The prisoner was removed to the hospital, and through an interpreter he made a statement to the effect that on the morning in question a man spoke to him at the corner of Backchurch Lane about work; when he returned to the house he saw the man and another on the first floor, and they took him by the throat, opened his mouth, and poured some poison down, saying, 'That is the brandy you asked for.' They asked him whether he had any money, and he replied only the sovereign he had given for the brandy. They asked him where his gold chain was, and he said it was in pawn – they said, 'If you don't give us it you will be as dead as the woman'; They threw him down and put a piece of wood in his mouth – one of the men said, 'Don't you think he is quite dead?' and the other answered, 'Yes, he does not want any more,' and they then drew him under the bed and left him for dead. Mr Poland pointed out the improbable nature of this statement and said that with reference to the sovereign spoken of by the prisoner he had asked the landlady to lend him five shillings that morning, but she refused. It was difficult to conceive a clearer case against the prisoner.

The first witness, Sergeant Bitten, was called. The testimony set out in the following passages is taken from the transcript found in the Home Office files, prepared at the request of the Home Office from the shorthand notes of Messrs Barnett and Buckler, 'shorthand writers to the Court'.[27] Since there was no right of appeal at the time, there would have been no transcript if the Home Office had not ordered one. It did so because of the controversy following the verdict.

Sergeant Bitten produced diagrams of the Angels' room, the house and the surrounding neighbourhood. The evidence was routine. Mathews conducted the examination.

It is a house of three storeys, consisting of a ground floor, first floor and second floor?
Yes.
The ground floor I think is composed of two rooms, one a bedroom, and behind it a kitchen?
Yes.
And there is a passage running along, through which you can get into the back yard without going into one or other of these rooms?
Yes.

Then there is a short staircase leading up to the first floor?
Yes.
Of seven or eight stairs only I think?
About nine or ten.
And the first floor, again, is composed of two rooms, one front, and one back?
Yes.
Then there is another short staircase which leads to the top floor, and that is composed of one room?
One room only.
Can you tell me the height of the first-floor window from the pavement?
Twelve feet: that would be from the window sill to the pavement.
You made a particular examination of that window sill, did you not?
Yes.
Could you discover any marks on it?
None whatever.
As though it had been in any way roughly used?
No.

The prosecution was, of course, trying to counter a potential argument by Lipski that the real murderers locked the door from the inside and escaped through the front window. This would have been an impossible theory to rely on, because a later witness testified that after discovering the body he could not raise the window to call the police. Moreover, a workman in a front room in the house opposite number sixteen gave evidence that he had not seen anything unusual.

The prosecution then asked about a side window which gave anyone going to Lipski's room a view of the Angels' bed. The little window is of considerable significance because Mr Justice Stephen became preoccupied with the idea that Lipski watched Mrs Angel in bed and entered her room to satisfy his 'lust'.

Did you go up the staircase leading from the first floor to the second floor?
Yes.
It is a fact, is it not, that there is a small window through which you could look on to this bedstead from the staircase outside?
Yes. Commanding a full view of the bed.
A muslin curtain was there?
Yes, but it is a very thin muslin, so you had just the same view.

Thin muslin you say?
Very fine muslin.
Did you see it?
I saw through the muslin.
You could see through the muslin, and get, as you have said, a full view of the bed?
Yes.
And of any one who was lying on it?
Yes.

McIntyre then conducted some inconsequential cross-examination as to the times the diagrams were made.

Isaac Angel, the deceased's husband, gave evidence through the interpreter, Mr Karamelli, whose knowledge of Yiddish, many persons later said, was inadequate:

Are you a boot riveter?
Yes.
Are you a native of Warsaw?
Some distance from Warsaw, from Poland.
Have you been about twelve months in England?
Ten months, longer now, ten months at the time.
When you came to England were you accompanied by your wife, Miriam Angel?
Yes.
Who at that time was between twenty-one and twenty-two years of age?
Yes. Twenty-two.
About a week before Whitsuntide this year did you go to live at 16 Batty Street, towards the end of May?
Yes.
And did you there occupy with your wife a room which you furnished in the first-floor front?
Yes.
Were you then working at George Street, Spitalfields?
Yes.
And was it your custom to leave home to go to work about half past six every morning?
Sometimes six, sometimes half past six, sometimes seven, on that day a quarter past six.
Up to this day, 28th June, had you known the prisoner to speak to?
I did not know him.

34

And to your knowledge did your wife know him?
Also not.

No witness at the trial gave evidence that Lipski either knew
or had even spoken to Mr or Mrs Angel. On the face of it, this is
hard to understand. All three were recent immigrants from
Poland, from Warsaw or near Warsaw. None spoke much
English, conversing instead in Yiddish. All were observant
Jews. They had lived one floor away from each other for almost
two months, no doubt passing each other on the stairs or
meeting in the only kitchen in the house on many occasions.

The trial continued with Angel giving evidence about the
evening before the murder and his leaving the house the next
morning.

*On the Monday night, 27th June, did you return home about nine
o'clock?*
Yes.
Did you see your wife?
She was waiting for me at the door.
Did you go to bed about twelve?
Half past eleven.
*When your wife and you went to bed that night was she in her usual
spirits?*
She was well.
Next morning about a quarter past six was it that you got up?
At six o'clock.
Did you speak to your wife whilst you were getting up?
Yes, I said 'Here you are, here is your breakfast, what shall I
prepare for your dinner?'
*Well, there was some conversation between you. You left the house at
what time?*
Quarter past six.
Was your wife awake at the time you left the room?
Yes, she was awake when I went away.
Your wife was in bed when you left, was she?
Yes.
With her chemise or night dress on?
Yes.
Did she seem perfectly cheerful and in her usual spirits?
She was well.
Did you notice the position of the table in the room at the time?
The table was at the window as usual, I said my prayers

there; her face was as splendid and red as that scarlet [no doubt pointing to Stephen's robes] when I left her.

The condition of the lock on the door was then explored to establish that it was in good working order. The prosecution's most powerful piece of circumstantial evidence was that Lipski was found in the room with the door apparently locked from the inside. It was important, therefore, to show that the lock was functioning properly.

Did you shut the room door when you left the room this morning?
Yes, the same as usual.
Do you remember whether the key was in the door or anything about the key?
It was stuck in the lock inside.
Had you locked the door that night when you went to bed?
Yes.
Had you to unlock the door in order to get out?
Yes.
What kind of lock was it, a good lock?
I have lived there six weeks, and eight days; after that they put the lock on, a new lock.
You said it was a good lock?
Yes.
And it worked properly, did it?
It locked well.

Angel testified that he was called home around noon by Mrs Levy, but was not permitted to enter his room.

When you got home did you find that your wife was dead?
Yes, they would not let me go into my own room.
Did you afterwards go into the room on that day?
No, not on the same day.
Your wife was six months gone in pregnancy, was she?
Yes.

Once again McIntyre conducted a brief, perfunctory cross-examination.

The evidence of Phillip Lipski, the landlord, given in English, was not controversial. In cross-examination Mr McIntyre stressed Israel Lipski's good character.

You say he had lodged with you for about eighteen months altogether?

Altogether about two years.

Was he a well-behaved young man?

Oh yes, he was.

Steady and industrious?

Steady and honest so long as he was in my place.

Although he has the same name that you have, I believe he is not any relation of yours?

Oh no, he is not.

No relation at all?

No.

Do you know that he was engaged to be married to a young woman?

Yes.

And had been engaged for some time?

Yes, I cannot tell you how long.

The landlord also testified that the lock had been put on by a Mr Peters, the landlord's own landlord, who was a retired tailor, thereby raising the possibility that it may not have been correctly installed, was not functioning properly and therefore was not, in fact, locked from the inside.

Simon Rosenbloom was then sworn and gave evidence through the interpreter. His evidence was crucial: he was one of the two persons Lipski said committed the crime and then attacked him.

Mr Poland conducted the examination-in-chief. Rosenbloom described the events leading up to 28 June.

Do you live at 27 Philpot Street, Commercial Road?

37.

Are you a native of Poland?

Yes.

And have been in England something over eighteen months?

Yes, not quite eighteen.

(Rosenbloom had been married for ten months.)

Do you work as a stickmaker?

Yes.

At one time did you work for a Mr Mark Katz?

Yes.

Of Watney Passage, Commercial Road?

Yes.

During the time you were working there was the prisoner working in the same employment?

Yes.

Did the prisoner continue to work there up to Monday 20th June or thereabouts?

Till the Jubilee week.

And was the boy Pitman also employed at Mr Mark Katz's?

Yes.

On Saturday 25th June, the Saturday in Jubilee week, did you meet the prisoner?

The same Saturday of the Jubilee week.

What conversation passed between you?

He said that he had made for himself a workshop and he said, 'You come to me to work', he did not earn much at Mr Mark Katz's; he said he would give me regular wages and I went to work at his place on Tuesday morning at seven o'clock.

Had you been to Lipski's on the Sunday before the Tuesday?

Yes, and they were making samples.

It was then arranged, was it, that you should come on the following Tuesday at seven o'clock to work?

Yes.

The events of the morning of 28 June, up until Rosenbloom said he last saw Lipski, were then described.

And at seven on the Tuesday morning the 28th did you go to the front door of 16 Batty Street and knock at it?

Yes.

What time was it you got there?

Seven o'clock.

Who opened the door to you?

He came down having been at work and he opened the door.

How was he dressed?

Trousers, shirt and bare-footed as they go to work.

Did you go into the house and go with him up to the top floor?

Yes.

Was anybody else there then besides yourself and the prisoner?

Only he and myself.

Did he give you some work to do?

Yes, he gave me points to bend.

Handles or what?

They were not then made, they were in a raw state.

Were they to be put on the top of the sticks?

On the top, handle.

Had they to be filed?

Yes, I filed them.

38

And did the prisoner at that time commence to do some work himself?
He commenced to work but only worked a few minutes.
At that time was there one vice in the room?
Yes, there was one in the room.
Was there only one?
One, the second one he went to buy.
What did he say before he went out to buy the second vice?
He said 'There will come another man, a filer, and he will require another vice.'
Anything more?
He would go and buy a sponge for the boy to varnish with.
Did he say anything more about the filer?
No.
Did he not say anything as to who had recommended him the filer?
He only said that he would come to the work and that was all.
Then did the prisoner put on any clothes before he went out?
He put on his boots, a shirt-coat and a hat.
Was it such a coat as that that he put on? (handing one to the witness)

The coat produced had acid stains on it. The precise location of the stains and the quantity of acid that would produce such stains would become the subject of great controversy after the trial.

Yes, such a one, that is the coat and that is the same hat. There were no stains on the coat then.
Did you hear him shut the street door as he went out?
No, that I did not hear.
After a short time did the prisoner return?
Yes, he came back and said, 'The shop is still closed.'
Did he say what shop was still closed?
That Marks, where he went to buy the vice.
About how long was he out?
I cannot tell because there was no clock.
Could you say about?
I cannot tell.
When he came back did he begin to do any more work?
No, he went up and down the stairs till the boy returned.
And did no work?
No.
Until the boy came?

39

Until the boy came to work.
About what time was it that the boy came?
Eight by the clock.
Was the prisoner upstairs in the room when the boy arrived?
No, he came up directly after the boy came, and he said 'I am going to buy a sponge for the boy to varnish.'
Was that the boy Pitman?
I don't know his name. (The witness Pitman was here called into court.)
Is that the boy you have been speaking of?
Yes, that is the boy.
Then where did the prisoner go?
He went to buy for the boy a sponge.
Was he dressed in the same way as he had been when he went out on the last occasion?
Yes.

Rosenbloom claimed that this was the last time he saw Lipski until Mrs Angel's body was discovered.

Rosenbloom, according to his testimony, remained in the attic room and Schmuss, the other person Lipski said committed the murder, came up to the attic. The lad Pitman was still there. The Crown asked Rosenbloom questions to show that he and Schmuss did not know each other. Rosenbloom's evidence was to the effect that Schmuss stayed only a few minutes and left, leaving him (Rosenbloom) and Pitman together in the attic. Rosenbloom testified that Pitman remained with him for an hour or an hour and a half, and that he (Rosenbloom) did not leave the attic from seven until Mrs Angel was discovered dead some time after eleven. Pitman's evidence, on the other hand, as we shall see, will be that he (Pitman) left at about nine o'clock, before Schmuss left, and did not come back for almost an hour. Poland continued his examination of Rosenbloom.

After the prisoner had gone do you remember a man coming up into the room?
After he had gone away the last time a man came, the boy was there. (The witness Schmuss was here called into court.)
Is that the man who came?
Yes.
Had you some conversation with that man?
He did not speak much, as he did not stay long.

40

But what he did speak, did he speak in your own language?
Yes, Yiddish.
Did that man wait there a little time?
Yes.
About how long?
I cannot say how long, either fifteen minutes or longer, I cannot tell.
During that time did the prisoner return?
No.
The prisoner did not return and the other man went away, did he? (Mr McIntyre objected to this as a leading question).
Did the prisoner return during that time or after that?
No, he did not return again.
And did Schmuss leave?
Yes, he went away.
Where was the boy when Schmuss went away?
With me in the room.

According to Rosenbloom, therefore, he and Schmuss were never left alone in the room.

When did the boy leave, how long after the man left did the boy leave?
I cannot think, there was no clock.
Cannot you say about?
I cannot say whether it was an hour or an hour and a half.
When the boy left how long did he remain away before he returned?
I cannot say.
Could you say about how long?
I cannot say, I won't tell any lies.
But the boy did go away for his breakfast?
Yes.
During the whole of that morning did you leave that upstairs room at all?
When I heard the disturbance downstairs I went down.
Up to then had you not left the room from the time you went there at seven in the morning?
From seven till the time I heard the disturbance.
After the prisoner went out the second time did he ever return to the room?
I did not see him any more.
What disturbance was it you heard downstairs?
Clapping, knocking and screaming, and the boy ran down the stairs.

41

Mr Justice Stephen: *He has not told us yet when the boy came back, he went to his breakfast, did he return, when?*

I cannot think.

Mr. Poland: *Did he come back?*

Yes.

And when he came back, did he come up into the room at the top of the house?

Yes.

And did he stay there with you until your heard the disturbance downstairs?

Yes, I was filing the handles.

When you heard the screaming and the knocking, did you and he go downstairs together?

Yes.

And did you go together or nearly together into the front room first floor and there see Mrs Angel lying dead on the bed?

Yes, and the women were inside in the room.

In cross-examination, Rosenbloom maintained that he did not know Schmuss and did not speak to the lad Pitman.

Did you know him [Schmuss] *before?*

No, I did not know him.

Did you ever see him before?

No, that was the first time I had seen him when he came up.

Did you tell the boy that you had known him before?

I did not say that to the boy, because I cannot speak English.

Do you mean to say that you did not speak to the boy in English?

No, I could swear that I did not speak with him in English.

Not a word?

No.

Did you tell the boy that the prisoner had gone for a vice?

No, I did not say [anything] to the boy at all.

Just be careful about this, did you not in English tell the boy that Lipski had gone to buy a vice?

No, I did not.

And did you tell the boy that you knew the strange man that came, before?

No, I did not say that to the boy at all.

And that you had been in the man's company before?

I did not say that, I could swear it.

Did you see the man before he came into the room?

I only saw him in the room for the first time.

42

McIntyre tried to get Rosenbloom to agree that brandy was used in stickmaking in order to explain why Lipski might have asked him to fetch some brandy, as Lipski claimed to have done in his statement to the police. The request for brandy so early in the morning, and particularly at a time when Lipski obviously had much on his mind and was short of money, strikes the hearer as very odd. McIntyre had no success in eliciting an explanation from Rosenbloom and, surprisingly, never asked any other witness about the brandy nor called expert evidence on the issue.

In this business of stickmaker, is shellac used?
Shellac and varnish.
Is the shellac dissolved in spirits?
The shellac is put into the varnish.
But is it dissolved in spirits of wine?
No, they call it varnish.
They call it varnish, don't they, when the shellac is dissolved in the spirits; that makes it varnish, does it not?
In the varnishing.
Mr Justice Stephen: *How do you make varnish for the sticks?*
I do not know.
Do you know what they do with shellac?
I was told by my old master that they put the shellac into the varnish.
Do you know what the varnish is made of?
No.

It was later established by another witness that Lipski had purchased two pounds of shellac the day before the murder, and so if McIntyre was correct, as he appears to have been, that shellac and spirits make varnish, this would explain the need for the brandy.

Mr McIntyre: *Have you been engaged in this business of stickmaking any length of time?*
Since I have been here.
How long?
About eight months.
Don't you know that sometimes brandy is also used for the purpose of dissolving shellac?
I do not know anything about the brandy.
Did not Lipski ask you to get some brandy?

No, he did not ask me.

Do you know whether Lipski used to take brandy in his coffee for breakfast?

I do not know that.

Did not Lipski give you a sovereign to buy a quartern of brandy for him?

A sovereign is a gold coin worth one pound. Later evidence will show that Lipski had borrowed twenty-five shillings from his future mother-in-law the previous day.

He did not give me a farthing. I could swear it.

And did not Lipski tell you when he gave you the sovereign to buy the small quantity of brandy, that he wanted change?

He never said anything to me, he did not send me for brandy, I went upstairs and I went to work.

McIntyre was equally unsuccessful in establishing that Rosenbloom knew that Lipski had a watch and a chain.

You have been working with Lipski I think for some time, do you know that he had a watch and chain?

He did not say so to me.

Do you know that he had?

No, I do not know.

Have you not seen him on the Sabbath wearing a watch and chain?

No.

McIntyre then led Rosenbloom through Lipski's statement. The entire cross-examination was remarkably restrained and polite, considering that Rosenbloom was the person Lipski said committed the murder. The style of cross-examination seemed to be that of a careful civil lawyer, not that of a vigorous defence counsel trying to break down the witness's story. It was completely ineffective.

Be careful and think how you answer this question: were not you and the strange man standing at the door of Mrs Angel's when Lipski came back?

No, no, I did not know who lived down there.

Mr Justice Stephen: *Ask him this again that there may be no mistake.*

A juror: *Repeat the question, please.*

Mr McIntyre: *Were you not, and the strange man, standing by Mrs Angel's door when Lipski returned?*

No, I was not.
Were you there standing by Mrs Angel's door when Lipski returned?
No.
And was not the door of Mrs Angel's partly open at that time?
No, I did not see.
Will you swear that you were not there when the door was partly open?
Yes, I will swear, in the Temple I will swear it.
Mr Justice Stephen: *Did you at any time that morning stand before Mrs Angel's door?*

(It is unusual for a judge to intervene in the cross-examination to the extent the Mr Justice Stephen did.)

No, I was not before the alarm took place.
Mr McIntyre*: Were you not standing just outside the door and the strange man just inside the door of Mrs Angel's room?*
No, I was not out, and I had not seen the man before he came up.
Did you have any small parcel in your hand when Lipski came up the stairs the last time?
No, I did not have any parcel, I can swear.
And did you not throw the parcel down and say to the strange man 'He is here, come on' as Lipski was coming up?
I can swear I had no packet and I saw no packet.
Did you say 'He is here, come on'?
That is all lies, I did not say that.
Did not the strange man catch hold of Lipski?
No.
And did you yourself catch hold of Lipski by his two hands or his wrists?
I did not catch hold of him at all, that is all lies.
And did not you and the other man throw him down?
Mr Justice Stephen: *Is not this useless? I can always allow a prisoner to make a statement.*

This is a strange intervention by the judge on this crucial part of Lipski's case – and even stranger that McIntyre, after a few more questions, followed the judge's suggestion and stopped his cross-examination.

Did not you yourself force open Lipski's mouth?
No, I did not, I am not such a strong man as to do that.
Whilst the other man held him?
The other one was not there; all lies, all lies.

What part of Poland do you come from?
From Plotz.
Is that near Warsaw?
Seventeen or eighteen Polish miles.

The cross-examination of Rosenbloom had concluded. Mr Poland did not wish to re-examine the witness and indicated to the Bench that this might be a convenient time to have a break for lunch. Mr Justice Stephen agreed. Lipski was taken to one of the tiny holding cells[28] below the Old Bailey. Mr Justice Stephen probably followed the custom of lunching with the Lord Mayor and the Sheriff, Sir Henry Isaacs, a leading member of the Jewish community and future Lord Mayor, at the Sherriff's personal expense, in the room provided for the judge at the Old Bailey.[29] Counsel probably remained in the small barristers' robing room. Poland, no doubt, had his usual small brown loaf, large pat of butter and jug of milk, which one contemporary says was all, in his forty years' knowledge of Poland, he ever saw him take for lunch.[30] And, no doubt, Geoghegan had one or more drinks.

Harry Bodkin Poland from 'Spy' cartoon in *Vanity Fair*, 1886

Chapter Three

The Trial: Afternoon

THE FIRST WITNESS called after the lunch break was the lad
Pitman. Pitman, who claimed he was sixteen but whose mother
later gave evidence that he was only fourteen, testified that he
had known Lipski for about a month, having worked together
with him at Mark Katz's. About a week before the murder,
Lipski had asked Pitman to come to work for him and for three
or four days he had been helping Lipski furnish his workshop.
Pitman's evidence of events during the morning of the 28th
differed in several significant respects from Rosenbloom's.
Mathews conducted the examination.

*Now let us go to the Tuesday morning, the 28th. What time did you get
to number sixteen that morning?*
Eight o'clock.
That was your regular hour for coming, was it?
Yes.
Did you go upstairs to the room on the top floor?
Yes.
Was the prisoner there when you got there?
No.
Anybody else?
Simon Rosenbloom.
Had you seen Rosenbloom before that morning?
No.
*After you had got up there, and were there with Rosenbloom, how long
did you stay there before you left?*
About an hour.
*You arrived about eight o'clock and stayed there till somewhere about
nine?*
Yes.
During that time did the prisoner come into the room?
Yes, sir.
Did he say anything when he came into the room?
He said 'I have been to buy a vice and the shop was shut up.'

Anything more that you remember?

Yes, in a little while after that he went out again and said, 'I am going to have another try and see if I can buy the vice.'

And then did he go out?

Yes.

Can you tell me at all about what time it was he went out?

About five minutes past nine.

When Lipski went out?

Yes.

After he had gone do you remember any strange man or any third person coming up into the room?

Yes, sir.

The witness Schmuss was here called into court.

Look at that man, is that the man who came up?

Yes.

Did he speak to Rosenbloom?

Yes.

They had some talk together, had they?

Yes.

Was it in a language that you understood?

No.

How long did Schmuss remain?

About five minutes, no longer.

And then what became of him?

He went out.

Did you go out after him?

No, before him.

It will be recalled that Rosenbloom had said that Schmuss left before Pitman. Pitman's evidence that Rosenbloom and Schmuss were left alone in Lipski's room obviously hurt the Crown's case. Pitman stuck to his story.

You have just said that Schmuss remained about five minutes and then went out?

Yes.

Were you there when Schmuss left?

No.

You left him behind you?

Yes.

You left, going downstairs, leaving Rosenbloom and Schmuss upstairs?

50

Yes.
You went home to breakfast, did you?
Yes.
About how far off are Whites Gardens from this house in Batty Street?
About a quarter of a mile.
You walked, of course?
Yes.
Can you tell me what time you got home?
No.
Your mother is here, I think?
Yes.
You saw your mother when you got home?
Yes.
Had your breakfast?
Yes.
And came back to Batty Street?
Yes.
Did you come back straight?
No, I had a little game in the street and then went back.
How long were you playing in the street?
About a quarter of an hour.
And then you went back?
Yes.
When you went back, did you go up to the workshop?
Yes.
Who was there at that time?
Simon Rosenbloom.
Any one else?
No, sir.
And did you stay there with Rosenbloom?
Yes.
How long?
About an hour.
And then what happened: anything to call your attention downstairs?
In about half an hour Lipski came in.

Mathews was expecting that Pitman would refer to the finding of Mrs Angel's body. Pitman's answer obviously caught Mathews by surprise.

Half an hour after you got there the prisoner came in, you say?
Yes.
Was Rosenbloom there still at that time?

51

Yes.
What did the prisoner say, if anything?
He did not say anything.
What did he do?
Nothing.
What became of him?
He stood still in the room.
How long did he remain?
About five minutes.
Standing still?
Yes.

Again, this last section of evidence harmed the Crown's case. There is a major inconsistency between Pitman's evidence and Rosenbloom's testimony that Lipski was last seen in the attic workroom shortly after eight o'clock.

Cross-examination of Pitman by McIntyre was designed to show that Rosenbloom knew Schmuss. At the preliminary hearing Pitman had said that Rosenbloom had told him that he knew Schmuss.

Was Rosenbloom talking to the strange man who came in while he was there?
Yes.
Did you ask him whether he knew the man?
No.
Did he say whether he knew the man?
Yes.
What did he say?
I did not understand if he knew the man. The reason why I thought he knew the man was speaking in his own language. [*sic*]
Mr Justice Stephen: *But did he tell you that he knew the man?*
No, sir.
Mr McIntyre: *Did Rosenbloom tell you that he knew the man?*
No, sir.
Did not Rosenbloom say to you 'I know that man; I have been in his company before'?
Yes, sir.
He did say that?
Yes.

52

Mr Justice Stephen: *Just now you said that he did not tell you, now you say he did tell you?*
I forgot my words.
Do you now remember that Rosenbloom did say that – did he?
Yes.
Mr McIntyre: *And did he tell you that, speaking the same language you did, which we call English?*
Yes(crying).
Did he also tell you a second time that he knew the man a little time?
Yes, sir.
Did he tell you that twice?
Yes.
Did Rosenbloom tell you that Lipski had gone for a vice?
Yes.
Were those the words that he said in English?
Yes.
'Lipski has gone for a vice?'
Yes.

Pitman's evidence clearly helped Lipski by showing that Schmuss and Rosenbloom were not strangers, as they claimed to be, and were left alone in the attic, thus making it more possible that Lipski's story that they killed Mrs Angel was true. The re-examination – which would today be considered improper cross-examination of one's own witness – undertaken by Poland, again with considerable assistance from the judge, ridiculed Pitman's evidence that Schmuss and Rosenbloom knew each other.

Do I understand you to say that the prisoner told you he was going to buy the vice?
Yes.
You have just told my friend that Rosenbloom told you?
Rosenbloom told me afterwards, when I came in at first at eight o'clock, when I came in to work.
Told you what?
That he had gone to buy a vice and a sponge.
How did he speak to you?
In English.
What sort of English?
Half his own language and half our language – I just understood him.
Could you understand him always?

Not always, sir.

You said at first that you thought Rosenbloom knew this man that came because he spoke the same language?

Yes.

Is that right?

Yes.

Then you afterwards said that Rosenbloom told you he knew the man. Just say what he said to you.

He said 'I know this man.'

As if he was speaking to you, now tell us what he said.

He said 'I know that man because I have been in his company before where he used to work.'

Did he say that all in English or part in the foreign language?

Half in English and half in his own language.

Mr Justice Stephen: *Which part of it did he say in English?*

He said as much English as his own language.

There are only a few words, can you tell us which words he said in English and which in his own language?

He had been in his own company before.

He said that in English, did he?

Yes.

Then in what language did he say 'I know that man'?

He said it in half English.

But you said that the half of all he said was in his own language.

Yes.

Do you mean that he talked like a foreigner, or a man who did not know English, or did not know much?

He did not know much of English; he just told me what I could understand.

You could make out what he meant?

Yes.

Mr Poland: *Could you make out all that he meant?*

Yes.

The part that was in English, of course, you understood?

Yes.

But the part that was in the foreign language you could not understand, I suppose?

No.

Are you quite clear that they did speak together in a foreign language?

Yes.

Did you think they knew each other when they spoke in the foreign language?

Yes.
Before you were told anything?
Yes.

Pitman's mother was then called. She confirmed that Pitman came home for breakfast that morning at about a quarter past nine.

Lipski went to buy a vice on Tuesday morning from Mark Schmidt, the hardware dealer in Backchurch Lane, which was next door to the shop where the Crown alleged Lipski bought the nitric acid. Schmidt gave evidence that Lipski had been in his shop on Monday, the day before the murder.

On Monday the 27th of June were you at your shop?
Yes.
What time was it? Did you see the prisoner that day?
Yes. It was in the afternoon.
Had you known him before?
I did know him.
For how long had you known him?
I suppose for a year before.
When he was in your shop were there some other men there?
There was a couple of workmen there.
Was one of them a man named Schmuss?
Yes.
What did the prisoner say to you on that afternoon?
He asked me if I could send him a man to work.
Did he say to do what work?
I knew that.
What was it?
Stickmaker.
You knew the prisoner was a stickmaker?
Yes.
Did he say what part of the work this man was to do?
Filing.
What did you then say to him?
I said 'There are four men here; you can have which you like.'
Who were the four men? Schmuss was one?
Yes.
Who were the other three?
I can't tell their names.

Have you seen them outside?
Yes.
Do you know their names now?
Yes, but not from memory.
Are they here?
Yes.
(Schmuss and Rosenbloom were here called into court.)
Barsook is not here.
(Barsook was here brought in custody from the jail.)

Barsook, who was then in custody on a petty theft charge, was to play a prominent role in the case after the trial.

Are those three of them?
Yes, they always came to me. I can't tell exactly this time those are three of them. [*sic*]
Which is Schmuss?
The middle one.
Look at Barsook: is that one of them?
Yes, one. He did not work for me, only he was with them together.
When the prisoner asked you about this man who he wanted as a filer, what did you tell him?
I told him 'You can have one of those four.'
Then what took place; did you hear what he said to them?
I did not send them, he went outside with them and talked with them. I don't know what they talked.
Did you see him afterwards the same afternoon, did he come into the shop again?
No. I saw no more of him.
Did you see anything of the four men?
Yes, they came tomorrow as well and they were there all day Monday afternoon.

This evidence, if correct, shakes Rosenbloom's claim that he had never seen Schmuss before the 28th. Did the shorthand reporter make an error in stating Rosenbloom was there? There is a question mark beside this evidence in the Home Office copy of the transcript. The Old Bailey record also says that Rosenbloom was identified, but this record was prepared by the same shorthand reporters. Stephen's own notes prepared by him during the trial do not indicate who was indentified. Schmuss's later evidence refers to a fourth person as Robinski, and it is likely that Robinski, not Rosenbloom, was, in fact, the person in Schmidt's shop on Monday. If it was Rosenbloom, one would have expected more to have been made of the point during the trial and afterwards.

Schmidt's evidence confirmed that part of Lipski's statement about the vice.

When did you last see the prisoner?
On Tuesday morning when he offered me [money] for the vice. He was then outside the shop and there I left him.
About what time was that?
I suppose it only took about five minutes altogether.
About what time was it you last saw him?
About eight. I don't know exactly.

Schmidt gave evidence about seeing Schmuss at noon on the day of the murder. His testimony makes one wonder where Schmuss was on the morning of the murder.

On that Tuesday did you see Schmuss again?
Yes.
What time?
About twelve o'clock.
Where did you see him?
At my shop.
He came to your shop?
Yes.
You must not say what was said, but at that time did you know that Mrs Angel had been killed?
I heard it.
You had heard the report that Mrs Angel was killed?
Yes.
Schmuss was in the shop about what time?
About twelve.
Did you have some conversation with him – talk to him?
Yes.
Was that talk about Mrs Angel's death?
Yes – I told him.

It is odd that Schmuss would not have noticed the very large crowd (later estimated by Dr Kay as two thousand people) milling around Batty Street and asked a bystander what had happened. According to his later evidence, he came to

57

Schmidt's from his lodgings, and the route back to Schmidt's would have passed Batty Street.

How often did you see him after that Tuesday?
I saw him about five or six days.
Every day?
Yes, he was there every day – he came to ask for a job.
Do you know that he left London – he came and said goodbye to you?
Yes, he told me he should go to Birmingham.

This line of questioning was designed to show that Schmuss did not flee from London. The Crown then tried to establish through Schmidt, with only limited success, that nitric acid was used by stickmakers.

Do you understand stickmaking, have you been a stickmaker?
Yes. Seventeen years I was a stickmaker.
Do you know what aqua fortis or nitric acid is used for?
Some use it for sticks; I do not know what sort it is, if it is aqua fortis or vitriol. I do not know what it is. I do not use it.
But is aqua fortis or nitric acid at all used in the stick trade?
Mr Justice Stephen: *Do people make any use of aqua fortis in making sticks?*
Yes, they do.

McIntyre cross-examined Schmidt.

That depends upon the sort of stick, I suppose?
Yes, they use it – not every one. It is used for staining or burning out sometimes.

No questions were asked in cross-examination to establish that brandy was also used by stickmakers. The cross-examination went on to show that the four men that had been in his shop on Monday were locksmiths.

You seem to know these four men, what are they – what is their business?
Lockmakers – they make locks and do general jobs.
What we call locksmiths, are they not?
Yes.
All of them?
Yes. They told me that. I do not know.

The fact that Schmuss was a locksmith raises the suspicion
58

that he might have been able to lock the door, somehow leaving the key inside the room.

Isaac Schmuss's evidence was given through the interpreter. Lipski's statement, of course, had implicated Schmuss in the crime. Mathews conducted the examination.

Do you come from Elizabethan Graff, near Odessa?
Yes, in Russia.
Up to recently have you been working at 42 Gough Street, Birmingham?
Yes. I am lodging at that place in Birmingham.
And did you work in Ince Street, Birmingham?
Yes.
Are you a locksmith by trade?
Yes.
But have you been recently employed as a slipper maker?
Yes.
Did you come to England about seven or eight months ago?
Yes.
Among other places did you go to Mr Schmidt's in Backchurch Lane in the hope of finding employment?
Yes, and also to work at jobs.
Did you meet there with other Russian Jews?
Yes.
Was Totakoski one?
Yes.
Barsook another?
Yes.
And also Robinski?
Yes.
Do you remember being at Mr Schmidt's shop on a Monday afternoon?
Yes.
Were you there with Totakoski and other persons?
Yes.

Could one of these persons have been Rosenbloom, even though Mathews left the impression by his line of questioning that it was Robinski?

Whilst there, did the prisoner come in?
Yes.
Did he speak to you, or to you all, as you stood there?
59

Yes.

What did he say?

He asked where they came from, and what trade they were – he asked what they were, and whether they wanted work.

What trade did you say you were?

I said I was a locksmith.

What did the prisoner say to that?

'Do you think you can file sticks?'

What did you say?

I said 'I will see, I never filed them, I will try'; he said 'Come with me and I will show you the door, and tomorrow you will come to me, and I will engage you.'

Upon that did you go with him to the door of number sixteen Batty Street?

Yes.

And there did the prisoner tell you to come the next morning?

Yes.

At what time?

About eight.

Schmuss then described the events of 28 June.

Do you remember going next morning, Tuesday, the 28th, to Schmidt's?

Yes.

At what time?

Eight o'clock.

Was Totakoski there?

No, he had not come.

Totakoski later gave evidence that he had arranged to meet Schmuss there, but Schmuss did not show up at Schmidt's until noon.

Did you wait there a little time?

Yes.

And then did you go to number sixteen where you had been shown the day before by the prisoner?

Yes, I waited fifteen minutes and then went to the door there.

About what time was it that you got to the door?

It must be about a quarter past eight.

Was the door open or closed?

It was open.

Did you go into the passage?

60

As I came to the door, the man came to me.
Which man?
Lipski, the stickmaker.
Is that the man [the prisoner]?
Yes.
You had some conversation with him, tell us what.
He said to me, 'You shall go upstairs, wait a little, and I will come upstairs and then I will give you something to do.'
Where did he then go?
I don't know.
How was he dressed at that time?
I did not know how it was.
Well, where did you go?
I went upstairs.
When you got upstairs, did you go to the top of the house?
Yes.
And in the room upstairs did you find two persons, a man and a boy?
Yes. (Rosenbloom and Pitman were called in.)
Were they the two?
Yes.
Did you speak to Rosenbloom?
I did not speak much to him.
What did you speak to him, in what language was it?
In Yiddish.
How long did you remain there?
Ten or fifteen minutes.
Did the prisoner come into the room while you were there?
No.
Which of the three first left the room, you, the boy, or Rosenbloom?
The boy.

Schmuss thus disagrees with Rosenbloom's evidence that Schmuss and Rosenbloom were never alone in the attic.

How long did you stay after the boy left?
About a minute's time, not more.
And then did you leave?
I went to eat my breakfast.

Why did Schmuss, who was very poor and obviously needed work, not wait for Lipski to return?

That same day did you return to Mr Schmidt's?
Yes.

61

What time was it that you went there?
About twelve midday.
While you were there, did Totakoski come in?
Yes.
Did you return after that at all to sixteen Batty Street?
No, I did not.
While you were at Schmidt's, did you first hear that the woman was dead? When was it that you first heard that the woman was dead?
Mr Schmidt told me.
When?
When I came there.
That was about twelve?
Yes.

McIntyre's cross-examination did not shake Schmuss's testimony. Indeed, McIntyre barely cross-examined the witness. The entire cross-examination – once again, adopting the polite, deferential manner used in examining Rosenbloom – was as follows:

Is slipper making a new trade to you, or an old trade?
Only since I went to Birmingham.
Do you speak English?
No.
Not at all?
Not at all.
Not a word?
I can say not one word.
Did not you see the prisoner at all after you left the shop on the morning of the 28th?

An experienced criminal lawyer would not refer to his client as 'the prisoner'.

No, I had not seen him.
Did not you yourself go into the room that belonged to Mrs Angel?
What Mrs Angel? I did not go in.
The first floor in the house where you went to work?
I went in nowhere.
Were you not standing in the doorway of her room when Lipski was coming up the stairs?
No, I was not there, I was nowhere.
You were not with Rosenbloom?
No.

Did you know Rosenbloom?

I saw him once, then I saw him for the first time.

Do you mean that you never saw him till you saw him in Lipski's room?

I saw him never more I saw him the first time there. [*sic*]

Mr McIntyre: *My lord, I do not propose to go through all the same cross-examination as with the last witness, as this man denies being there at all.*

Mr Justice Stephen: *No, there is no use in doing that.*

Once again McIntyre failed to cross-examine a key witness on the crucial issue in the case.

Mr McIntyre: *Have you been brought up as a locksmith?*

Yes, I learnt it at home.

Before you went to Birmingham, did you hear that Lipski was taken up by the police?

Yes.

Did you hear it the very day that you had been to Lipski's place?

Yes.

Did you hear of the inquiries before the magistrate?

Where is the magistrate?

Well, by the judge?

Yes, I heard it by the newspaper.

You heard it from the paper, did you, before you went to Birmingham?

I can't read.

Did you have it read to you?

Mr Schmidt told me that they had locked him up.

Did you hear that he was to be taken before the magistrate?

I did not hear that.

Can you fix the day when you say you went to Birmingham?

Yes.

What day was it?

Sunday night.

But how long after you had been at Lipski's?

Eight days, or ten days.

Was it the Sabbath, or Sunday?

Sunday night.

Up to that time were you seeing Mr Schmidt every day?

Yes.

Why did not you go back after you had had your breakfast?

I saw that I should not have a great chance of work there, so I did not come back.

McIntyre did not ask any questions about why Schmuss did not wait at Batty Street for more than ten or fifteen minutes, or where he was for the rest of the morning.

Leah Lipski, the landlady, gave evidence that she saw Lipski at about eight thirty in the morning, when he asked her to fetch his coffee and also tried to borrow money from her. Lipski's request for money was, of course, used by the Crown to suggest one possible motive for entering Mrs Angel's room. Mathews continued the examination in English.

What did he say?
He asked me for five shillings.
What more?
I said I had not got it.
What more?
I said, 'I have not got it. Go to your young girl's mother, she lends you so much she will lend you the five shillings too,' and he said to me, 'I am ashamed to go to her, she only gave me last night twenty-five shillings.'

She then went to a neighbouring shop to have her coffee pot filled, as she did every morning.

You brought it back and got back to the house about what time?
About twenty minutes I was away.
That would bring you back somewhere about ten minutes to nine?
Yes.
What did you do with the coffee?
I put the coffee pot on the table and went to call him down.
Who?
Israel Lipski, the prisoner. I called out, 'Come down and have your coffee.'
Was there any answer at all the first time you called?
No.
You called a second time, did you?
Yes, and the boy answered, 'He ain't here.'
Then you had your breakfast?
Yes.
And sent your children off to school?
Yes.
And was it about half past nine your mother, Mrs Rubenstein, came down?

Yes.

She lodged in the same room with Mrs Levy?

Yes.

The coffee was still on the table, was it?

Yes.

The coffee remained in the same place?

Yes.

About ten did you go out with Mrs Levy to shop in Petticoat Lane?

Yes.

Had you seen the prisoner up to the time you left at ten o'clock?

No.

The coffee was in the same place?

Yes.

And you left with Mrs Levy about ten?

Just ten.

Between the time you returned and ten that morning, had you seen anybody come in or leave the house?

I could not say. I was busy with my children for school, I did not see anybody.

You were away about an hour in Petticoat Lane?

Just an hour.

You came back with Mrs Levy, therefore, somewhere about eleven?

Yes.

When you came back, did you see your mother?

I saw my mother sitting on a chair in the passage outside in the street.

The landlady's evidence hurt Lipski. Why did Lipski not drink the coffee that the landlady got for him? Where was he from nine to ten o'clock?

The landlady then described the finding of the body. Mrs Dinah Angel, the deceased's mother-in-law, came to the house about eleven o'clock and went upstairs looking for her daughter-in-law. Mrs Angel called down and was joined by the landlady and Mrs Levy. Mathews continued the examination:

And in consequence of that you went upstairs?

I threw everything down and ran upstairs.

In what condition was the door of Mrs Angel's room?

I did not try the door. I only looked through the little window.

You went up beyond the first floor and looked through the little window. Could you see through from the staircase?

Yes.

Was there any curtain over it at that time?

A muslin curtain.

Could you see through the curtain?

I saw a little like fainting she was. She was lying like fainting she looked to me.

Mrs Angel?

Yes.

Did you then come down to the first-floor landing?

Yes.

What did you three do?

I burst open the door.

Was the door fastened or open?

This was, of course, one of the central issues in the trial.

I did not try much about the door because Mrs Levy said it was locked.

Did you burst the door open?

The three of us.

The three of you altogether?

Yes.

Was the door locked at that time before you burst it open?

I did not try so much.

But having to burst it open, the three of you, did you do it together?

Yes.

Was it fastened?

Yes, shut.

Was she lying on her back or how?

Sideways.

Were the bed clothes over the whole of her or was any portion of her person exposed?

Half over.

Was any portion of her body exposed?

I did not see.

Mr Justice Stephen: *I thought you said part of her was exposed?*

Half covered.

Then was the other half uncovered?

Yes.

Cross-examination by McIntyre brought out Lipski's good character and the fact that the Angels did not have any money.

The prisoner has been lodging with you for nearly two years?

Yes.

Was he a steady, respectable young man?

Yes.

And always bore a good character with everyone?

Yes.

Was Mrs Angel the very day before obliged to borrow money to pay her rent?

Yes.

Borrowed five shillings to pay you her rent?

Yes, from Mrs Levy.

McIntyre tried to elicit information from the witness that the new lock did not fit well; he was not successful, but he did get evidence that a hole had been left where the old lock had been, thus suggesting that the door could have been locked from the outside.

Was not the box of the lock higher than the lock itself?

No, it would just fit, the two of them.

Do you recollect the old lock being on before the present lock was put on. Is this correct: 'Where the old lock had been a hole was left large enough for three fingers and the box of the lock was higher than the lock itself'?

Yes.

Is that correct?

Yes.

Is this correct: 'With the key inside I could catch the key from the outside through the hole left from the old lock'?

Yes, you could just touch it.

Once again, Stephen took over the cross-examination.

Mr Justice Stephen: *Could you have locked it from the outside?*

No.

When the key was inside you could not, by putting your hand through the hole, lock it from the outside?

I could not.

All you mean is that when you were outside the door you could put your hand through and touch it?

Yes.

But not enough to lock it?

Not by the fingers.

Further cross-examination established that Lipski had a silver watch and a gold chain, both of which had been pawned.

67

The landlady possessed the pawn ticket for the gold chain, no doubt because Lipski owed her money.

Mrs Levy's evidence confirmed the landlady's testimony, adding the fact that she, Mrs Levy, had looked through the keyhole and saw the key inside in the lock before the three of them pushed the door open.

Mrs Dinah Angel stated that her daughter-in-law usually came to her for breakfast 'sometimes at half past eight, sometimes at nine', never later. She had arrived at Batty Street at about eleven and went upstairs with Mrs Levy. The landlady, she testified, was not there when she and Mrs Levy broke open the door after looking through the side window; Mrs Levy had already tried the handle and said, 'The key is inside.' Mr Mathews, through the interpreter, continued the examination.

How did you get the door open?
We knocked it mostly with the hand.
What way?
With force with the hand.
Was Mrs Lipski there at that time?
No, only Mrs Levy.
Who went into the room first?
Me and Mrs Levy, both together.
When you got into the room did you see your daughter-in-law?
I and Mrs Levy ran to the bed and I thought she was fainting, she laid with her hands so, with her head aside and we put her hands in front and moved her head thinking she was fainting. I then saw she was dead and went out and created an alarm.
Did you see how she was lying on the bed?
On her side, her hands behind, and uncovered.
What part of her was uncovered?
The whole.
How was her night dress or chemise?
Up.

Mrs Rubenstein, the landlady's mother, who was almost blind, gave evidence that she remained in or just outside the house when her daughter and Mrs Levy left to go shopping. McIntyre brought out in cross-examination that she had her hands full looking after the children and thus might not have seen strangers leaving the house.

Did not one of the children run away to the back?
Yes, and went into the yard.
You had some trouble in catching the child, had you not?
Yes, I was afraid it had run away.
And were you in the back yard some time looking after the child and trying to catch it?
Only a few minutes, I did not take particular notice, I did not think I should be asked about it.
You cannot tell how long it was?
I do not know.

Another witness confirmed that Mrs Rubenstein was sitting outside the house when he came at nine thirty or ten o'clock to pick up some boots that the Angels were repairing for him, but Mrs Rubenstein would not let him in.

Harris Dywein, a general dealer, whose shop was round the corner from Batty Street, knew the Angels and, hearing shouts, came to the house shortly after the body was discovered. He went in to the Angels' room and saw the deceased lying on her back with her face towards the wall and her hair 'disarranged all over the bed'. The examination continued.

Did you notice anything on the right side of her face?
Yes, there were several marks here, I could not tell whether scratches or not.
How was her chemise or night dress?
It was right up, up to the breast, just here. (Describing)
Was her person exposed?
Yes.
Were there any signs of struggle in the room?
No, I could not see any signs of struggle.
Did you cover her up in some way?
Yes.
After you had done that, did Mr Piper, Dr Kay's assistant, come?

Dywein then described how Piper cleared the room. Piper, he said, took the key with some difficulty from the inside of the lock, after first turning the bolt back. Piper then locked the door from the outside.

Dywein testified that he came back into the room shortly after this with Piper and Dr Kay.

When you got back was something said about a bottle?
Yes.
That was said by Dr Kay?
Yes.
In consequence of that, what did you do?
We were looking for a bottle.
Mr Justice Stephen: *You looked for a bottle?*
Yes, and Mr Piper and Dr Kay said we should take everything from underneath the bed. We took away from underneath the bed an old coat.
You did yourself?
Yes.
What did you do?
Took away from underneath the bed an old coat, and then pulled away an old egg box, several old clothes were in that, and Mr Piper and Dr Kay said, 'Is there anything underneath the bed'? I looked underneath the bed and said 'There is something underneath the bedstead'; and Mr Piper or Dr Kay, one or the other, said 'Go and see what it is.' I laid down and felt like a hand; while I was coming back Dr Kay jumped on the bed and took away the pillow which was towards the wall and said 'Why, it is a man.' So he told me I should call for the police. [*sic*]
Mr Mathews: *At that point was anything done to the bedstead?*
The bedstead was pulled away.
What did the doctor do to the prisoner in your presence?
Slapped his face; he felt his pulse and then slapped his face.
Mr Justice Stephen: *How was the prisoner got out from under the bed?*
He was lifted up by two constables.
Afterwards . . . ?
Mr Mathews: *Was he still on the ground where the doctor had first seen him when the doctor felt his pulse and slapped his face?*
Yes, still on the ground.
Mr Justice Stephen: *You felt a man's hand?*
Yes.
Dr Kay jumped on the bed, threw off some of the bed clothes and said 'Why, it is a man'?
Yes.

Tell us particularly how the man was found after that, what was done, who it was who did it, and how he was brought out?

He was lying on his back and his shirt sleeves were tucked up, his guernsey sleeve was down, his waistcoat was unbuttoned.

Mr Mathews: *Had he any coat on?*

No.

Had he any boots on?

Yes.

You say he was lying there, in what condition did he seem? In what state?

He was like unconscious.

Lipski's condition was an important issue at the trial. Was he, in fact, unconscious or was he, as the Crown would suggest, faking insensibility? There was considerable controversy on this question after the trial.

Then Dr Kay told you to call a constable, and you went to the window; you could not get it open because it was so tight?

The bottom window.

Then you called the constables over the top of the window and they came in?

They came into the room.

What did they do when they came?

They lifted him up and . . .

And brought him where?

Dr Kay told him 'Look what you have been doing to the poor body.

Obviously, Dr Kay had instantly concluded that Lipski was guilty.

Where did they put him?

Held him against the wall.

Leaving him still between the bed and wall?

No, just took him in the corner; they just lifted him into the corner.

They lifted him out from behind the bed?

Yes.

And put him up in a corner?

Yes.

Now go on.

Mr Mathews: *Could he stand when they put him in the corner?*

71

I could not tell that because the two constables were still holding his hands.

They still held him?

Yes.

Then?

Then Dr Kay told the constables to take him to the station.

Mr Justice Stephen: *What did Dr Kay do to the man?*

He slapped his face when he was lying on the ground.

Mr Mathews: *And felt his pulse?*

Before he slapped his face.

Mr Justice Stephen: *Did the man speak?*

No, he did not speak much.

Not after his face was slapped?

No, he opened his eyes, he never spoke.

With regard to the bottle spoken of by Dr Kay; you were told to look for it under the bed in the first instance; you looked for it there. Did you find it there?

No.

Were you present when it was found?

Yes.

Who found it?

The bottle was seen by a constable. I pulled the bed off, prevented the bed falling down from the bedstead, I put the feather bed on the bedstead so I found the bottle as it was lying and showed it to the constable.

Did you see it before the constable, or the constable before you?

I saw it before the constable.

Where was it when you first saw it?

On the bed.

Where on the bed?

Just the middle part of the bed.

Was it on the wall side or on the room side?

On the wall side.

And about the middle of the bed, do you say?

Yes.

Mr Justice Stephen: *I understood you to say it was under some part of the bed clothes?*

When we pulled the bedstead away for Dr Kay to come in there to see the man, the feather bed fell away and then I saw the bottle.

You lifted up the feather bed and then you saw the bottle under the feather bed?

72

Yes, my lord.
It was a bottle without a cork?
Yes.

No fingerprints were taken. The technique of fingerprinting
was not used by Scotland Yard until 1901. Today, fingerprint
evidence, as well as other scientific evidence, such as
identification of blood, hair fibres and spermatazoa, would play
a key role in the solution of a similar murder.[1]

McIntyre's cross-examination tried to link Rosenbloom with
the finding of the bottle.

Before you went into the room, were other people in it?
Yes.
About how many?
I could not tell you, sir.
Was Rosenbloom there?
I can not tell you.
Did not you see him there?
I did not see him in the room.
Did Dr Kay say there must be a bottle somewhere?
Yes.
Then did Dr Kay and Mr Piper tell you to look under the bed?
Yes.
And then did you and Simon [Rosenbloom] look under the bed?
Yes.
Then he was there?
Yes, afterwards.
At any rate before the bottle was found, Simon was there?
Yes, the first time I entered into the room I did not see Simon
there.
*At all events he was there before the bottle was found. Did not Simon
hand the bottle to the doctor?*
No.
Did not you see Simon with the bottle at all?
No.

Dr Kay's assistant, William Piper, gave evidence that he had
been stopped in the street shortly after the body was found.

*You were stopped in the street; you went there at once? What time did
you get to the house?*
About half past eleven.

73

Did you go at once upstairs?
Yes.
Did you go into the front bedroom on the first floor?
Yes.
At that time can you tell me who were in the room?
Dywein, the last witness, and Rosenbloom and two or three women and perhaps another man.
Did you see the woman lying on the bed?
Yes.
Describe her position.
She was lying on her back with her head inclined to the right, with her right arm more or less over her breast.
Her parts exposed?
Yes.
The chemise?
Drawn up.
Rolled up so that you could see the lower parts exposed?
Yes.

He then described his actions in locking the door.

When you went to the door to leave the room, did you see the lock and the key of the door?
Yes.
Where was the key?
On the inside, in the lock.
Did you take it out?
Yes.
Did you see whether the bolt of the lock had been shot – whether it was fastened?
I did not find that out until I got outside the door.
You took the key out and then went to shut the door?
Yes.
Then did you find the lock had been locked so that the bolt was shot?
Yes.
So that it had been shot?
Yes.
Did that prevent you from shutting the door completely?
Yes.
Mr Justice Stephen: *Did you unlock it?*
It had a queer look so I went back and unlocked it from inside.

74

Piper then gave evidence that Rosenbloom was the person who found the bottle.

Did you see who actually found it?
Well, it was not exactly found, it was pointed out by Rosenbloom to the constable.
Where was it then lying?
In one of the folds of the feather bed.
We have heard it had no cork, and it was taken possession of?
Yes, I put a cork in.
Who took it?
Dr Kay took it.
Did you look at it at the time?
Yes, we both had a look at it, and smelt it.
Was there any stuff in it?
Yes, just a little.

The first policeman to appear on the scene, Arthur Sack, described taking Lipski from under the bed and finding the bottle.

Did he seem to be conscious at this time?
He seemed to know a little.
How were his eyes, opened or closed?
They were open when we lifted him up.
After you assisted him up, what happened to him?
He fell down backwards again.
In consequence of what the doctor said, did you get a cab and take him first to Dr Kay's, and then to the police station?
Yes.
And afterwards to the London Hospital?
Yes.
And leave him there in charge of a police constable?
Yes.
Did he speak during the whole of this time?
No.
Did he seem to be in pain?
No, he did not seem to be in pain.
He was asked his name, was he not?
Yes, and he wrote it down.
He wrote the name of Lipski?
Yes.
When was that?

When he was in the hospital.
How long after you had left sixteen Batty Street?
About three quarters of an hour.
Were you present when the bottle was found?
Yes.
Who actually picked it up from the bed?
Dr Kay.
Or was it Dywein?
Dr Kay.

On cross-examination Sack stated that Harris Dywein pointed out the bottle to Dr Kay.

Another policeman, Alfred Inwood, who had been called to the scene, gave evidence about Lipski's coat.

Where did you find that?
I found that at the foot of the bed near the wall, underneath the bed on the floor.
Was anything over it?
There was another coat over it, a newer coat.
Look at the coat that was over it. (This was handed to the witness.)
That is the coat, the coat that was covered over.
The newer coat was lying on the other coat, the other coat being on the floor?
Yes.
Did you see anything the matter with the good coat at the time?
I did not notice anything particularly the matter; I noticed it was lying as if it had been laid down, as if it had not fallen.

The leaseholder of the house, Charles Peters, described how, a few weeks before the murder, he had put on a 'brand new lock, and a very good lock'; that he had been doing those type of repairs for almost twenty years; and that he was satisfied that it was 'in perfectly good and working order'.

The final witness that day was a person from across the street who gave evidence that he did not see anything unusual occurring. He saw Lipski only once.

Did you see him go in or out of the house that morning?
Once that morning.
About what time was that?
I should think about a quarter to nine, sir.
Did he then go into the house?

76

He had his hat and coat on.
Was he going in or coming out?
Going in.
Hat and coat on?
Yes.
Was he carrying anything at the time?
He had a little, small parcel, very small.
After that hour you did not see him come out?
Never saw him after.

The trial was then adjourned until Saturday morning at ten o'clock. The jury were not allowed to separate overnight, but were 'locked up' at the nearby Cannon Street Hotel.[2] The Jews in the public gallery walked home sadly to 'celebrate' the approaching Sabbath.

The corner of Batty Street and Commercial Road today. The doorway to
Dr Kay's surgery is still visible.

Chapter Four

The Trial: The Second Day

EVEN MORE PEOPLE than on the previous day – mainly Jews whose shops were closed on the Sabbath – came to the Old Bailey for the second day of the trial. Lipski was brought into court. Throughout the proceedings, according to the newspaper reports, he looked calm, but showed anxiety by the constant twitching of his fingers and lips.[1] The jurors were called, each answering to his name, and the second day of the trial began.

The first witness called by Mr Mathews was Inspector David Final of the Metropolitan Police.

On 28th June this year, about a quarter to one, was the prisoner brought to Leman Street police station?
Yes.
In what condition was he at the time?
He appeared to be partially insensible.
Was he seen by Mr Phillips, the divisional surgeon?
Yes.
And after that was some mustard and warm water given?
Yes. I gave him some and Dr Phillips ordered him some afterwards.
It had not the effect of making him sick?
No.
After that, was it, you searched him?
Yes.
What did you find on him?
Two shillings or three shillings in silver, and some coppers and a pawn ticket.
What became of that pawn ticket?
I put it back in his pocket and the money.
And he was then sent to the London Hospital?
Yes.
And did you yourself go to sixteen Batty Street?
I did.

Did you go into the room and examine the lock?
Yes, I did.
Did you notice anything about the box of the lock?
Yes, the screws were about a quarter of an inch drawn from the wood, as if the door had been forced.
How was the wood at that time?
Split.
As it now is?
Yes.
What was the condition of the lock?
In perfect order except that the bolt was shot.

It is not clear why the bolt (the sliding piece of the lock) would still be shot, that is, extended beyond the door in a locked position, considering that Mr Piper had already locked and then unlocked the door from the outside to let Dr Kay in.

Later on did Police Constable Inwood bring you this coat and hat?
Yes.
You searched the coat pockets?
Yes.
In one of them did you find anything?
Yes.
What?
'J. Lipski, United Stick and Cane Dressers Protection Society', and a pawn ticket for a silver Geneva watch pawned in the name of John Lipski on 23rd June, and the amount six shillings – Merdle Street.

Final then described going to the hospital about seven thirty that evening along with Sergeant Thick and the interpreter, Smedge, and taking a statement from Lipski. A further statement was taken at the Arbour Square police station the following Saturday, 2 July, after Lipski was officially charged with the murder.

McIntyre in cross-examination asked about Lipski's condition when he was first brought to the Leman Street station on the 28th.

When you first saw the prisoner on the 28th of June was he insensible?
Partially so.
When he was brought to your station, did he not appear to be insensible?
Partially so. I will explain it. I slapped his face and he
80

acknowledged it, and then I gave him an emetic, mustard and water, and he was not sick, and I also opened his eye and touched the pupil and he acknowledged it.

On your oath before the magistrate, did you swear he appeared insensible?

Partially so.

You did not say 'partially'?

The word 'partially' was not put in.

That was in examination-in-chief to the gentleman conducting the prosecution, you swore that he appeared insensible?

I say so now.

No, you qualify it now, 'partially'.

Yes, partially.

Mr Justice Stephen: *He qualifies it, he says about opening the eye and slapping the face.*

Again, the judge intervened during an important part of the cross-examination. Inspector Final was then asked how the statement in the hospital came about.

You took the interpreter with the intention of getting a statement from the prisoner?

Yes, I had been told he wished to make one.

Who told you that?

Miss Lyons, his young lady; she came to the police station.

Although the police had not charged Lipski, he was obviously their prime suspect and, according to Inspector Final, would not have been allowed to leave the hospital.

The interpreter, Smedge, was now called to prove the circumstances surrounding the taking and translating of the two statements. In both cases the interpreter claimed to have cautioned Lipski, stating on the first occasion: 'You are not bound to say anything, but what you do say will be taken down in writing by the Inspector and may be used as evidence against you at your trial.'

McIntyre's cross-examination brought out the fact that at the magistrates' court the interpreter had not said that the evidence would be used 'at your trial', but only that 'what you say will be put down'.

Whether McIntyre was trying to have the statement excluded on this technical basis is not clear. Then, as now, statements had to be voluntary before being admitted. Indeed at that time it was easier to have a confession excluded than today. No mention is made in the transcript or in any newspaper report that Mr McIntyre attempted to have either statement excluded. It would have been surprising if he had done so because both denied the accused's guilt. One wonders, therefore, what the point of the cross-examination was.

Inspector Final was then recalled to introduce the two statements. Mr Justice Stephen took up the questioning.

Mr Justice Stephen: *Is this a copy of what you are going to read? Is it?*

Yes.

Of what was taken at the bedside at the hospital? Will you read it, what you took down at the bedside translated to you as the prisoner having said?

The trial transcript then notes that the statement that Final was about to read 'was translated to the prisoner sentence by sentence', implying the none of the other evidence given in English at the trial was translated into Yiddish for Lipski, thus making it impossible for him adequately to instruct his counsel on much of the Crown's evidence. Inspector Final read Lipski's statement (previously set out in Chapter One), which also included some further interrogation by Inspector Final.

At seven am a man working for me came. He asked me for work. I told him to wait. I would buy a vice for him so as he could work. I went to purchase a vice. I went to the shop but it was too soon. As I was going along I met another workman whom I knew at the corner of Backchurch Lane. I went back; the shopkeeper wanted four shillings, I offered him three shillings, he would not take it. I returned and came into the passage, and I saw the man that I met in Backchurch Lane. He asked me, 'Will you give me work or not?' I said, 'Go to the workshop. I am going to get my breakfast, then I will give you work.' I then told my landlady to make some coffee. I then told a man [meaning the first man] that called at seven am to fetch some brandy. I then went to the yard. I went upstairs to the first floor. I then saw both these men. I saw them open a box; they took hold of me by the throat and threw me to the ground; there on the ground opened my mouth and put in some poison, and said, 'That is the brandy.' They got my hands behind me and asked me if I had any money. 'I have got no more than the sovereign that I gave you to get the brandy with.' He then asked, 'Where is your gold chain?' I said 'It is in pawn.' They said, 'If you don't give it to us you will be as dead as the woman.' They put a piece of wood in my mouth. I struggled; they put their knees against my throat. One said to the other 'Don't you think he is quite dead.' The reply was, 'He don't want any more.' They then threw me under the bed and there I lay for dead.
Do you know who those two men are?

I know one who formerly worked with me.
Do you know his name and where he lives?
His name is Simon, I don't know where he lives.
Do you know anything of the other man?
I don't know him, he is a stranger to me.
Is his name Simon Rosenbloom?
I can't say.
Do you know if Simon lives in Philpot Street?
I think so. I have nothing further to say.

Mr Justice Stephen then asked Inspector Final about the second statement on the following Saturday at the police station.

Mr Justice Stephen: *What question did Mr Smedge ask him at the police station? Will you say what question Mr Smedge asked him at the police station? You read over the charge to him at the police station?*
Yes.
And cautioned him?
Yes.
What did he say in reply to that?
He said, 'I have not murdered her, and I have not done it.'
Did he speak in Hebrew or English?
He said '*Ich habe nicht gehalhret, ich habe nicht getahren*' – 'I have not murdered her, I have not done it.'

Dr Kay, who practised at the corner of Commercial Road and Batty Street, described his activities after he was called to 16 Batty Street on 28 June.

On the bed, did you see the woman lying there?
Yes.
Just describe what position she was in.
She was lying on her back, dead, with her hair dishevelled.
Her mouth?
Her mouth had a stream of yellow coming from the corner on the left-hand side.
Her neck?
Her neck had two or three splashes, her breast had a splash.
Her hands?
Her hands were covered with the stains of nitric acid.
What were they, those yellow stains, what were they?
Nitric acid.
Commonly called aqua fortis?
Yes.

Mr Justice Stephen: *Her hands were covered with it, you say?*
Yes, covered with it.

Mr Poland: *How was she covered?*
She was covered up to her breast with one of the German feather beds.

Did you remove that?
I turned it down to see if any violence had been offered to her.

How was the body, exposed? How was the chemise?
The chemise was pulled up to the breast and the body was exposed.

Besides the marks of the acid in the places you have mentioned, did you notice any marks of blood anywhere?
I noticed blood on the feather bed, splashes of blood and acid mixed.

Would the effect of the administration of this stuff cause a person to cough?
Yes.

Violently?
Very violently.

There were no marks of violence on the body, the lower parts?
No marks of violence.

On the person at all. Did you form an opinion at that time as to how long she had been dead?
I formed an opinion about three hours.

Was the body cold?
Not quite cold.

Had what is termed 'rigor mortis' set in?
It was absent, no rigor mortis.

Supposing about three hours, were you able to say with any degree of certainty as to the time?
It must be pretty near it.

What sort of habit was she, stout woman or thin woman?
Stout woman.

You have taken into consideration the state of the room, and the weather, and her condition of body in forming your opinion as to the three hours?
Yes.

Did you notice on her face at all at that time any marks?
No, not at that time, except the mark on it of the acid.

Dr Kay testified that he pulled the bedcover away from the

84

wall in search of the bottle, but discovered Lipski lying on his back.

The prisoner?
The prisoner lying on his back.
Could you see him without moving anything?
Yes.
In what state did he appear to be?
He was in his shirt sleeves; he looked pale, and his eyes were partially open; you could see the white of his eye and part of the pupil.
What did you do to him?
I felt his pulse and then I said, 'He is alive.' Then I put my finger on the cornea to see if he was unconscious, and he was unconscious.
And then?
Then I slapped him on the face, and he opened his eyes wide.
At that time did he say anything to you?
No, sir.
What took place then?
I called for police to help me out with him, out of the corner, near the window.
How was he got out, was he lifted out?
On each side of him – took hold of his arm and pulled him out. The bed was pulled round and he was taken round the end.
Pulled round on the floor?
Yes.
Bare floorboards?
Yes, boards.
Pulled him near the window?
Yes.
What was next done?
I looked in his mouth and saw he had taken some of the nitric acid – not so much as the woman.
Mr Justice Stephen: *What position did the police put him in after getting him round the bed?*
They held him up standing.
Did he fall down again?
No, the police had hold of him.
Mr Poland: *Did you notice anything more about him then?*
I asked him some questions, and shook him, but he did not answer anything.

Did you ask him in English or German?
Both.
Can you tell whether he could understand what you said to him then?
I don't think he could.
Then did the police take charge of him?
The police took him.

A post mortem examination of Mrs Angel was later made by
Dr Kay. He found no evidence of recent intercourse.

Afterwards did you make a post mortem examination?
Yes.
A well-developed young woman?
Yes, a well-developed woman.
About six months gone in the family way?
Yes.
On the lower part of the body you saw no signs of violence?
Yes.
No signs of recent connection?
No.
*You saw some discharge, that was the natural . . . What was the date
of the post mortem?*
Next day, Wednesday the 29th.

The post mortem examination revealed that there had been
violent blows to the head.

What did you notice about the right eye?
That it was discoloured black and swelled.
What else?
I noticed this yellow stain at the corner of the mouth.
As to external injuries?
No other external injuries.
Did you examine the scalp?
Then I reflected back the scalp and saw over the right temple
extraversated blood.
You cut the scalp and turned it back?
Yes.
In what state was the muscle?
The muscle was lacerated and bloody, and in a pulp from
violent blows.
*Could you tell whether the violence . . . do you say whether more than
one blow?*
Must have been more than one blow.

And were they such that they might have been given with a man's fist?
Yes.
How many blows, could you judge at all?
I should think at least four blows.
What sort of blows?
Very violent blows.
Was the brain congested?
No, sir.
Does that come on at once from violent blows?
Not immediately, it must have time.
Could you tell from the appearance of those blows whether she would be rendered unconscious?
She would be rendered unconscious by such blows.
How would you describe it?
She would be stunned.

Dr Kay's post mortem examination indicated that the nitric acid had been administered when Mrs Angel was unconscious. A portion of the acid had 'gone into the stomach' and another portion had gone 'down the windpipe', indicating, according to Dr Kay, 'that it had been poured down her throat while she was insensible'.

Where would the greater portion of the acid appear to have gone?
The greater portion appeared to have gone down the windpipe.
Could you at all estimate the amount of stuff – acid – at all?
Approximate estimate about half an ounce.

The quantity of acid administered was a matter of considerable controversy after the trial.

And her hands?
They were stained with the acid.
Whereabouts?
All over the back and front, all over.
Now what was the cause of death?
Suffocation.
Was that produced by the acid acting on the . . . ?
Acting on the windpipe.
Would that be acid acting on the windpipe and closing the passage for the air?
Yes.
How would it act? Would it produce convulsion of those parts?

87

Great convulsion.

And how soon after the administration would it close the windpipe?

About three minutes.

Dr Kay confirmed in cross-examination that there was no evidence of recent intercourse. McIntyre's questioning concentrated on Lipski's condition when he was found.

I believe the post mortem examination you made completely convinced you that there had been no recent connection?

That and putting the discharge under a microscope.

You came to the conclusion there had been no recent connection?

No evidence of it.

You say the man did not understand you, was unconscious, was that from the effect of poison also?

No, not from the poison. I attributed it to mental perturbation.

Surely a man who does not flinch when you put your finger in his eye must have been unconscious?

He was not very unconscious, a slap roused him.

Mr Justice Stephen: *Do you say a man from mental causes could be thrown into such a state that you could put your finger in his eye without his flinching?*

I have seen a woman that I could put my finger on the cornea, I don't remember a man.

I suppose if a man was both in a state of mental perturbation and had drunk a certain quantity of nitric acid, one would help the other to make him unconscious?

Yes, but the nitric acid was not sufficient in my opinion to cause unconsciousness.

You saw this man about twelve o'clock, I understand, between that and one.

Mr McIntyre: *About a quarter to twelve.*

Mr Justice Stephen: *There had been a quantity of people in the room and a good deal of noise; for how long would a mere fainting fit – what is the longest period that you have ever known a man remaining unconscious from mental causes, or a woman?*

I frequently have known a woman remain unconscious from mental causes for two hours in spite of all restoratives, mustard plasters, and ammonia.

That is a long time?

Yes, but I have known them.

What about men?

I have not seen a man unconscious from mental causes.

Mr McIntyre: *Suppose this man had been seized, and men had knelt on his chest, would that have produced, with the poison that was taken, such unconsciousness as you saw him under?*

Violence would tend to produce unconsciousness.

William Calvert, the house surgeon at the London Hospital where Lipski was taken, said that he examined Lipski carefully shortly after he was brought in, to determine the extent of any injuries.

Did you see his fingers and his finger-nails?

Yes.

What did you find on them, if anything?

On the fingers of his left hand I saw some yellow stains, also on the nails of the left hand, and on the second joint of the . . .

Mr Justice Stephen: *Which fingers?*

Nearly all his fingers; I think also on the nails of the same left hand, and a slight stain on the second joint of the third finger of the right hand.

Mr Mathews: *Were they such stains as would be produced by nitric acid?*

Yes.

Did you notice anything more on the hands?

I noticed some trivial scratches on the backs of both of his hands.

Anything on one of the wrists?

A scratch larger than the rest.

On which wrist?

On the back of the right wrist.

Anything on the forearms?

There were some slight scratches on the forearms.

The elbows?

The skin was rubbed off both elbows, partially rubbed off, abraided.

The condition of Lipski's elbows also became the subject of controversy after the trial. Was the skin rubbed off Lipski's elbows because of an assault by Schmuss and Rosenbloom, or was it caused in some other way? Mathews then asked questions designed to show that Lipski had not been assaulted.

The forehead?

There were one or two slight scratches on the forehead, and notably one on the right temple.

Were the appearances you saw indicative of any serious violence of any kind?

I think not.

Did you examine the mouth?

Yes.

From your examination of the mouth, what opinion did you form?

I thought the injuries were produced by the application of some corrosive fluid.

Such as nitric acid?

Yes.

Were those injuries serious in their character?

No.

Did you examine the throat upon the outside?

I did.

No marks of violence upon it?

I found none.

Were there any marks of violence or of injury on the body beyond those you have given us?

None.

You have spoken about the injuries on the person. Were they such in your opinion as would prevent a man crying out?

There were not of such a nature I should think as to prevent a man crying out.

McIntyre then cross-examined the doctor about the abrasion on the inside of Lipski's mouth. Lipski, it will be recalled, had told the police. 'They put a piece of wood in my mouth.'

Now was there not an abrasion in the inside of the mouth?

Yes, there was.

Did that indicate to your mind that some foreign substance had been thrust into the mouth?

Yes.

On re-examination, Poland brought out the fact that the abrasion could have been caused by a stomach pump.

Whereabouts was it?

At the back part of the palate, back part of the mouth.

Was it in such a position that if a stomach pump had been used, it would have made a mark?

90

Yes, I should think in the condition of palate and condition of mouth, a stomach pump would have produced this injury because it was in the locality of one of the white patches, the mucous membrane was there softened.

Thomas Redmayne, another house physician at the London Hospital, gave evidence that around noon on 28 June he had used a stomach pump on Lipski.

Mr Justice Stephen: *Do you think it likely that you could have produced such an abrasion as was spoken of by the last witness?*
Very probably, yes; we had to use a gag to get his mouth open and he broke that.

Charles Moore, the manager of the shop in Backchurch Lane next door to Mark Schmidt's, described selling a bottle of nitric acid on the morning of the 28th.

On Tuesday the 28th of June, do you remember a man coming to your shop with a bottle?
Yes.
What sized bottle?
Two ounce phial.
A bottle similar to this? (Showing one to the witness.)
Yes, similar one to that.
You have seen the prisoner before the magistrate, to the best of your belief, is he the man who came with the bottle?
Yes, the prisoner is the man to the best of my belief that I served the nitric acid to, and that I saw before the magistrate.
About what time was it?
About nine o'clock in the morning.
What did he ask you for?
A pennyworth of aqua fortis.
What language did he speak in?
English.
He produced the bottle and did you supply him with the pennyworth of aqua fortis?
Yes.
About how much would that be?
About one ounce, I weighed it to him.

Could a single ounce of nitric acid have produced all the results described in the evidence?

Did you say anything to him about what it was wanted for?
I asked him for what purpose he wanted it.
What did he say?
He said he was a stickmaker, he wanted it for staining sticks.
And then did you say anything to him about it?
I cautioned him that it was poisonous.
Do you remember what you said to him?
That is what I said to him.
Did you wrap it up in anything?
The bottle?
Yes.
No.
He took it away?
Yes, just as it was.
You corked it and he took it away with him?
Yes.

On the Friday morning after the murder, Moore was taken to the London Hospital where he identified Lipski, a matter of considerable controversy after the trial. Was the identification fair or was it such that Moore would be steered to Lipski?

Were you taken into wards where there were a number of patients in the beds there? – that was the Friday.
Yes.
You went from bed to bed?
Yes.
Did you come to a bed where the prisoner was?
Yes.
What did you do when you came to that bed?
I pointed him out to the Inspector.
And had you previous to that given a description of the person who had made the purchases at your shop?
Yes.

McIntyre questioned the fairness of the identification in his cross-examination.

When you went to the hospital and into this ward, was there a police constable in plain clothes sitting at the head of this bed?
There was a man in plain clothes sitting by the side of the bed; I could not say whether he was a constable or not.
Was that the only bed in the room where a man was sitting by the side of the bed?

92

I believe so.

Were you in the ward about ten minutes?

Yes, about ten minutes.

Were you walking up and down the ward during that time?

I walked down once and back again.

You walked from one end to the other?

No, I walked as far as the prisoner's bed and back again.

Was his the end bed?

No, I think it was near the fireplace.

Did you not walk to the end of the ward?

No.

Was the Inspector with you when you went?

Yes.

He was in uniform?

Yes.

What did the man sitting at the head of the bed do when the Inspector came up to the bed with you?

Did he get up?

Yes.

I did not take any notice of that; I could not say positively whether he did or not.

You were taken there to identify the man who had bought the aqua fortis, were you?

Yes.

Were you told you would most likely see him there?

Yes.

Mr Justice Stephen: *Who told you that?*

I could not say whether it was the Inspector or the detective.

Mr McIntyre: *But either the Inspector or the detective told you that?*

Yes.

And you expected, of course, did you not, to find the man there when you went?

Yes.

At the time you sold this aqua fortis, were there many people in your shop?

About six people I should say.

Were you very busy at the time?

Yes.

Serving these people with different things?

Yes.

Do you sell all the things that are requisite for these stickmakers?

Yes.

Everything?
Yes.

Lipski's future mother-in-law, Anna Lyons, giving her evidence in English, described lending money to Lipski.

Have you a daughter named Kate?
Yes.
Was your daughter engaged to be married to the prisoner?
Yes, six months.
Do you remember the prisoner coming to your house on the Monday, the 27th of June?
Yes.
What time in the day did he come?
About one o'clock, to eat his dinner.
Did he say anything to you about money?
Yes, he said I shall be so kind enough as to lend him money, how much he did not say.
What did you say?
I said I got no money to lend him, I take borrow money [*sic*].
What did you take and where did you go?
I went in Church Street and took a brush and ring and pawned them.
For how much?
Twenty-five shillings.
To whom did you give that money?
I took it there.
Where?
To his house.
To whom did you give it?
To Mr Lipski.
Did he say anything as to repaying you?
I gave him the money – yes, he said, 'Saturday, please God, I will take in the work, or finish the work, I shall pay you all I owe you.'
Had you lent him any money in the week before this?
Yes, there is the ticket.
How much?
One pound.
Has he ever paid you any portion of that two pounds five shillings back?
No.

94

McIntyre in cross-examination questioned her about Lipski's character and his new business.

Had you known him some time?
Known him when he was working at my son-in-law's, I have known him two years.
Was he a man of good character?
So far I cannot give him a bad character, he always behaved himself.
Did you know when you lent him this money that he was fitting up his room for the purpose of turning it into a workshop?
I think so.
Did you know he was having the money for the purpose of fitting up a workshop?
Yes.
And did you know he was working at home and employing that boy that has been called, Pitman?
Yes.
And did you know he was going to employ other men as well?
I don't know that, I was not there.
Did you know he was doing work for people in the city, that he had to take home and get his money for it?
No.
You don't know what work he was doing?
Horn work.
Stick work?
Yes, stick and horn work.
Do you know whether he was working for a Mr Lewis in Aldermanbury?
I don't know.
Mr McIntyre: *These are the names, your Lordship* (handing papers to the judge).
Mr Justice Stephen: *These are the names of the people for whom he worked. No doubt he was a stickmaker.*
Mr McIntyre: *And those are the persons for whom these sticks would be made.*

'That concludes the case for the Crown,' announced Mr Poland. Mr McIntyre said he did not intend to call any witnesses for the defence. The court adjourned early for the lunch-break, resuming at one o'clock, when counsel would address the jury.

McIntyre's decision to call no evidence meant that Poland would address the jury first and that the defence would have the crucial last words before the judge's charge to the jury. If the defence had called a single witness – for example, to show that brandy was used in stickmaking or that the lock might have been defective – the rule of criminal procedure at that time was that the Crown would be entitled to address the jury last.

The accused could not be called as a witness on his own behalf in criminal trials for most offences in 1887; it was not until 1898 that the general law was changed to permit the accused to enter the witness box in a criminal case.[2] Mr Justice Stephen, however, like some of his colleagues, permitted an accused to make an unsworn statement from the dock before his counsel addressed the jury. His practice was well known to lawyers.[3] Indeed, earlier in the trial, it will be recalled, the judge had said to McIntyre, when Rosenbloom was being questioned: 'I can always allow a prisoner to make a statement.' The jury heard this statement and may well have improperly drawn an unfavourable inference from the fact that Lipski did not later make a statement.

McIntyre commented after the trial that the 'prisoner declined to make a statement although invited to do so'.[4] Should McIntyre have encouraged Lipski to make an unsworn statement? There is no simple answer. It is difficult to know what would be gained by Lipski giving evidence in Yiddish, which would have to be translated for the jury. In any case, his story was already before the jury. Moreover, if Lipski had given an unsworn statement, the Crown would, it seems, have been able to address the jury last.[5] Still, Lipski, without having to face cross-examination by the Crown, might have amplified his case for the jury, as he did after the trial. And he may have impressed the jury with his sincerity, as he impressed many of those close to him.

After the adjournment for lunch, Mr Poland addressed the jury. The transcript does not contain the addresses of counsel or the judge's charge; for these one has to rely on newspaper accounts. The fullest description of Poland's jury address is the following brief account contained in *The Daily Telegraph*:[6]

Mr Poland, in summing up the case for the prosecution, argued that the facts were so simple and clear that on the evidence the jury could form only one conclusion. He said it was clear that at the time the deceased lost her life she and the prisoner were the only persons in the room, and that on the very day on which the occurrence took place the prisoner had purchased the acid which was undoubtedly the cause of death. The question of motive was not material, but upon the facts it was reasonable to suppose that the accused might either have intended to outrage the deceased or to commit a robbery. The prisoner's answer to the charge was that the crime was committed by Rosenbloom and Schmuss. He, therefore, asked the jury to believe that, although they were unknown to each other, these two men combined together to kill Mrs Angel first, in broad daylight, and that, too, when the woman was unknown to them, and was in such poverty that she had had to borrow five shillings the day before to pay her rent. The prisoner was an active young man, and if he had struggled for dear life with those two men, did not the jury think he would have marked them in some manner while they were seizing him and opening his mouth. But neither man had any mark, neither did the prisoner have any marks such as he would have had had there been such a struggle as he alleged. The marks he did bear were such as he would be likely to get in a struggle with a woman, and this was all the more likely to be the most feasible explanation when they remembered that he uttered no cries for help. At first there was a little mystery in the case, the man Schmuss having gone away, but it was now proved that he went to Birmingham for work, that he made no secret about his going, and that he was quite ready to return to give evidence when wanted.

Lipski, according to the Yiddish weekly *Die Tsukunft*, listened with greater concentration to what he could understand of Poland's address and his usually calm face changed drastically.[7]

It was now McIntyre's turn. Again the report in *The Daily Telegraph* contains a fuller description than that in any other paper:

Mr McIntyre, in addressing the jury on behalf of the prisoner, said it was a painful duty to have to put forward a defence which implicated others, but he had to submit that the prosecution had not made out such a case against the accused as would justify his conviction upon this fearful charge. What motive could the prisoner have had? He at first thought the imputation was that he had entered this young married woman's room for an immoral purpose, but the medical evidence entirely destroyed that contention, and the prosecution had given it up. Mr Justice Stephen, interjecting, observed that the prosecution had not given up the motive of immorality, but they had not attempted to prove that adultery took place.

Mr McIntyre said the alternative motive suggested was robbery, but the accused bore an exemplary character, he did not conceal his movements on the morning in question, and must have been aware that there was not much to be gained by plundering the deceased's room. All the circumstances seemed to indicate that the murder was the work of two men. If the prisoner had attempted to outrage the deceased she would have struggled and screamed for assistance, and could not have been easily overmastered. But had there been two men one could easily have gagged the woman while the other administered the blows, which the prisoner alone would have been unable to give her while preventing her from giving an alarm. It was said that the door was locked on the inside when the prisoner was found under the bed of the deceased woman. The evidence, however, showed that the door was easily got open by the women pushing outside, which would suggest that the lock had merely stuck. If the door were locked, what reason could there possibly be for the prisoner locking himself in? The fact that the accused was found under the bed in an insensible condition was to his mind far more in keeping with his statement that he was attacked by two men than with the theory of the prosecution. He contended that the evidence for the Crown, which was in some respects contradictory, was too inconclusive to justify the jury in finding the prisoner guilty upon a charge of this awfully serious character.

There is no indication in the Press reports of the impact McIntyre's address might have had on the jury. Certainly, Stephen's very unusual interruption might seriously have affected McIntyre's concentration and delivery and destroyed the effectiveness of his jury address.

'Mr Justice Stephen summed up at great length,' stated the *Daily Telegraph*[8] 'remarking that he had never known a case which presented so many remarkable and singular features.' One remarkable feature was Stephen's summing-up itself. He steered the jury more forcefully than even he was accustomed to do. Stephen did not have a high regard for juries. A year earlier he had said that 'jurors are usually ignorant, good-natured men, quite unaccustomed to the administration of justice, and willing to receive any plausible statement consistent with a prisoner's innocence as being enough at least to raise a reasonable doubt on the subject.'[9] He obviously wanted to guard against that happening in this case. The report in *The Times* contains the fullest synopsis of his charge.[10]

Mr Justice Stephen, in summing up, said whoever caused the death of the deceased, the act was one of wilful murder. There was no doubt that between the hours of six and eleven on the morning in question the deceased woman was murdered by some person or persons. There were only two motives which could be put forward for the commission of the crime – passion and avarice. There was nothing taken from the deceased's room, because there was nothing to take, and the circumstances did not seem to support the motive of avarice. His Lordship pointed out that it was more probable that passion was the motive for the crime, and that if that were so it would rather be the act of one man than two. It was shown that the prisoner had not been acquainted with the deceased and her husband, and consequently if it was the prisoner who committed the act it must have been under the influence of a sudden temptation, there being a window from which a view of the deceased's room could be obtained from the stairs. The prisoner was a man of good character and was engaged to be married, and these were circumstances which the jury should take into consideration in favour of the prisoner. The man Schmuss remained in London for several days after 28 June, and then went to Birmingham for work, writing from there to London, and his conduct certainly did not look like that of a man who had committed a horrible murder. There was evidence that the prisoner had nitric acid, but that no one else had. His Lordship read the evidence in detail and the prisoner's statement, referring also to the denials given by the men Schmuss and Rosenbloom to the questions put them in cross-examination. The prisoner's statement was a highly important part of the case, and the witnesses Schmuss and Rosenbloom had been cross-examined as to its truth. One could hardly imagine that two men who were strangers to each other should walk down from the workshop and go into the deceased's room for the purpose of committing an assault upon her, and it was almost as difficult to imagine that they should go into the room of a woman as poor as themselves for the purpose of taking a few clothes, which after all they did not take, and why should they rob the prisoner? How could they reconcile the prisoner's statement with the fact that the door was locked on the inside? The locking of the door was a circumstance of very great importance supposing the jury were of opinion that it was locked. The observations made on the part of the defence as to the improbability of the prisoner having committed the crime were of very great importance, and should be carefully considered by the jury. If the jury came to the conclusion that the prisoner was the person who committed the offence, then the natural inference was that he attempted to commit suicide afterwards.

Stephen's statement that 'it was more probable that passion was the motive for the crime and that if that were so it would rather be the act of one man than two' was a strong invitation to the jury to convict.

The jury retired at 4.43 pm and returned just eight minutes later at 4.51. The foreman announced that the jury found the prisoner guilty of the murder as charged.

Lipski was asked by Stephen if he had anything to say why sentence of death should not be passed. His reply in Yiddish was translated by the interpreter: 'I did not do it.'

Stephen then donned the traditional black cap and said: 'Israel Lipski, you stand convicted of the crime of wilful murder. By the law of England the punishment of that crime is death. I have only to say to you, prepare to die.'[11] He then pronounced sentence of death:

And the sentence of the court is that you be taken from hence to a place of execution, that you be there hanged by the neck till you are dead, and that your body be buried within the precincts of the prison in which you shall have been last confined – and may the Lord have mercy on your soul.

The sentence was translated for Lipski, who was said to have received it 'with composure'.[12] He was taken by the two warders back to Newgate Prison – this time to the cell for the condemned, which was twice as large as the normal cell – to await his execution.

Henry Matthews, M.P., Q.C. from an engraved portrait c. 1880

Chapter Five

The Fight for a Reprieve: The First Two Weeks

STEPHEN HAD NO doubt about the verdict and sentence. On Monday he wrote to his wife, who was staying in the country for the summer:[1]

> I finished trying Lipski on Saturday. He was convicted, and sentenced, and will be hanged I think. It was a horrid business, but there was morally no doubt about it. It was exactly the story of David and Bathsheba, except that poor Mrs Angel was virtuous, and Lipski brutally murdered her when she disappointed him. I never remember a worse or more curious case.

Stephen was still convinced that Lipski's motive was lust. In the Old Testament story, it will be recalled, David had spied on Bathsheba from a balcony and had then seduced her.

The Home Office, as was the usual practice, requested the judge's notes to assist in the analysis of whether there were circumstances warranting a free pardon or a commutation of the sentence. It also ordered, as it did in exceptional cases, a transcript of the evidence recorded by the shorthand reporters.

If no recommendation by the Home Secretary for a reprieve or a temporary respite were made, Lipski would be executed on Monday morning, 15 August. The practice then was to allow three intervening Sundays before the hanging, which normally would take place, in the case of those tried at the Old Bailey, at eight o'clock on Monday morning in the yard of Newgate Prison.[2] On Tuesday, Lipski was officially informed by the Sheriff, Henry Isaacs, of the time of execution; the *East London Observer* contained the following report:[3]

> Since his removal to the condemned cell, Lipski has scarcely seemed to realise his position, but conducts himself in a nonchalant manner, and even when, on Tuesday afternoon, he was visited by the sheriffs and chaplain and informed through the medium of the interpreter that the dread punishment would be carried out on Monday, August 15th, the condemned man appeared to be scarcely concerned, and certainly not surprised. Mr Duffield, the chaplain, asked him if there was any statement he wished to make – any person he wished to see – in the meantime, but the prisoner merely shook his head and intimated in Hebrew that he was guiltless.

103

Before Victoria became Queen in 1837, it was the Sovereign who made the real decision whether to reprieve a prisoner, guided in earlier days by the Privy Council, often referred to as the 'Hanging Cabinet', and then later, during Sir Robert Peel's tenure in the Home Office, by the Home Secretary.[4] But when Queen Victoria came to the throne, the practice changed because, to quote from Stephen's own *History of the Criminal Law of England*, 'it would have been indecent and practically impossible to discuss with a woman the details of many crimes then capital.'[5] The result was that the Queen acted on the advice of the trial judge, who would send his recommendation to the Queen through the Home Secretary. In 1861, however, the judge's *de facto* reprieving power was eliminated, and it was the Home Secretary himself, after the consultation with the judge, who made the recommendation.

The Home Secretary was, in effect, a 'Court of Criminal Appeal', reviewing the facts of the case, gathering new evidence and judging the seriousness of the prisoner's conduct. An actual Court of Criminal Appeal was not established until 1907.[6] Sir William Harcourt, the Home Secretary from 1880 to 1886, described the three main principles used in reaching a decision:[7] 'compassion'; 'a possibility of an unjust conviction'; and 'mercy . . . where there was no intention to kill'. During the 1880s about half of all those sentenced to death had their sentences commuted.[8] In 1887, for example, there were only three people hanged at Newgate out of six Old Bailey convictions for murder. As previously pointed out, there were far fewer people convicted and hanged than is now thought to have been the norm in Victorian times. The Home Secretary's practice was to announce his decision at least forty-eight hours before the execution, which in Lipski's case would be on Friday evening, 12 August.

Henry Matthews (no relation to Mathews, the prosecutor) had become Home Secretary when Lord Salisbury, the Tory leader, formed his second government in 1886.[9] The choice of the recently elected, wealthy sixty-year-old bachelor, described as 'one of the strangest and most brilliant men that ever entered English politics',[10] caused much surprise because Matthews had not been in the House of Commons since 1874, when he had lost to a Liberal Home-Ruler. It was also a surprise to Matthews, who claims that he had initially refused it on the ground of his 'want of experience and unfitness for the office'.[11] There were a number of factors which caused Salisbury to turn to him. One reason that is often stated is Matthews' friendship with Randolph Churchill, then a key member of Salisbury's administration. Another is that Matthews was a very good lawyer. *The Times* obituary in 1913 referred to his tenure at the Home Office as 'an unexpected episode in a brilliant forensic career'. Salisbury wanted a good lawyer in the position because he anticipated serious legal questions arising in his attempt to hold Ireland in the United Kingdom; he had already offered the post to Webster, later Lord Chief Justice Alverstone, and to Macnaghten, later a Law Lord, but both had turned him down.[12]

Matthews had several months earlier made a name for himself as the devastating cross-examiner of Sir Charles Dilke in the Crawford divorce case. In addition, Matthews was a strong supporter of the Union and, perhaps, most importantly, was a Catholic, which would appeal to the Irish Catholics, both in and out of Parliament. He was, in fact, the first Catholic to be a cabinet minister since the seventeenth century. As a Catholic he was unable to attend Oxford or Cambridge and so had gone to the University of Paris, before returning to England to study at the Bar.

His role in the Government became crucial to the survival of Salisbury's administration. In February 1887, Matthews had threatened to resign on an issue relating to Ireland. Salisbury wrote to the Lord Chancellor, Lord Halsbury: 'Can you do nothing to persuade him? The loss of him at this time would very seriously imperil the Government, and I think I am not rating our value too high when I say that the fall of the Government at this moment would probably be fatal to the Union.'[13] Halsbury succeeded in talking Matthews out of resigning. In July 1887, Matthews again tendered his resignation because of a rebuke by the House of Commons for his inept handling of the Cass case, discussed below. Matthews may have been a very good lawyer, but he was, by all accounts, a bad Parliamentarian – 'a Parliamentary failure', according to the *Dictionary of National Biography*. *Vanity Fair* described him as 'a lawyer-minded man, with more knowledge of courts and cases than of human nature'.[14] Still, Lord Salisbury refused to accept the resignation.

Matthews' symbolic importance to the Government later

blocked his appointment as a Law Lord. In January 1891, Lord Salisbury wrote to the Queen saying he had hoped to appoint Matthews as the new Law Lord, but a number of key members of the Government objected because 'Mr Matthews' seat at Birmingham would certainly be lost; and their view is that just now, when opinion is forming upon fresh bases, and the convictions of many Home-Rulers are materially shaken by passing events, it would be a serious public evil to have a great Unionist defeat in so conspicuous a constituency as Birmingham.' Salisbury went on to say that 'they think it the lesser of two evils to bear, during the remainder of this Parliament, whatever indiscretions Mr Matthews may commit in the House of Commons, rather than run the risk of the effect upon opinion, at this juncture, which the loss of the seat would exercise.'[15]

The Cass case should be briefly noted. Miss Cass had been charged with soliciting, and although not convicted, had been given a strong rebuke by the magistrate. It appeared to many that she was an innocent victim of circumstances and Matthews was asked in the House of Commons to set up an inquiry. He refused to do so and as a consequence was censured by the House. This was undoubtedly a humiliating experience for Matthews and he tendered his resignation, which, as we have seen, was not accepted. Matthews was strongly criticized by the Press and the public. The attack was led by W. T. Stead and the *Pall Mall Gazette*, who were to be the principal supporters of Lipski in the fight for a reprieve.

Stead's possible motivation for attacking Matthews will be explored in detail later. It is clear that he was hostile to Matthews (as a Unionist, a Conservative and a Catholic) from the moment his cabinet appointment was announced. Stead's leading article in the *Pall Mall Gazette* of 30 July 1886 was entitled *Who is the New Home Secretary?* and stated:

But the most astonishing appointment is that of Mr Henry Matthews as Home Secretary. Mr Henry Matthews, to begin with, is a Roman Catholic. What a shudder of horror will run through the pious ranks of the Orangemen when they see, as the first fruits of their exertions for the Protestant cause, the establishment of a Papist in the very Holy of Holies of the Constitution! All the prisons of the United Kingdom, to mention only one point, with the religious and moral welfare of the prisoners, will be absolutely at the mercy of this representative of Anti-Christ ... Immediate steps should be taken to organise a special Liberal electoral committee in East Birmingham for the specific purpose of ridding the

106

town from the reproach of returning a Tory to Parliament. There is no time to be lost. We look to the Birmingham Liberals to do their duty.

This appears to have been a crusade in the literal sense, to remove the infidel Matthews from the 'Holy of Holies'. Harry Poland later said, with reference to the Lipski case: 'I don't say that Stead took all the trouble he did because Matthews was a Roman Catholic, but he took a lot.'[16]

Matthews and the Permanent Under-Secretary, Godfrey Lushington, reviewed the transcript of the evidence after it arrived on Monday morning, 8 August. They also read the judge's notes, which had arrived at the end of the previous week, transcribed by Stephen's clerk because of the Judge's notoriously indecipherable handwriting. The fifty-six pages of notes provided a good summary of the evidence, although Stephen pointed out in his covering letter that there were omissions in his notes of 'matters which turned out to be of more importance than appeared at the moment'. The evidence was first read by Lushington.

Godfrey Lushington, whose reaction to the evidence is contained in the file, would normally offer his analysis of the evidence before the matter was dealt with by the Home Secretary. A barrister, and former Fellow of All Souls, Oxford, he had joined the Home Office as counsel in 1869 with the reputation of a radical, and had become the Permanent Under-Secretary of State in 1885, holding the office until 1895. Lushington had once stood unsuccessfully as a Liberal candidate and still appeared to some to favour Liberal policies. He was known for his ability and his remarkable capacity for hard work.[17] A contemporary government official's description of Lushington was, however, not particularly flattering: 'He had about him much of the schoolmaster – honest, laborious and painstaking, but lacking in personal interest on subjects which came before him.'[18]

There is nothing in the file to indicate that Lushington's reaction to the evidence was not shared by Matthews:

I am satisfied as to this man's guilt.
1 He was found in the bedroom of the murdered woman, hidden away behind the bed. The door was locked on the inside. The woman was exposed, with her chemise rolled up to her breasts: the man had scratches on his temple; those on his arms seem to have been not recent.
2 The woman was poisoned by nitric acid and the prisoner himself

107

swallowed some. The prisoner has to my mind been sufficiently identified as the purchaser of the nitric acid in the morning.

Some of the 'difficulties in the way of the prisoner's guilt' are then analysed by Lushington, including the following:

> Why after killing the woman did he not run away? And why did he drink the nitric acid?
>
> I can only answer this by conjecture. I believe that the murder was unpremeditated: that a sudden passion seized the prisoner when he looked through the window and saw the woman in bed, that he went into the room and on the woman resisting him he struck her with blows till she was insensible, and then poured the nitric acid which he had with him down her throat to kill her, violated or thought of violating her person, was seized with utter remorse, and drank what remained of the nitric acid. Another conjecture might be that he was disturbed by the mother-in-law, Angel, coming, was struck with terror at the certainty of his capture, and tried to kill himself with the rest of the stuff in the bottle, and tried to hide behind the bed, drawing the pillow over the space between the wall and the bed.

Lushington's view that the motive was lust was the view that Stephen had emphasised at the trial, although Stephen had not added the possibility of necrophilia.

During the first week after the conviction Lipski's solicitor, John Hayward, had been busy on Lipski's behalf. Indeed, on the very evening of the day of the conviction, he wrote to the editor of the *Jewish Chronicle*, stating:

> Sir, – The poor fellow Lipski has this day been found guilty. I spent a considerable time with him in prison.
>
> I tested a statement made by him most severely, and his plain, straightforward demeanour and his excellent character fully convinced me that he was not guilty of the charge brought against him.
>
> There are one or two points that are especially noteworthy. First, that his landlady, who pushed open the door, is not at all sure that the door was locked. Secondly, that the one ounce of nitric acid stated to have been purchased by the prisoner was, according to the doctor's evidence, all consumed in poisoning the woman, and it must have taken at least another ounce to have destroyed the coat. Also that the man's elbows had the skin rubbed off them, and the skirt of the coat was burnt in such a way as to indicate that the man must have been lying on his back at the time.
>
> I do hope that these things may be considered, and that some efforts may be made to spare the man's life.
>
> Yours obediently,
>
> John Hayward,
> Solicitor for Defence

27, King Street, E.C. 30th July, 1887.[19]

108

No doubt similar letters were sent to other papers. Monday's *Pall Mall Gazette* had a brief note on the case, echoing Hayward's points:

> The result of the trial of Lipski leaves several points unsettled. Was the door of the murdered woman's room locked or not? The whole matter hinges on that. The landlady is not sure that it was. And the solicitor for the defence raises a good point this morning by the inquiry where the second ounce of nitric acid came from, as two were apparently employed and Lipski only bought one. The case is one which calls for consideration at the hands of the authorities before the death sentence is enforced.

Hayward went further and published, towards the end of the first week after the trial, a six-page pamphlet, which was widely distributed, arguing that Lipski was wholly innocent, stating:

> I visited the prisoner Israel Lipski several times in prison before his trial. I took down his statement most carefully and tested the truth of it in every possible way. I am fully persuaded from the straightforward answers he gave me, borne out as they were by certain facts, that he told me the truth, and that he is wholly innocent of the dreadful crime for which he has been condemned, and that if he could have been cross-examined on his statement in Court his innocence would have been most manifest. He is a young man, only twenty-two, slightly built, most modest and retiring in his demeanour, and bears an excellent character for industry and good conduct. It does seem a shocking thing that such a man should die for a crime of which it is to say the least possible, that he is not guilty. I do hope, therefore, that you will use the influence that you possess to have his life spared, at all events until further investigations have been made.[20]

Hayward's pamphlet analysed the evidence in some detail, raising a number of points in the prisoner's favour. The defence, Hayward stated, had been taken by surprise by the judge's theory of Lipski's motive:

> No outrage had been committed on the woman, and the prosecution quite declined to suggest any motive for the commission of the crime. A motive, however, was suggested by the judge in his summing-up. He said that the prisoner might have seen the woman in bed through a window on the staircase; that he suddenly determined to enter the room for an immoral purpose; that being foiled by the resistance offered he became furious, and then beat the woman insensible with his fists, and afterwards poured down her throat the acid which he had purchased for his business. He then might have taken the remainder of the acid with the view of destroying his own life, and crawled or fell under the bed, where he was found . . . This theory, which no doubt led to the conviction of the prisoner, came upon the defence by surprise, and when there was no opportunity of commenting on it to the jury.

Why, Hayward asked, did Rosenbloom not hear anything, considering that fact that he was in the room above and the

109

partition dividing the Angels' room from the staircase leading to Lipski's room was only a quarter of an inch thick? Why did Schmuss leave after a few minutes when 'there were plenty of raw sticks lying about and he was a man apparently in abject need'? Can one have confidence in Moore's identification of Lipski in the hospital as the person who purchased the acid when 'according to the statement of the hospital nurse, he was taken straight up to the bed where the prisoner lay and on which a detective was sitting'? In any event, Hayward pointed out, Moore sold only a single ounce of acid, and Dr Kay said 'one ounce of acid at least' had gone down Mrs Angel's throat and Dr Calvert said an ounce had been spilled on Lipski's coat. How could Lipski have covered up his own coat with Mr Angel's coat and then crawled under the bed, dragging an eggbox after him? Were not the abrasions on Lipski's elbows because of his struggle while on his back? How is it that Mrs Angel's bedding was marked with acid mixed with blood, but acid mixed with blood was not found on Lipski or his coat?

Hayward then turned to the crucial question of the 'locked' door. Was the door to the room, in fact, locked? Before the trial Hayward had the lock examined by a locksmith who concluded that 'the lock was very badly put on' and that a person could think that it was locked 'when in fact it was held by the handle latch alone and not by the bolt of the lock . . . If held by the latch alone it would account for the door being so easily pushed open and so little damage being done.' Assuming that the door was locked with the key inside, the locksmith stated, anyone knowing how to do it could easily turn the key from outside'. Hayward went on to point out that, 'Schmuss was a locksmith, and therefore skilled in such matters.' These facts, said Hayward, were fully set out in the counsel's brief.

Hayward included a further statement by Lipski to the one that had been given to the police:

According to the statement made by Lipski to his solicitor, he had been out to buy a vice and returned, and had gone down to the yard to have a wash, and afterwards proceeded to Petticoat Lane to buy some sponges from the hawkers for varnishing.

On his way he met a hawker at the Whitechapel end of the Commercial Road. He bought a shillings worth of sponge off him and returned. He described the sponge hawker as an old man of about sixty, with a beard. A man answering this description has been seen selling sponges, but he is a foreigner, speaking English most imperfectly, and says he recollects nothing of the matter; he refused to give his address.

110

He then returned home, and on his way upstairs to his workshop he saw the man Simon standing half way in the doorway of Mrs Angel's room. The other workman, Schmuss, who is a tall powerful man, was standing behind him. Schmuss immediately seized him by the throat and put his hand over his mouth; Simon laid hold of his hands and held them behind him, they then pushed him backwards; in the struggle and fall, his coat was pulled off his left arm by the man Simon, who had hold of him from behind. Schmuss then knelt on his chest or stomach until be became nearly insensible.

He was just able to tell them in answer to their questions that he had no money, but was not strong enough to cry out, and if he had cried out there was no one at that time in the house.

Simon then forced his mouth open with a piece of steel used for scraping sticks, and poured some stuff into his mouth. He says the stuff gave him very little pain at first. He saw them drag his coat off his other arm and feel in the pockets. He remembers them pushing him under the bed. He then became insensible, and must have lain in that condition for about three hours when he was discovered.

The pamphlet concluded with a note that Hayward was working on Lipski's behalf at his own expense.

A paragraph having appeared in an evening paper of this date to the effect that the wealthy Jews have subscribed liberally towards the efforts now being made by me to save Lipski, I beg to say that this is entirely a mis-statement. The money subscribed for the defence was barely sufficient to cover counsel's fees, and since the prisoner's conviction no contributions have been asked for or received.

I am working for this man with all my might and energy, and at my own expense, simply because from the facts before me, and my intercourse with the unfortunate prisoner, I am thoroughly convinced he is not guilty of the crime for which he is condemned.

Very little information is now available on John Hayward. The Law Society was not required to keep records before 1907 and so all that is recorded about him is that he 'was admitted a solicitor in November 1876 and took out his first Practising Certificate on 16 November 1876. From 1876–1909 he practised alone, and ceased to practise in 1909.' He died in 1917. No obituary notice has been found, but with so many deaths occurring during the war, this is not surprising. The successor to Hayward's firm has no papers relating to Hayward or Lipski. Hayward's practice was in Cheapside, outside the East End, from 1876 until 1905. How he became Lipski's solicitor is not known. Perhaps it was because his managing clerk, Solomon Myers, also a solicitor, was Jewish. John Hayward was not.

Hayward's pamphlet arrived at the Home Office on

Saturday, one week after the conviction, having been forwarded by an aged Liberal MP, A. McArthur, who wrote to the Home Secretary:

> I have known Mr Hayward, the solicitor in the case, for many years past as a highly respectable man, and I am perfectly certain he would not state anything he did not believe to be strictly true and accurate . . . I believe Mr Hayward to be incapable of telling a falsehood and thus he is actuated by the purest and best motives.

Matthews instructed Lushington to send the pamphlet to the 'learned judge for his observations'. This was done, but Stephen had already received a copy, which had been sent to him by Hayward on the advice of Sir Edward Clarke, the Solicitor General. Hayward had shown a copy to Sir Edward, an expert in murder trials (the successful defence counsel in the Adelaide Bartlett murder case the year before), who strongly urged him to send a copy to the judge. 'It is altogether against legal etiquette', Hayward is reported to have stated, 'for a solicitor to communicate with the judge.' 'Never mind that', the Solicitor General replied, 'you had better do it.'[21]

The judge's copy also arrived on Saturday. He wrote to his wife that same day:

> I have got a letter from that wretched Lipski's solicitor, about his client, which I foresee will give me a great deal of anxiety and worry, and perhaps keep me in London, after I meant to leave.

The following day, Sunday, he again wrote to his wife about the case:

> I have employed half the morning over that dismal Lipski story, which makes me anxious and unhappy whenever I think of it. The man was not quite properly defended and I myself did not exactly hit the right point in summing up. To be sure, if his story is true, and if he has to be hanged because two villains tried to murder him, and all but succeeded in doing it, he is the most luckless human being that ever lived. I never saw a case which so completely proved the truth of my views about enabling accused people to give evidence. I do not know what to do about it. I have however written to his attorney to come to see me tomorrow, at the rising of the court, and talk the matter over.

Stephen wrote to the Home Office the same day, stating:

> I have carefully considered Mr Hayward's pamphlet of which I received a copy from him before I got Mr Lushington's letter. I propose to see Mr Hayward myself and discuss several points with him as I think that in some particulars he is inaccurate. I should like also to see his brief for Mr McIntyre. Until I have done this I think it will be best for me to defer the observations which I have to make.

112

Stephen suggested that in the meantime the Home Office might examine a number of points raised by Hayward. He wished Drs Calvert and Kay to be asked 'whether they can say with any confidence that an ounce of nitric acid could not have produced all the effects which they observed on Mrs Angel, on the prisoner and on the clothes'. Secondly, he wanted a chemist to examine the coat, 'who might say how much acid would be required to burn it as it is burnt'. Further, he wanted the lock 'to be inspected by the Secretary of State'. Finally, he wanted Dr Kay's evidence that Lipski's insensibility (such that the cornea of his eye could be touched without blinking) was caused by his 'mental agitation' to be tested by experts in the field.

Stephen summoned Hayward to meet him at the Law Courts on Monday afternoon, 8 August, after the court adjourned. (This was the start of the second week of a long complicated patent case which Stephen was trying.) 'Never in the whole course of my experience,' Hayward later stated,' 'had I heard of a judge sending for a solicitor in this way before.'[22] Stephen was impressed with Hayward. He wrote to Matthews about him the same day:

> I must begin by saying that I was very favourably impressed by Mr Hayward himself. He discussed the matter with great candour and calmness and it was impossible not to feel that he personally was convinced of his client's innocence by the clear manner in which, as he said, Lipski gave his account of what had happened and answered the various questions put to him.

Moreover, and more importantly, he wrote that the points raised by Mr Hayward 'appear to be deserving of the most careful attention and I shall be willing to discuss them with you whenever you please. In fact I should wish to do so.'

The judge had changed his mind on the crucial question of motive, in which respect, it will be recalled, his charge to the jury virtually assured a conviction. His letter to Matthews states:

> First as to motive. I do not on full reflection think that much can be said on this subject. Lust and robbery are the only conceivable motives. I think each is about as likely to have actuated one man as to have actuated two. At the trial I suggested that if lust was the motive it was more likely to have actuated one man, but on reflection I am disposed to think that no reliance ought to be placed on any speculation of this sort. Someone did commit a murder for some reason or other. Do the circumstances suggest one man or

113

two as having been the criminals? The murderers as the evidence stands must have been either Lipski or Rosenbloom and Schmuss.

Stephen tested these two possibilities by looking at the 'comparative general probability of the two stories.' Of course, this is not the proper test in a criminal case, where the Crown must prove its case beyond a reasonable doubt. He then went over the grounds on which Hayward attempted to show that the murder was committed by two men, stating that 'they were indicated by Mr McIntyre in his speech, but were put forward somewhat slightly and in a way which did not at the time impress me.'

Stephen was now impressed. For example, with respect to the abrasions on the elbows he now observed that 'no explanation of them consistent with his guilt occurs to me, unless they were self-inflicted when he got under the bed, which if guilty he must be supposed to have done.' Hayward's argument about the acid on Lipski's coat being the result of a struggle with Rosenbloom and Schmuss worried Stephen: 'The burning of the coat is certainly a remarkable incident and as I think favourable to the prisoner.' Stephen was also concerned about the quantity of acid used, Moore's identification of Lipski, the fact that Rosenbloom said he did not hear any noise in the room below, and the possibility that the door was not locked, but on the latch, when the women pushed it open.

Another meeting between Stephen and Hayward was arranged for Thursday, 11 August, after court. This time the prosecutor, Harry Poland, was present. The meeting lasted over an hour. After that meeting, which will be discussed in more detail later, Stephen had a two-hour meeting with Matthews at which Dr Stevenson, a chemist from Guy's Hospital, was present. Stephen described the meeting with the Home Secretary in a letter to his wife the next day:

I have had my dismal conference with Matthews. He behaved very well, so far as I was concerned. He merely discussed this matter in every possible point of view, showing an exceedingly minute and accurate knowledge of the whole case, and he did not, in the least degree, ask my advice as to what was to be done. From what he said, I have no doubt he has decided not to interfere, but he did not say so to me. He was perfectly satisfied of the man's guilt, and I am not at all dissatisfied with his decision. If the case had been properly argued before the jury, and they had convicted, I should not have felt the least anxiety. The painful thing was, the new case being sprung upon me after the trial. Several points were brought out before Matthews which made much against the prisoner, and were not known before.

In particular Dr Stevenson, a leading chemist, said that he had analysed the acid, and found that it was not nitric acid at all, but a mixture of nitric and sulphuric acid, and that, having bought a specimen of what was sold as nitric acid, at the shop where Lipski was said to have bought his, he found that it was mixed in the same proportion with the same ingredients. I have little real doubt of the man's guilt, and Matthews has none. It is a sad and anxious case, but I shall think of it no more. I shall go to Froude's tomorrow, unless I hear from Matthews that he wants me to stay, which I do not expect at all.

The Home Secretary had received additional material for the meeting with Stephen. Inspector Final submitted a further report on a number of matters. Final argued that Mr Angel's coat, which was found on top of Lipski's coat, 'did not appear to have been placed there purposely', but 'had fallen down on the coat of the prisoner'; that 'a person in Angel's room could not be heard speaking when anyone was at work in Lipski's room filing horn handles for sticks'; that Pitman 'did not speak the truth' in saying that Rosenbloom said he knew Schmuss; that no 'piece of wood (broom handle) or steel of any description' was found in Angel's room; and that the person guarding Lipski in the hospital at the time of the identification was not sitting on the bed and was a 'very young looking person and being in a ward at a hospital no person would have an idea that he was a constable'. Further, with respect to Schmuss, Final stated that Schmuss 'has not the appearance of a person being in abject need' and that Schmuss informed him through an interpreter that 'Lipski's place being so small and very little business being done he thought it was no good for him to waste his time by waiting for Lipski.' In general, the police evidence added very little to the case. Obviously, the police were still firmly convinced of Lipski's guilt.

Other evidence, however, supported Lipski. Dr Calvert, the house physician at the hospital, signed a declaration stating:

1 I examined the prisoner Lipski when he was brought into the hospital on the 28th of June last. I found among other injuries abrasions on each of his elbows. In my opinion such abrasions were caused by his elbows rubbing against some hard substance such as the floor of a room. The struggles of a man on his back in his shirt-sleeves would be likely to produce such abrasions.

2 I examined the prisoner's coat at the trial and I consider it would take an ounce of nitric acid to produce the damages and stains which I saw

upon the coat, but as I have made no experiment I cannot speak positively as to this.

3 I acquainted the prisoner's solicitor with these facts on the first day of the trial of the said prisoner and previous to my examination. I was asked no questions as to the cause of the abrasions or as to the amount of acid spilt upon the coat.

A doctor, whose name had been obtained through the Lunacy Commission, and who had been asked to comment on Lipski's 'insensibility', concluded his report to the Home Secretary by stating:

The causes of the unconscious condition (not necessarily fainting) in which Lipski was found were in all probability complex – sudden fear or shock acting in conjunction with physical violence. No other explanation, under all the circumstances of the case, appears to me to be reasonable.

This evidence, referring to physical violence, and therefore very favourable to Lipski, made no impact on the Permanent Under-Secretary, Lushington, who noted on the file:

I am not sure what Dr Gover intends to be inferred from this opinion. But I cannot attach importance to it if it is intended to point to Lipski's innocence . . . I cannot help thinking that the proof of actual insensibility in this case is far from satisfactory.

It was Dr Stevenson's evidence, however, which was of crucial importance to the Home Office. Stevenson, the renowned chemist at Guy's Hospital, who was later to be the editor of the still widely used *Taylor's Medical Jurisprudence*,[23] had been asked to examine Lipski's coat. The Home Office officials were not surprised that he was of the opinion that 'half an ounce of a strong corrosive acid might amply suffice to produce all the results met with on Lipski's coat.' They were surprised, however, that the nitric acid found on the bed, the coat, and in the bottle was 'not ordinary commercial nitric acid, but an adulterated article, containing sulphuric and nitric acids in the proportion of two parts nitric acid to three parts of sulphuric acid.' 'The mixed acids, sulphuric and nitric,' Stevenson went on to say, 'are used for the manufacture of explosives, but do not form an ordinary article of retail commerce.' Nitric acid bought from Moore's shop, where Lipski was said to have bought the acid, contained the same two-to-three part mixture of nitric and sulphuric acid.

The Home Office officials were greatly impressed with this evidence. It proved, according to them, that Lipski had bought

116

the acid from Moore. But, of course, it did *not* prove that it was Lipski who bought the acid. Why would he buy acid 'used for the manufacture of explosives'? Is it not possible that Schmuss, a locksmith, would buy that type of acid? Is it also not possible that the supplier had delivered this adulterated nitric acid to a number of places and the fatal dose could therefore have been bought at another shop?

On Friday, 12 August, two weeks after the trial, a question was asked in the House of Commons directed at Mr Matthews, asking 'whether representations had been made to him concerning the case of Israel Lipski, now lying under sentence of death; and, whether he could hold out any hope of reprieve.'[24]

The Home Secretary's reply is an important one because it established the precedent which was used by subsequent Home Secretaries over the next seventy-five years, until capital punishment was abolished in 1965, to justify a refusal to discuss the question of a reprieve in advance of the actual decision:

> I must begin my answer by saying that I think it highly inexpedient and injurious to the administration of justice that the circumstances of a criminal case, on which the exercise of the prerogative of mercy depends, should be made the subject of discussion or of questions in this House. The case of Israel Lipski has been for some days under my most anxious consideration; and the advice I tender to Her Majesty will be made known in due time in the usual manner.[25]

In 1961, for example, R. A. Butler, then Home Secretary, in refusing to discuss the controversial Riley case, stated that Lipski was:

> the first case which I have been able to trace in which a Home Secretary was asked, in a case involving the death penalty, to give information before he had given his advice to the Crown or, where he decided to tender no advice for a reprieve, before the sentence had been carried out . . . That is of some importance as a basis, but it might be less important if it had not been so frequently followed up.[26]

If Parliamentary pressure could not be put on the Home Secretary, other pressure could. Hayward's pamphlet was widely distributed and petitions were circulated. Earlier that week Hayward had forwarded to the Home Secretary a petition of about a hundred sheets containing several thousand signatures, which, according to Hayward's estimate, were mainly from the Jewish community. Advertisements were placed in a

117

number of papers. The one in the *Jewish Chronicle*, which appeared on Friday, 12 August, stated:

THE CASE OF ISRAEL LIPSKI

ANOTHER PETITION in FAVOUR of the prisoner, with 2,000 signatures, goes up to the Authorities today. A Pamphlet setting forth facts not brought out at the trial and which conclusively prove the innocence of the man condemned, to be executed on Monday next, will be forwarded to any address upon application to John Hayward, 27, King Street, Cheapside, E.C., Solicitor for the Defence.

Although the prestigious *Jewish Chronicle* ran the advertisement and raised some questions about the justice of the sentence, for the most part it stayed out of the controversy. However, the English-language weekly, the *Jewish World*, took up Lipski's cause, as did the major Yiddish paper, the East End weekly, *Die Tsukunft* (*The Future*), which had commenced publication in 1884 under the title *The Polish Yidel*. *Die Tsukunft* was probably primarily responsible for the success of the petition. The paper explained to its readers in Yiddish its three reasons for supporting Lipski: 'the death penalty is unjust'; 'the punishment of criminals should not be motivated by revenge taken by society'; and thirdly, because 'it is no great honour for Jews when one of them is hanged.'[27] The paper pointed out that 'from the time England became civilised no Jew was hanged except for Marks about ten years ago. For Jews are by nature peaceful people and do not kill. And we must constantly make effort to keep our reputation clean and unblemished.' (In fact, a number of other Jews had previously been hanged, including some for murder.)[28] The paper then pointed out the danger of a rise of anti-Semitism:

When an ordinary person kills a person everything is quiet. It will not occur to anyone to call another person by the name of the murderer. But when Lipski is sentenced to death, the ordinary people taunted other Jews 'Lipski'! Two weeks ago Saturday it happened in Brick Lane. Last Saturday in Church Lane there was a great fight between Jews and locals, and all because of Lipski.

It was only later that the paper took up Lipski's cause on the ground that 'it was factually proven that Lipski was being hanged innocently.'[29]

The petitions, the new evidence and whatever doubt the judge now had were not enough to convince the Home Office. On Friday evening, 12 August, Matthews wrote on the subfile containing Stevenson's report on the acid the fateful word 'Nil', which meant that no action would be taken to recommend a pardon or a commutation from hanging to imprisonment. The Home Secretary's decision was communicated that evening to John Hayward, and to the governor of the prison, the judge and a number of other persons connected with the case. Lushington wrote to Hayward stating that the Home Secretary 'has most carefully considered all the circumstances in this case, and he regrets that he is unable to discover any sufficient ground to justify him in advising Her Majesty to interfere with the due course of the law.'[30] Lipski would, therefore, be hanged on Monday morning.

W. T. Stead, editor of the *Pall Mall Gazette*

Chapter Six

A Fight for Time

HAYWARD DID NOT give up. He immediately sent a telegram to Queen Victoria, who was then at her summer residence on the Isle of Wight:

> To Queen Victoria, Osborne, – Israel Lipski absolutely innocent of the crime for which he is condemned, will be hung on Monday. Secretary of State will not interfere. May I implore your Majesty to stay execution? John Hayward, solicitor for the defence.[1]

And he inserted advertisements to appear the next day in the morning papers:

> Israel Lipski – The jury who sat on the trial of this man, who, although condemned, is, from facts known to the solicitor for the defence, undoubtedly innocent, are requested to call before twelve o'clock today (Saturday), at the office of John Hayward, 27, King Street, Guildhall, E.C.[2]

The authorities would not, understandably, provide Hayward with a list of the addresses of the jurymen.

It was now Saturday morning, two days before Lipski was to hang. There was a Saturday sitting of the House of Commons. The Parliamentary session of 1887 was said to have been the longest continuous session that had been known for fifty years; and the average time of rising was after two o'clock in the morning.[3] So it was not surprising that the House sat on Saturday. The House met at noon for question time. The second question dealt with Lipski. The same MP who had attempted to ask a question on Friday, R. B. Cunninghame Graham, the radical Scottish socialist and literary figure, who was later jailed for his part in the November Trafalgar Square riots, again asked the Home Secretary about Lipski. Hansard records:

> Mr CUNNINGHAME GRAHAM (Lanark, N.W.) asked the Secretary of State for the Home Department, if he has seen the statement contained in the *Pall Mall Gazette* of the 12th August as to the statement of Mr Justice Stephen's belief in Israel Lipski's innocence?
>
> The SECRETARY of STATE (Mr Matthews) (Birmingham, E.): The

121

only statement I have seen in the *Pall Mall Gazette* of the 12th instant, in reference to the case of Israel Lipski, is that Mr Justice Stephen and Mr Poland laid great stress on certain portions of the evidence; but admitted, it is reported, that there was something to be said in the prisoner's favour.

Mr CUNNINGHAME GRAHAM asked, whether the Right Hon. Gentleman had seen the fifth edition of the same paper, which contained a full statement with regard to Lipski's case?

Mr MATTHEWS: No; I have not.[4]

The fifth edition of that Friday's *Pall Mall Gazette* contained a remarkable article by its editor, W. T. Stead, under the headline HANGING AN INNOCENT MAN: CONVERSION OF MR JUSTICE STEPHEN. The article opened:

Lipski must not be hanged. Why not? – For a very simple but very sufficient reason. Mr Justice Stephen, who tried Lipski, and whose summing-up contributed not a little to his conviction, has since been converted, and is aghast at the prospect of hanging a possibly innocent man.

Stead then outlined how Hayward had first met Stephen the previous Monday and was later summoned for a second meeting on Thursday:

This second interview took place yesterday evening: Mr Poland, who conducted the case for the prosecution, being also present. The matter was thoroughly thrashed out, with the result that two out of three persons present were in Lipski's favour. Mr Justice Stephen had been converted.

It was in this way. Many small facts which came out in evidence were yet not commented on by Lipski's counsel, and still less were they strung into any consistent theory. This was what Mr Hayward did to Mr Justice Stephen – making out what to himself seemed an 'irresistible' case on Lipski's behalf. 'Well, hardly irresistible,' replied Mr Justice Stephen; 'I should rather call it very strong.' Mr Hayward, as may be imagined, was well satisfied with the words. 'But how was it,' naturally asked the judge, 'that all this was not brought before me at the trial?' 'It was not my fault,' replied Mr Hayward – adding, however, that it was not an afterthought, nor a case of straws clutched at to save a hanging man, as the judge would see by looking through the leading counsel's brief, which the judge had specially instructed Mr Hayward to bring with him. Every fact stated in the pamphlet was, Mr Hayward says, contained in the brief, except one very important circumstance, to which we need not here allude, and which came out in the evidence in court. 'I do not complain,' Mr Hayward added, 'either of the summing-up or of the verdict. On the case as presented nothing else was possible. But I do ask you to give weight to the new facts and theories now adduced.' And Mr Justice Stephen did; he admitted, as we have seen, that the case was 'very strong.'

What makes this conversion all the more remarkable was the whole bearing of the judge. Sir James Fitzjames Stephen has not the reputation of being a very impressionable or soft-hearted man. But 'his anxiety, his

122

agony of mind almost,' says Mr Hayward in describing his interviews, 'were obvious. "It would be a terrible thing," he said, "to hang this man, when in reality he may have been half killed by the real murderers, who by that means endeavoured to hide their guilt. Why was not all this," he asked again, "submitted to me before? I cannot tell you what I think. But I can tell you this, that if I were not I, I should heartily wish you success".'

With these words Mr Hayward's interview came to an end – Mr Poland remaining behind. Mr Poland was, of course, not converted; Mr Hayward's theory, he had said, would seem ridiculous to a jury. 'No, Poland,' Mr Justice Stephen had replied; 'there I don't agree with you.' On leaving Mr Hayward happened to speak with Mr Justice Stephen's clerk. What the clerk said entirely corroborated the impression which Mr Hayward had formed from his interview. 'The governor is terribly worried about it,' the clerk said. 'I've never known him so bothered about a case all the forty years I've been with him.' Mr Justice Stephen has, Mr Hayward believes, himself been down to the scene of the murder, to make observations and inspections for himself.

The article shocked Stephen who heard about it on Friday evening. If anything, it converted Stephen into firmly believing in Lipski's guilt. He wrote to his wife the next day:

I dined at Twickenham yesterday and I heard an unpleasant thing from Evelyn. He said he had read in the *Pall Mall Gazette* a long article headed 'Mr Justice Stephen – converted to the innocence of Lipski', setting forth a long communication from Hayward, the solicitor, to the effect that he had had a conversation with me, in which I was 'terribly upset' and admitted repeatedly that I was convinced of Lipski's innocence.

I need hardly tell you that it was a wicked lie from beginning to end. I have not yet seen the article, but I shall see it today, and shall consider what to do. Of course the *P.M.G.* is beneath contempt or notice, but I shall write to Hayward, and as, fortunately, Poland was present, I shall be able to get a contradiction from him if I want it. Meanwhile, as I understand from the H.O., the man is to be hanged on Monday morning. The more I think over the matter, the more fully I am convinced that he did it. My doubts – such as they were – or rather my hesitations are all at an end.

(There was at one time a Home Office sub-file under the heading *Judge writes on Pall Mall Gazette*, but, unfortunately, this file was later destroyed.) Stephen was particularly upset about the reference to his clerk. The judge took the unusual step of writing a letter to *The Times* about the matter, explaining his concern to his wife as follows:

Poor Dyke [the clerk] is, I am convinced, absolutely innocent of what the vile Stead imputed to him. You will see in Saturday's *Times* a letter in which I say that I have examined into the matter, and am clearly convinced that the story is a mere falsehood. It would, if true, have been so bad that I should have had a great mind to dismiss him. Did you notice, the liar said, 'in all the forty years I have been with him, I never saw him so bothered and on.' Why, in 1847 I had not gone up to Cambridge, and Dyke cannot have been seven years old.

The letter, which appeared in *The Times* on the following Saturday, is worth setting out in full because of what it reveals of Stephen's character:

Sir, – At the end of last week an evening newspaper published in two consecutive numbers a long account of a confidential interview between myself and Mr Hayward, the solicitor of the convict Lipski. Of what was stated in that account about myself I shall not say one word. But the interests and character of another person are attacked in that article, and those interests I feel bound to protect, though it is reluctantly that even for such a purpose I notice such a publication. The article contains the following passage: 'On leaving, Mr Hayward happened to speak with Mr Justice Stephen's clerk. What the clerk said entirely corroborated the impression which Mr Hayward had formed from his interview. "The governor is terribly worried about it," the clerk said. "I've never known him so bothered about a case in all the forty years I've been with him".'

Such language would have been not only vulgar but a gross breach of confidence. I made every inquiry of both my clerks, and received from each of them explanations which convinced me that the statement in question, whoever was responsible for it, was absolutely false and unfounded. It is, indeed, false upon its face. Forty years ago I was just going up to Cambridge, and had not even chosen my profession. One of my clerks has been with me fifteen and the other twenty-three years. It was to the latter that Mr Hayward 'had occasion to speak on leaving.' My clerk tells me that on that occasion all that passed was that Mr Hayward had taken up a wrong hat by mistake; my clerk said, pointing to another 'That is your hat, Mr Hayward.' Before the interview with me a little conversation passed between Mr Hayward and both my clerks. He asked which was the senior and which the junior clerk, and in return was told that one of them had been with me fourteen (it should have been fifteen) years and the other twenty-three, but no such expressions as are mentioned in the newspaper in question were used by either of them. If used, those expressions would have been wholly untrue.

I have written this because my clerk tells me that his character has suffered, and that he has incurred censure in consequence. He has served me faithfully for twenty-three years, and I never once had occasion to blame him either for disrespectful language or breach of confidence.

I am, Sir, your obedient servant.

J. F. STEPHEN

32 de Vere Gardens, W., Aug. 18.[5]

Stead commented in the *Pall Mall Gazette* on Stephen's letter: 'Mr Justice Stephen's letter to *The Times* this morning about his clerk and Mr Hayward is an amusing instance of the way in which an official position – and most of all perhaps a position on the Bench – tends to puff a man up in his own conceit.'[6] The previous year Stead had, with specific reference to Stephen, commented on 'the growing tendency among the judges to travel beyond their sphere, and to invest themselves with an extra-judicial importance, which they do not possess in anyone's eyes but their own.'[7]

Stead acknowledged in the *Gazette* that Hayward had, indeed, insisted that the interviews with Stephen were confidential. Hayward, wrote Stead, 'could not and would not permit one word that passed at those interviews to be published. He had only mentioned them to induce us to call attention to the case of the doomed victim. The conversation was private, and must remain so.'[8]

He agonised in print over his decision to publish the interview. Again, it is worth quoting in full:

> When Mr Hayward left, the editor of this journal was placed in one of those difficult positions in which all the commonplaces of ethics seem to point one way, and paramount and imperious duty in another. To save Lipski – to prevent a judicial murder of the most aggravated kind – one way lay open, and only one way. Publish the fact that Mr Justice Stephen is, to say the least, haunted by a terrible doubt as to whether Lipski is not as innocent as the poor woman for whose murder he is to be hanged, and his execution becomes morally impossible.
>
> But then the conversation was private, the interview confidential. We were in precise terms interdicted from using it. If we published it, Mr Justice Stephen might be very angry. Mr Hayward would fall into disgrace, and we should have to face the odium of a breach of confidence. 'You have no right to use a private conversation.' 'If you don't, an innocent man will be hanged.' 'You may ruin Mr Hayward.' 'But save Mr Hayward's client.' 'And no one will trust you any more.' 'Well, when a life is at stake they had better not tell me anything that would save that life and expect me to keep it secret.'
>
> And so, after many arguments pro and con, we decided that our first instinctive conclusion was the true one, and we publish the above statement just as we received it.
>
> When going to press a boy brought up a letter from Mr Hayward, couched as follows:
>
> Dear Sir, – I do most sincerely trust you will not report my private conversation with the judge; it would ruin my professional standing, and, what is of more consequence, it would be adverse to the interests of my poor client. Yours very truly, *John Hayward*.
>
> Once more a pause. Should we blast Mr Hayward's professional reputation to save an innocent man from the gallows? Certainly, if necessary; but Mr Hayward is not to blame. He had no idea that we would violate his confidence. But what about injuring his poor client? How can it injure him to convince the public that the judge who tried him is no longer certain of his guilt? In any case, we take the responsibility of our decision, and publish the statement as we received it.[9]

One competitor of the *Gazette* claimed early the following week that there was, in fact, no breach of confidence by the *Gazette*, that 'this story of Mr Stead was nothing but a journalistic ruse invented to give spice to a commonplace attempt to excite public sympathy on behalf of a condemned man.'[10] Considering that Stead was a firm believer that newspapermen should not breach confidences ('his ear should be as sacred as that of a confessor,' he had once said),[11] it is just possible that there may be something to this speculation.

Stead, one of the most fascinating and important characters in the history of journalism,[12] is not an easy man to understand. The details of his life have been well documented by a number of authors,[13] but the motivation for his actions are far less clear.

He was thirty-four years of age when in 1883 he took over the editorship of the *Pall Mall Gazette* from John Morley (the statesman and, among other things, biographer of Gladstone), who was about to enter the House of Commons. Stead had joined Morley as an assistant editor several years earlier after making a name for himself as the editor of a daily paper in northern England. The *Pall Mall Gazette* had been established in 1865; the name was borrowed from the journal in Thackeray's fiction. The *Gazette*, then a sedate evening paper, was transformed by Stead into an innovative, sensational paper by adopting some of the techniques then being used by Joseph Pulitzer in the *New York World* and William Randolph Hearst in the *New York Journal*. Stead was the first journalist in England to use some of the techniques we now take for granted, such as headlines, illustrations and interviews. He used these techniques very effectively and in a serious manner to influence the course of English public life. Lord Esher once said that Stead 'came nearer to ruling the British Empire than any living man';[14] he was, for example, responsible for sending Gordon to Khartoum, and had a substantial impact on the policy of the British navy.

Stead had paid special attention to social conditions among the London poor. The impact of the famous pamphlet of 1883, *The Bitter Cry of Outcast London*,[15] was in part due to the publicity it received in the *Pall Mall Gazette*; Stead wrote:

What the evil is every one knows. It is the excessive overcrowding of enormous multitudes of the very poor in pestilential rookeries where it is a matter of physical impossibility to live a human life. Men, women, and

126

children are herded together in filthy styes; there is a family in every room; morality is impossible, and indeed has ceased to exist.[16]

Thus, it is not surprising to find Stead interested in a case in the squalid East End of London. In fact, Stead had written the year before the Lipski case that 'good copy is oftener found among the outcast and the disinherited of the earth than among the fat and well-fed citizens.'[17]

Not everyone, of course, was happy with the *Pall Mall Gazette*: the establishment papers, and much of the establishment, disliked 'the New Journalism', a term first used by Matthew Arnold, in relation to Stead, a few months before the Lipski case, in an article in a monthly review. 'The New Journalism,' Arnold wrote, 'has much to recommend it; it is full of ability, novelty, variety, sensation, sympathy, generous instincts; its one great fault is that it is *feather-brained*. It throws out assertions at a venture because it wishes them true; does not correct either them or itself, if they are false; and to get at the state of things as they truly are seems to feel no concern whatever.'[18] Nevertheless, the *Gazette* was widely read by influential members of English society. Even Queen Victoria read it and sympathised with some of Stead's crusades;[19] and Lord Chief Justice Coleridge once sent in five pounds to Stead in answer to a story about two ladies in distress.

Stead held a very exalted view of the role of the editor. This was set out in an article by Stead in 1886 entitled *Government By Journalism* which no doubt did not endear him to politicians or civil servants. He saw 'the newspaper as a substitute for the House of Commons'; it was 'becoming more powerful than all the other estates of the realm'; 'it may yet become a much greater power in the State'; 'an editor is the uncrowned king of an educated democracy'; 'even, as compared with the office that is highest of all, that of the Prime Minister, such an editor would have to think twice, and even thrice, before changing places with its occupant.'

The newspaper, according to Stead, was 'the great court in which all grievances are heard, and all abuses brought to the light of open criticism . . . the great inspector, with a myriad eyes, who never sleeps.' Moreover, he wanted 'the great inspector' to enlarge his vision to include some of the areas for which the Home Office had responsibility: 'The sphere of this inspection needs to be enlarged so as to include such official

127

establishments as lunatic asylums, prisons, workhouses, and the like. An editor of a daily paper, or his representative, should be *ex officio* vested with all the right of inspection enjoyed by a visiting justice or a Home Office inspector.'[20] One can picture the reactions of Henry Matthews and Godfrey Lushington to these ideas. Stead's campaign in the Lipski case, which he himself described as 'Trial by Journalism',[21] was one that was not welcomed either by the Home Office or the legal establishment.

Stead's views on the role of a newspaper as 'the great court in which all grievances are heard' helps to explain the philosophy behind his involvement in the Lipski case. Stead's hostility towards Matthews as a Conservative, a Unionist and a Catholic has already been mentioned. A great number of editorial comments in the *Gazette* during the summer of 1887, personally directed at Matthews, show Stead's animus towards the Home Secretary: 'unprecedented fiasco'; 'incorrigible bungler'; 'the cruelty of a coward'; 'devoid of the moral instincts common to most creatures of the human species', to mention just a few.

The other personalities involved in the case may also have provided some possible incentive for Stead's involvement. Stephen's pomposity, which can be seen in his concern over his clerk calling him 'governor', would not have been attractive to Stead. Stead, according to Frederick Engels, 'though full of it himself, hates respectability and middle-class cant.'[22] It is, perhaps, ironic that Stephen, one of the objects of Stead's attack, had been one of the major contributors to the *Pall Mall Gazette* in the 1860s: in 1868, for example, he wrote over two hundred articles for the paper. He even submitted a pro-atheistic article to the *Gazette* when he was a judge in the early 1880s that Morley wanted to publish, but Stead did not. Indeed, Stead threatened to resign if it were published and the article was rejected. How that episode affected the relations between Stephen and Stead is not known. Stephen certainly did not like Stead's *Gazette*. In a letter to his friend Lord Lytton a few months before the Lipski case, he remarked that 'the *Pall Mall* is too impudent and contemptible for any further notice. . . . Put it in the fire.'[23]

There may well have been bad blood between Stead and Poland because Poland had vigorously prosecuted Stead in the so-called 'Maiden Tribute' episode two years earlier.[24] That case cannot be ignored in any discussion of Stead because it was probably the single most important crusade in his life. In brief, Parliament had been procrastinating over a Bill to raise the age of consent from thirteen to sixteen. Stead was anxious to see the Bill passed, and, in order to show that there was an immoral trade in young girls in London, he arranged, with the support of some influential religious leaders, such as Bramwell Booth (the son of the founder of the Salvation Army), to 'purchase' a thirteen-year-old girl, Eliza Armstrong, for five pounds from her parents; he had her examined to prove she was a virgin and had her taken to France for her protection. These facts were prominently set out in a series of articles in the *Gazette* under the heading *The Maiden Tribute of Modern Babylon* which had two important consequences: Parliament quickly passed the Criminal Law Amendment Act in August 1885; and in the month after the Act's passage, Stead and a number of others were charged with abduction. Stead defended himself, but was convicted, and even though the jury concluded that Stead was misled by some intermediaries and throughout 'was animated by the highest motives',[25] he was given a sentence of three months' imprisonment. Poland not only prosecuted Stead, but immediately after the case he took the extraordinary step of sending a letter to *The Times* taking up a collection 'to give a helping hand to the Armstrong family.'[26]

Coincidentally, Henry Matthews was also involved in the case (he was not in Parliament at the time) in defending one of Stead's co-defendants. Whatever may have passed between Stead and Matthews, it is clear as a result of this lengthy case that they knew each other well. Even Godfrey Lushington played a part in the case. After the sentence was announced, a large deputation went to the Home Office to ask for a pardon and the release of Stead and others. Twenty members of the delegation were admitted into the Home Office to present the case, but in the words of *The Times* report:

> At this point Mr Lushington, Permanent Under-Secretary, entered the room, and stated that it was contrary to the practice of the Office to receive deputations with respect to criminals. Much dissatisfaction was expressed when this message was delivered to the crowd outside the Office.[27]

The Armstrong case and Stead's imprisonment must have influenced Stead's views on the criminal law, in particular on the judge's role in directing the jury. Stead complained, with justification it should be added, about the judge's influence on the jury in his summing up in the Armstrong case, the same complaint that Lipski's supporters were to make about a trial in the very same courtroom two years later. Stead stated after the Armstrong case:

> The judge had spent the whole day summing up against us. His animus was undisguised. He constructed a series of questions, to which the jury would have to answer yes or no, with such care that it was simply impossible for them to do other than return the verdict of guilty.[28]

The judge, Mr Justice Lopes, obviously wanted Stead convicted. One can see this in the following excerpt from the charge to the jury, ostensibly meant to help Stead:

> I would warn you, although I feel it is not necessary perhaps to do so, not to be prejudiced against Stead because in our streets and throughout our provinces some months ago there were circulated, emanating from the *Pall Mall Gazette* offices, an amount of disgusting and filthy articles – articles so filthy and disgusting that one cannot help fearing that they may have suggested to the minds of innocent women and children the existence of vice and wickedness which had never occurred to their minds before.[29]

This view, shared by many Victorians, caused a long-term drop in the sales and profit of the *Gazette*, after an initial burst in sales. Stead assured his publisher from prison that 'we are not going Maiden Tributing any more. It is to be the old *Pall Mall*.'[30] No doubt this is why the sexual aspects of the Lipski case were not given major prominence in the *Gazette*.

Sex was, however, an important preoccupation for Stead. One sees it clearly in the Armstrong case and in Stead's concern about immorality owing to overcrowding in slum areas. It may be that the sexual side of the Lipski case helped draw Stead to it. Havelock Ellis, the sexologist, later wrote that Stead's 'repressed sexuality was, I consider, the motive force of many of his activities.'[31] Stead recorded in his diary in 1889 his sexual activity just before the conception of his sixth child:

> I will set forth simply what has taken place. I have from the birth of Willie [thirteen years earlier] practised simple syringing with water. Of late always withdrawal. We never used anything but this. Intercourse limited to twice a week, and withdrawal, taking place just before the supreme moment, never did me any harm. The pleasure I think is rather greater then when the emission takes place in the natural way. If thrice or four times in the week, I got deaf with apparent wax formation in the right ear.[32]

One wonders what conclusion Havelock Ellis would have

drawn if he had known about Stead's concern about 'wax formation in the right ear'!

One final point before we return to the Lipski story concerns the apparent oddity of Stead's championing the cause of a Polish immigrant Jew. Many Jews in the 1880s considered the *Pall Mall Gazette* to be anti-Semitic. As previously mentioned, the earliest serious outburst in English against 'pauper aliens'[33] was contained in a letter to the editor published in 1886 in the *Gazette* under the heading *A Judenhetze Brewing in East London*:

> The foreign Jews of no nationality whatever are becoming a pest and a menace to the poor native-born East-ender. They oust him out of all the decent habitations, and greatly lower the standard of living, as well as the general moral tone . . . Not fewer than fifteen or twenty thousand Jewish refugees, all of the lowest type, have planted themselves chiefly at the East End within the past three years, and have a greater responsibility for the distress which prevails there probably than all other causes put together.[34]

Stead was surely aware of what he was doing in choosing to publish the letter. Rabbi Simeon Singer, who will play a prominent role later in the Lipski story, replied to this letter, stating in part, 'so far from the Jews being a pest and a menace, they might more justly be styled a remedy and a promise.'[35]

The following year, several months before the Lipski case, the *Gazette* joined in the growing agitation against the poor Jewish immigrants:

> Hordes of Jewish paupers from their Polish breeding grounds are descending upon our shores without a penny in their purse, or anything in the world beyond the rags which cover their nakedness. They contrive to live by blacklegging the English workmen. They are our Heathen Chinese. We shall have an anti-Jewish riot in the East End quite as serious as the anti-Chinese riot in California, if we don't look out.[36]

And the following year, in his book *Truth About Russia* Stead stated: 'We have already made the discovery in London that the presence of a colony of Russian Jews is an all but intolerable nuisance. We can sympathise better now than of old with the unfortunate Russians, who have five millions of the poorest Jews in Europe encamped within their frontiers.'[37]

In spite of Stead's lack of sympathy for poor immigrant Jews, he took up Lipski's case with a determination seldom equalled in the history of journalism. It is possible to argue, of course, that Stead wanted to highlight the terrible conditions found amongst the immigrant Jews and, by establishing Lipski's innocence, to throw the blame on to two other Jews, one of whom, Schmuss, was clearly a 'pauper foreigner'. But if there was any evidence of this – and none has been discovered – it was forgotten in Stead's desire to save Lipski's life.

The *Pall Mall Gazette*'s revelation of the 'Conversion of Mr Justice Stephen' was read by Matthews on Saturday afternoon, 13 August, the day following its publication. Matthews informed the House late the same day:

> Since I have been in the House today I have learnt that an account of what passed at the interview between Mr Justice Stephen and Mr Hayward had appeared in print; and I wish to say that I have heard from Mr Justice Stephen this afternoon that such statements in the public Press are partly exaggerated, partly false, and altogether irrelevant to the inference drawn. He further informs me that he is in no degree dissatisfied, either with the verdict or with my decision. And, again, he says: 'I did not at the time feel so clear and strong in my opinion as you did, but your decision has not surprised me nor given me the least uneasiness.' Therefore, in what I have done, I hope my Hon. Friend will see that I have acted in entire accord with the learned judge.[38]

Matthews then left the Chamber to continue a meeting he was having with Hayward, the first time the two had met. The meeting had been arranged by Baron Henry de Worms, whom a young journalist assisting Hayward, L. J. Greenberg, had seen earlier that day. Greenberg later became a leading English Zionist (Herzl, the founder of the Zionist movement, described him as 'the most able of all my helpers') and much later took over the editorship of the *Jewish Chronicle* as well as the *Jewish World*.[39] Baron de Worms, the Parliamentary Secretary to the Board of Trade, was the most senior Jewish member of the Government. The preceding year, however, he had severed his connection with the Jewish community after one of his daughters had married a non-Jew;[40] for fourteen years before that, de Worms had been the president of the Anglo-Jewish Association. Matthews and de Worms would have known each other well: both were barristers and both had a close connection with Ceylon. Matthews was brought up in Ceylon, and the service the de Worms family rendered to the economic development of Ceylon (through coffee planting) was such that Queen Victoria allowed the family to use their Austrian title in England.

The meeting with Matthews, which was attended by Hayward, Greenberg, Baron de Worms, a number of MPs, Sir

Henry James (the Attorney-General) and Godfrey Lushington, lasted about an hour and a half. The Home Secretary concluded the meeting by stating that 'he would keep his mind open to the last moment and would not allow the law to take its course if he saw the slightest grounds for altering his decision.'[41]

On Saturday, the Queen asked Charles Ritchie, the Minister responsible for local government and the Member of Parliament for St George's-in-the-East, where the murder occurred, for a report on the case. Why she was interested in the case is not clear: perhaps it was because of Hayward's telegram to her earlier that week, or, more likely, Stead's revelation concerning Stephen's 'conversion'. Ritchie wrote to the Queen on Sunday, 14 August, saying that he had had a number of conversations with the Home Secretary and that he, Ritchie, 'is able to assure Your Majesty that Mr Justice Stephen does not doubt that the verdict of the jury was a just verdict', although, 'Mr Justice Stephen feels some regret that he did not more fully place before the jury certain portions of the case which tended in the prisoner's favour.'[42] Ritchie then referred to the acid, stating that 'in the course of the inquiry a piece of evidence of a very important character has transpired which was not before the jury at the trial.' The nitric acid was a mixture of nitric acid and sulphuric acid and 'such a mixture as this the chemist reported was of most rare occurrence.' The Home Secretary, reported Ritchie, 'after allowing full weight to the previous good character of Lipski and to all the facts that could be advanced in his favour does not entertain any doubt as to the justice of the verdict.'

Stephen, on the other hand, continued to worry. On Saturday afternoon, after communicating with Matthews, he left for Devon, to stay with his close friend, J. A. Froude,[43] the historian and literary figure (Carlyle's and Disraeli's biographer), at Froude's summer residence. No doubt, Stephen discussed the case that evening with Froude, who held a far more favourable view of Stead than Stephen did.[44] The next morning, shortly after nine o'clock, Stephen sent the following telegram marked *Most Important* to the 'Secretary of State Home Dept. Whitehall London to be delivered wherever he may be instantly':

I have anxiously considered Lipski's case. I retain opinion already expressed. I do not know what passed last night in House of Commons but suggest respite of one week with intimation that reprieve is not to be expected. This would remove any impression of haste from public mind and give Hayward opportunity of answering Stevenson.

Stephen wrote to his wife that same day:

I have decided to return to town tomorrow, after thinking over and over Lipski's case. I decided at last, this morning, to telegraph to Matthews to respite the man for a week; to satisfy the public and avoid the appearance of haste. I do not doubt the man's guilt, but I thought the execution was to follow too quickly on the consideration of the case, and I felt also that when we held our final conversation on Thursday night, I had been rather tired and hurried, and I wished to make assurance doubly sure. I shall therefore go back to town tomorrow, thoroughly restudy the whole case, from first to last, and probably come back to my first opinion, for I do not see how anything new can come out. I am dreadfully vexed about the whole matter, as you may imagine, and the worst of it is that everyone will say, I was bullied into it by that blackguard Stead. In fact his disgusting interferences tempted me violently to hold off from all interference at all, but that would have been a vile motive to act upon. I have tried to do right, but it has been a most trying time, and I shall not forget it for a long time.

Matthews had no choice but to grant the one-week respite. On Sunday afternoon, the governor of Newgate delivered the respite to Lipski, with the instructions the governor had received from the Secretary of State:

In communicating the enclosed Respite to Israel Lipski, be good enough to inform him distinctly that it is granted not from any doubt existing in my mind as to the verdict or sentence, but merely to enable his solicitor to make certain enquiries which he has asked to be allowed to make. The convict must clearly understand that unless these enquiries put a new aspect upon the case the sentence will be carried into effect.

I am, Sir, your obedient servant,

Henry Matthews.

Rabbi Simeon Singer

Chapter Seven

A Further Week

RABBI SIMEON SINGER, who had been acting as Lipski's spiritual advisor, translated the respite for Lipski late on Sunday afternoon. The thiry-nine-year-old Singer, who at one time had been a master at Jews' College, London, and was since 1879 the rabbi of the fashionable and wealthy New West End Synagogue,[1] had acted eleven years earlier as one of the advisors for Isaac Marks, wrongly thought by some to be the first Jew to be hanged in England for murder since the Jews had been expelled from England in 1290.[2]

After Lipski had been convicted, he was, it seems, passed from one rabbi to another. The rabbi who preached near Newgate was very old and could not undertake the task. Another rabbi saw him once or twice and passed him on to other hands. Finally, Rabbi Singer, perhaps because of his involvement in the earlier Marks case, took on the duty.[3]

The Jewish community did not receive the news about the respite until the next morning. The editor of *Die Tsukunft*, who had urged Jews to sign petitions, related his feelings:

> How many bad dreams people must have had. I myself dreamed about Lipski hanging, his body being buried, and angels taking his innocent soul to the Garden of Eden, as his spirit chokes those who permitted him to be hanged innocently. I hear as they scream 'Oh! brother Lipski! Have pity, do not choke me. I did not sign because I cannot write. Pity! Have Pity!'
>
> But night ended. The beautiful morning approached. Together with the rays of the sun came the report that Lipski will not be hanged. His sentence was postponed.[4]

Lipski was now to hang on the following Monday morning. During the week, the Lipski case was in every paper, almost every day. *Die Tsukunft* reported: 'The name Israel Lipski has in the past week been the universal topic of discussion among old and young, Jews and Christians, street children and small innocent children who know nothing more than that there is a Lipski that they hear of in their houses and on the streets.' The paper also described fights that had started to break out on the streets because of Lipski. A fight on the Wednesday of that week began when Jews retaliated to taunts: 'More locals came along and it turned into a Russian pogrom with English blows.'

During the week, Lipski, who was strictly observant, received kosher food for the first time. For his first two weeks in Newgate his only meals were said to be breakfast and tea.[5] Lipski also received a number of visitors. Singer came almost daily from the South Coast, where he was on holiday with his family. Miss Lyons, his fiancée, had visited him the previous week; there is no evidence, however, of a visit this week. Lipski's landlord and landlady visited him on Tuesday afternoon. Their conversation was reported in the Press the following day:

> *Lipski:* I have been in your house for two years. You two have been like father and mother to me, and I should like you to know that I am innocent. I swear by Almighty God, before him I shall stand on Monday, that I shall be hanged innocently; and I like to protest my innocence, though I know you cannot help me.
> *Landlord:* How can you be so indifferent under such horrible circumstances?
> *Lipski:* It is easy to be gay, and still easier to die, when you know that you will die innocently.[6]

Hayward visited him a number of times. On Friday, accompanied by an interpreter, he told Lipski of the efforts he and his friends were making on his behalf. Hayward told the Press of the following significant conversation:[7]

> *Hayward:* The week is going very, very fast.
> *Lipski:* Yes, but I have good hopes still.
> *Hayward:* You seem very cheerful.
> *Lipski:* Oh, yes, I think the Lord will not forsake me. I have done no wrong.
> *Hayward:* Well, it might be that your sentence will be changed into one of imprisonment.
> *Lipski:* Oh, I would rather die.

Hayward, who had left on Saturday evening to rejoin his family on holiday in Eastbourne, had received a telegram from the Home Secretary on Sunday evening with the news of the respite. The next morning he telegraphed Scotland Yard asking for assistance in his efforts to prove Lipski's innocence. When he returned to London on Monday, Hayward did not get the co-operation he expected – or deserved. On Tuesday morning, he received a telegram from the Home Office saying that an answer to his request would be forwarded at noon by

138

special messenger. It did not arrive until late that afternoon. Godfrey Lushington wrote: 'I am directed by the Secretary of State to acquaint you that the police have been instructed to give you all the information they possess as to the lodgings of Simon and Schmuss. They cannot part with the phial or lock, but these articles will be shown to anyone that you desire in the presence of the police, and can be seen at Scotland Yard at any time, and any experiments can be made there.'[8] A postscript was added stating that whenever the bottle or lock was shown or experimented upon, the presence of two police officers would be required and that the police should be assisted by a skilled locksmith.

When Hayward went to Scotland Yard to see the lock and the bottle, the police would not even show him the exhibits unless a locksmith was present. Hayward contended that the locksmith only had to be present if experiments were conducted. Inspector Final, Hayward stated in his complaint to the Home Secretary, would not even let him send in a photographer to take a picture of the bottle. Final, however, later told the Home Office that he did give Hayward permission to send in a photographer 'to photograph it in the presence of two police officers, but possession will not be given to him.' Final alleged that Hayward had been abusive, calling him 'a villain and a scoundrel', and stating: 'You have done all you possibly can and are doing to hang this man.' Another police officer reported to the Home Office that 'Hayward became enraged, stamped his feet and slammed the door.' In any event, the next day, Thursday, the matter was cleared up through the intervention of the Home Secretary, to whom Hayward had gone to complain, and Hayward was allowed to have the bottle photographed, but Hayward publicly complained: 'My feeling is that they gave me a week and have taken three days off.'[9] Hayward requested more time, stating that he felt 'fearfully overweighted in having to conduct my inquiries almost alone, and with the police standing in my way.' However, on Friday, the Home Secretary wrote that he 'must decline to grant any extension of time.'

Throughout the week, the Press, led by the *Pall Mall Gazette*, covered every new – and old – development in the case. The *Gazette*'s campaign was an unprecedented and, perhaps, since unmatched effort. Every day there was a leading article on the case with, from time to time, interviews, sketches, opinions

139

from other papers and investigative reporting. Indeed, the paper employed all the techniques for which Stead has become an important figure in the history of journalism. The titles of the articles give some of the flavour of the approach:

Monday August 15: *A Life for a Bottle*
Tuesday August 16: *The First Batch of Fresh Evidence*
Wednesday August 17: *On the Murderer's Track*
Thursday August 18: *Fresh Evidence and Further Clues*
Friday August 19: *Dare We Hang Lipski?*
Saturday August 20: *Spare the Man*

The Saturday edition contained almost four full pages devoted to the case. It put the issue squarely and properly: 'Let us see at the outset exactly what the question at issue is. It is simply this: whether there is or is not an element of reasonable doubt in the case. It is not whether the crime can or cannot be brought home to any other parties.' Stead ended his Saturday editorial with the plea:

Once more then, and for the last time, we repeat the juror's prayer, not to the Home Secretary, but to his master, and cry again, Spare, spare the man!

Stephen returned from his friend Froude's in Devon on Monday. On Sunday, just after sending the crucial telegram suggesting a respite, he wrote a letter to the Home Office which he expected would arrive on Tuesday. He explained in some detail why he recommended the respite:

I saw no reason to change the opinion I gave you that Lipski was guilty, but I also felt that I came to the conclusion so quickly and after having been so much pressed by other business (in particular by trying a patent case which lasted a fortnight and made great demands on my attention) that I could hardly be sure that I might not on full and quiet consideration of the case see ground to change my mind. I think the man guilty, but I have not as yet so fully grasped all the details and got the matter so comprehensively into my mind as I should wish.

'I shall be in London,' Stephen went on to state, 'the night before you receive this and I propose to devote the whole of my time for as many days as may be required, two or perhaps three I should think, to the preparation of a final report which will express clearly my ultimate views on the subject.' Stephen authorised the Home Secretary to place upon him 'if he sees fit the whole of the responsibility for the respite' because 'after receiving that telegram he could hardly act otherwise than he did.'

The judge spent the next three days going over the case, becoming as his letters to his wife show, increasingly convinced of Lipski's guilt.

Tuesday, 16 August. I have seen Matthews today, and have engaged to see him tomorrow, and I think he has acted quite right throughout. I will explain at length about the respite when we meet . . . I have just had a cold meat dinner here, and mean to go back to my Lipski papers. It is the least fatiguing way of getting such a job done. Well, all this will be forgotten before long, and I have at all events, and mean to keep, a perfectly clear conscience about it all.

Wednesday, 17 August. I have had another day of Lipski, and have carefully gone through all the papers in the case, with all the bits of additional matter, which have been brought to light, and I feel now fully satisfied in my mind of his guilt, and so I shall report to Matthews. I don't want to tell all the horrid story, which is disgusting and odious to the last degree. I hardly ever remember so infamous and horrible a story. However, I have pretty well done my part in the matter, but I shall stay here till the last. I was nearly one and a half hours with Matthews this morning, and I shall see him again this evening. Never did I know such a pother and worry, but it is far worse for him, poor man, than it is for me.

Thursday, 18 August. I sat at home all day writing Lipski for Matthews, and expressed a perfectly clear opinion that the man was guilty. Matthews has behaved very well in the matter, and I suppose the poor wretch will be hanged. It has been an exceedingly painful affair, but it is now out of my hands.

Stephen's letter to the Home Office, sent immediately after requesting the respite, contained a number of suggestions for further investigation, some of which the Home Office had already undertaken. For example, he wanted an impartial person (not Inspector Final) to question the nurse in the hospital, concerning Moore's identification of Lipski. He also wanted Hayward to be asked to provide 'any further observations he may wish to make.' 'His conduct,' Stephen said, 'has made it absolutely impossible for me to hold any further communications with him direct or indirect.'

One matter which was of particular concern to Stephen was Dr Stevenson's evidence concerning the composition of the acid found in the bottle and at the scene of the crime. It will be recalled that it weighed very heavily against Lipski in the Home Office deliberations. Stephen stated in his letter to the Home Office:

Too much weight was attached to Stevenson's evidence. It struck us all powerfully and myself in particular, but we did not consider that its weight would be diminished to almost nothing if it should appear that the substance commonly called nitric acid was in fact usually composed of sulphuric and nitric acid.

Stephen added an important postscript to his letter: 'I should also inform Hayward of Stevenson's evidence so that he might show, if he could, that the nitric acid of commerce is really a mixture of nitric and sulphuric acid' – in other words, to give Hayward the opportunity of showing that other shops sold the very same 'nitric acid'.

Stevenson's crucial report that the acid at the scene was precisely the same as the acid sold by Moore was *not* given to Hayward. The Permanent Under-Secretary, Godfrey Lushington, specifically notes on the file, after receiving the judge's letter: 'Dr Stevenson's report is not to be communicated to Hayward.'

Because they did not have this specific evidence, Lipski's supporters pursued a will-o'-the-wisp, searching for a chemist who might have sold nitric acid to someone other than Lipski. Indeed, this may well have been what the Home Office was hoping would happen. And Lipski's supporters found such a person, a reputable chemist by the name of Buchner, whose shop was in a nearby street, Houndsditch. He came to Hayward on Thursday saying that 'about the end of June a dark man, rather square built, hair dark brown, a foreign Jew by his face, purchased for two-pence, two ounces of nitric acid, in a bottle labelled *Bell and Co Camphorated Oil*. The description of the person did not at all match Lipski, who was tall, fair and of slight build. The evidence had the ring of truth to it; Buchner 'noticed the label, because the bottle being oily my label would not stick.'[10]

Hayward was, however, informed by the Home Office in general terms on Wednesday that the nitric acid sold by Moore and also that found on the scene contained more sulphuric than nitric acid, but Hayward took the position that 'its being adulterated was no proof that it came from Moore's shop.' The letter from the Home Office, which is not contained in any of the files, was obviously not very convincing; Hayward said on Wednesday night: 'The Treasury have a theory that the acid **was adulterated**.'[11] Hayward was not deterred. He took Buchner's evidence to the Home Office on Thursday. If Hayward had received Stevenson's report, he might not have pressed Buchner's evidence so strongly.

142

The Home Office quickly discovered that the acid could not have come from Buchner's shop because Dr Stevenson's laboratory at Guy's Hospital showed that Buchner's acid (which was from the same batch that was sold at the end of June) was of a somwhat different composition than that used at the scene. As Lushington noted on the file: 'The analysis is conclusive that Buchner's acid was not used in the murder.' But this fact was not communicated to Hayward or the Press and so the Buchner evidence was prominently featured in the newspapers, and Lipski's advisors continued to search for the person who may have bought the acid from Buchner. On Friday, for example, the young journalist helping Hayward, L. J. Greenberg, told the Home Office about a man in Birmingham who may have been the person who purchased the acid from Buchner. On Saturday, the *Pall Mall Gazette* contained a sketch of Buchner's shop under the heading *The Shop Where the Poison Was Bought* and stated: 'We give here a sketch of Mr Buchner's shop at 149, Houndsditch, where the bottle labelled *Camphorated Oil* was presented at the end of June, was filled with nitric acid by the chemist, and was found in the bed of Miriam Angel.' As late as Saturday night Hayward was telling the Press about the importance of Buchner's evidence.[12] If Stevenson's reports had been given to Hayward, this false lead might not have been pursued.

The fact that Moore's acid had the same composition as that used in the murder does not, of course, prove that it might not have come from another shop, although Dr Stevenson purchased acid from five other places and found none of them was mixed with sulphuric acid.

Even if the acid did come from Moore's shop, it may not have been Lipski who purchased it. Some effort was made by the Home Office, without success, to link Lipski with the bottle, apart from Moore's identification. The chemist at Bell & Co, whose label was on the bottle, had seen Lipski when he was brought into Dr Kay's surgery and told the Home Office that he 'did not recognise Lipski as a customer.' Mrs Lipski, the landlady, was shown the bottle and said: 'I never before saw that or any other bottle labelled *Camphorated Oil* in Lipski's room or any other room in the house.' Similarly, Mrs Levy said: 'I used occasionally to clean Lipski's room while he occupied it. I never saw a bottle labelled *Camphorated Oil* therein or any other bottle like the one you show me so labelled.' The Home

Office even checked hospital records to determine whether Lipski ever had a condition which might have called for camphorated oil, but all they found was a record of a cut finger several months earlier. The Home Office thus had difficulty connecting Lipski with the bottle, apart from the identification in the hospital.

Meanwhile, Hayward was offering additional evidence in Lipski's favour. He obtained evidence from Lipski's former employer, Mark Katz, where Lipski learned the stickmaking business, that nitric acid was not used in Katz's work, as nitric acid was used only for hard wood. Moreover, Hayward offered to obtain evidence that the sticks that Lipski had already worked on did not contain nitric acid. He wrote to the Home Office: 'Lipski never used nitric acid either when working for himself or his employer. Acid was not used for the kind of sticks made by them. I have one in my possession which can be tested.'

Moore's identification of Lipski in the hospital was therefore very important to the Crown's case. Inspector Final gave his opinion that the identification 'was not open to exception'; the constable guarding Lipski, Final said, 'was a young man in plain clothes, and not brash like a constable.' When Final, Thick and Moore went into the ward, the constable, who was sitting beside the bed, according to Final, 'did not rise.' This was also the constable's view. It will be recalled that Stephen wanted an independent person to examine the nurse on this question. Nurse Miles, who was in bed at the hospital with diphtheria at the time of the questioning, did not support Final's confident assertion about the identification:

> I saw Inspector Final, the detective and Moore as they entered the door. They were all together and it seemed to me went altogether direct to the foot of Lipski's bed . . . It was only after they had left that I knew the object of their visit.

Moore himself gave a full account of the identification, supporting Final's opinion that other persons in the hospital were looked at before they came to Lipski and that he 'did not know the man who was sitting there was a detective.' Moore was even more certain now that it was Lipski: 'I have seen the man since – at the police court and in the dock – and I have not the slightest doubt about his being the man who bought the stuff – the nitric acid.' Moore even added some details about the person who purchased the acid that had not come out at the trial: 'I noticed the creases on the arms were full of dust as if he had been filing wood. I meant to have mentioned this before, but I never had a chance.' Assuming that this was not imagined by Moore to confirm his identification, it does not necessarily help the Crown's case, because there was no evidence that Lipski had done any work himself that morning.

More importantly, Moore stated for the first time that the purchaser had a handkerchief around his neck:

I think he had a coloured handkerchief tied round his neck. I don't think he had a collar – a shirt collar I mean. I could not positively swear what the colour of the handkerchief was. It seems to me running in my head that it was a mixture of blue and red – but it was not tied even, same as we might – but it seemed to be put on any how.

The Home Office then investigated whether Lipski wore a handkerchief around his neck. No witness could be found to state that he did. The landlady and Mrs Levy said Lipski usually wore a collar and never saw him wearing a large handkerchief. Even Simon Rosenbloom said: 'He usually wore a collar. I never saw him wear a large neckhandkerchief.' The lad, Pitman, gave the same evidence and then added: 'Rosenbloom usually wore a neckhandkerchief and no collar. I do not remember the kind of handkerchief, but it was the same he was wearing at the trial when I last saw him.' On the other hand, Mrs Sarah Katz, Lipski's future sister-in-law, gave evidence that she had sold a one-foot-square silk handkerchief to Lipski:

About a year ago I bought a silk handkerchief from a shop in the Commercial Road. I think I paid two shillings and tenpence ha'penny for it. I bought it to wear round my neck but it was not long enough to tie into bows in front. It was a reddish coloured one. Sometime afterwards I sold it to Lipski for three shillings, I think. I never saw him wear it round his neck.

The handkerchief was important for a further reason, also not mentioned at the trial. Isaac Angel, the deceased woman's husband, went with his sister to his room in Batty Street two days after the murder to get some of his possessions. A constable let him in. Mr Angel told the police for the first time, almost three weeks after the trial, that he had found a dirty handkerchief on the bed: 'I saw lying on the bed from which the body of my wife had been removed, a dirty dark-coloured neck

145

muffler. This did not belong to me and I had never seen it before . . . The handkerchief was folded up for wearing around the neck and had the appearance of having been so worn.' Angel then claimed to have shown it to the constable, hung it on the bed rail, and left the room.

Angel's sister, Sarah Angel, who had accompanied him, confirmed this evidence: 'It was a reddish-brown or snuff-coloured one with flowers. It was dirty and had the appearance of having been worn round the neck . . . I should say the handkerchief as folded up was about a yard long.' Sarah Angel also said that she went back to the room with another brother a week after the murder to clear out the room. The police were no longer there. The handkerchief was, according to her statement, still hanging on the bed, and when Mrs Lipski, who had accompanied them into the room, saw it she said: 'Dear me, that is the murderer's handkerchief.' The Angels took everything but the straw mattress and the handkerchief, which they say was left on the mattress. The mattress was later thrown out, when the Angels said they did not want it, although its cover was returned to them.

The police could get no confirmation of this story. Mrs Lipski denied it: 'They never showed any handkerchief to me and I did not see one.' Nor could the constable recollect anything about a handkerchief:

> They spoke to me, but I could only imperfectly understand what they said. I did not hear them say anything about a handkerchief nor did I notice Angel with one in his hand or anywhere about the room.

Was a handkerchief found in the room? Who was mistaken or lying, the Angels or the landlady? If a handkerchief was found in the room, was it Lipski's? If not, where was Lipski's handkerchief?

Another new matter which emerged in the third week after the trial was that the landlady, Mrs Lipski, claimed that her box, which was kept in Mrs Levy's room, was broken open on the morning of the murder. Hayward wrote to the Home Secretary on the Tuesday of the third week:

> Mrs Lipski will prove that during her absence between ten and eleven on the morning of the murder her box was wrenched open; all the things had been taken out and returned in great disorder; a purse in the box contained only pawn tickets had been opened and left open; nothing had been stolen. The thieves, whoever they were, had evidently been seeking for money

only. She had told this to the police but they said it had nothing to to with the matter and did not ask her about it. She had told me also about this attempted robbery, but I had no idea that it took place on the morning of the murder.

If true, the evidence supports the defence that theft was the motive and not lust, and that anyone who may have thought that Mrs Lipski had money in the box and tried to steal it, also tried to steal from Mrs Angel.

The Home Office started a new round of examinations. 'I never said anything about the box,' Mrs Lipski told the officer investigating at the request of the Home Office, 'because I was not asked.' She claimed to have told Inspector Final about the box on the day of the murder, but he simply said: 'Never mind, he's found under the bed.' Mrs Levy supported Mrs Lipski, stating that Mrs Lipski had called out: 'It's open. I am robbed.' Mrs Levy also claimed her own box had been disturbed, but nothing taken.

The deceased woman's mother-in-law, on the other hand, stated that she 'did not hear Mrs Lipski or Mrs Levy call out that they had been robbed or that anything had been done to their boxes.' Inspector Final said that 'Mrs Lipski never said a word to me about the box which she now says had been broken open . . . None of my officers reported to me that any complaint had been made about it to them by Mrs Lipski or anyone else.' Constable Inwood, who was in the house shortly after the murder, said that Mrs Lipski mentioned the box only because she was worried that the large number of people – perhaps twenty – in Mrs Levy's back room were 'smashing my box'. He removed two people who were sitting on it, and saw that there was a crack in the lid 'where it had apparently been forced in by the weight'; and three hours later Mrs Lipski said to him 'I should not be surprised if those people have taken something out of my box.'

The Home Office gave no weight to the story of the box. Nor was the Home Office impressed with the new evidence – described by the *Pall Mall Gazette* as 'of an extraordinary character'[13] – given the same week by Mrs Levy that she saw the back of a strange man going out of the house about nine-thirty on the morning of the murder. She had intended to mention this in court, she said, but she forgot, and when she got home and told her landlord, he said that it was too late now to say anything. The Home Office also did not pay much heed to

147

the evidence of the landlord's employer, who claimed to have been at 16 Batty Street at seven o'clock on the morning of the murder and saw two strange men coming out.

Of far greater concern to the Home Office was the evidence concerning the abrasions on Lipski's elbows. It will be recalled that Dr Calvert, who examined Lipski at the hospital, had stated the week before the respite that in his opinion 'such abrasions were caused by his elbows rubbing against some hard substance such as the floor of a room.' This evidence did not come out at the trial, although Hayward said he asked McIntyre to ask Dr Calvert about it. After the respite, Dr Kay was asked about Dr Calvert's opinion. According to Dr Kay:

> Those abrasions were caused by the mob who tried to lynch Lipski as the police were taking him to the police station. I examined Lipski's arms when I found him under the bed at 16 Batty Street and there were no abrasions, there were only a few small scratches not recent. I looked out of the window of 16 Batty Street and saw the mob seize Lipski by his bare arms and try to drag him from the custody of the two policemen all the way up Batty Street.

Dr Kay then added that 'if Lipski is guilty, his accusation of the two men is worse than a murder committed under the influence of sexual excitement, inasmuch as the accusation was made in cold blood.'

Calvert disagreed with the mob theory stating, 'the fact of the abrasions being both of a similar character and on corresponding positions on each arm would tend to negate the opinion that they were produced by mere pulling-about or even by blows.' But Dr Kay stuck to his earlier opinion that the abrasions were not present when Lipski was at Batty Street:

> I saw nothing to attract my attention as to his elbows – but if there had been abrasions I should have seen them and made a note of them.
> I am able to say positively there were no abrasions on his elbows at that time.
> I saw the police taking Lipski up Batty Street and on to my surgery.
> There were two policemen – they were holding him by the shoulder or by the arm and when the mob tried to take him away, they got hold of him anyway they could. I should think there must have been two thousand. It was a howling mob – I have heard it estimated at two thousand. I could see some of the mob get hold of him by his arms, his arms were hanging down – the police had him by the shoulders – women were as bad as the men – they tried to drag him away. They never got him right away from the police who clung to him, and he never fell on the pavement. He might have been knocked against the wall of the street. I am certain the abrasions were caused in this struggle. They were because I saw him before and after.

148

The police confirmed that there was a large hostile mob, one constable stating: 'We then got him into the street where the mob tried to molest him, took hold of his hair and one or two kicked him on the legs. It was a very large mob and very excited. We tried to get him along but as the mob increased we found great difficulty in getting along and I suggested that we should put him in Mr Kay's surgery until I could get a cab.' But, he added, 'I noticed no injury to him in any way.' Two other constables denied that Lipski was even touched by the mob. One stated: 'The mob was very violent and attempted to strike him but did not succeed in doing so . . . I am quite sure the mob did him no injury.' The other confirmed this view: 'There was no struggle in the street. The crowd tried to get round him – no one touched him except myself and the other constable.'

Whose evidence was correct, the police officers' or Dr Kay's? The Treasury solicitor had no doubt that Kay's evidence should be accepted over the police officers', stating: 'Dr Kay's statement however is absolutely conclusive on that point. He does not admit the shadow of doubt on the subject. There were no abrasions on Lipski's elbows when he was found under the bed.'

On almost every point raised at the trial there were further investigations that week by the Home Office and by Hayward – and in many cases there was new evidence.

There was, however, very little new evidence concerning the lock, perhaps because it was so exhaustively dealt with before the respite. Hayward, however, continued to press the point, writing to the Home Office early in the week that 'a locksmith today has shewed me how a lock with the key inside could by means of a bent wire or a button hook be opened almost as easily as if the key were outside.' A number of cases came to light of earlier crimes committed where doors were locked from the outside. A London doctor wrote to the *Pall Mall Gazette* about cases in Newcastle and Manchester where robbers entered hotel rooms locked from the inside and then relocked the door with the key still inside after the robbery was completed. A Scottish solicitor wrote to the *Gazette* of the execution of a woman, found drunk in a locked room with a bloody poker in her hand, lying beside her dead husband, and the subsequent confession of an Irishman to the murder.[14]

Hayward continued to remind the Home Office that Schmuss was a locksmith.

Other possible solutions to the locked door were, no doubt, put forward by others. Could the door have been locked from the outside and the key slipped under the door, causing the persons who broke down the door to assume that the key had fallen when the door was burst open? This was one of the possible solutions raised by Israel Zangwill a few years later in his classic locked-door mystery *The Big Bow Mystery*, obviously inspired by, but not based upon, the locked door in the Lipski case. (In Zangwill's book the murder was committed by the policeman who broke down the door.) Arthur Conan Doyle's locked room mystery, *The Speckled Band*, published in 1892, is less easily traced to the Lipski case: in this Sherlock Holmes story the victim was poisoned by a snake trained to enter the victim's room. Locked room mysteries have become an important genre of mystery stories.[15]

Lipski's clothes were examined at Hayward's request, and with the permission of the police, by two chemical experts, who supported Lipski's story. 'The lower part of the left skirt of the coat,' they wrote, 'is most damaged and burned away, as well as the under part of the left sleeve, which is also very much saturated . . . The great spread and splash of the acid on this particular part of the coat could only be caused in two ways – (1) by being thrown directly upon it, or (2) by an attempt while lying on his back in a struggling position to ward off or push away some person or persons leaning over the body, probably in the act or attempt of pouring acid down the throat from the bottle.'[16] Spots on Lipski's shirt, according to their report, 'tend to show that the direction and flow of the acid could only be caused by the knocking or pushing away of the bottle from the throat or chest.' They also concluded that one ounce of acid was not sufficient to produce the results that occurred: 'We are also clearly of the opinion, taking into consideration the quantity of acid found in the stomach of the murdered woman, the acid stains on the floor, bedclothes, and other places, that at least two or three ounces of acid must have been used.'

Dr Stevenson conducted further tests. He had already given his opinion that one ounce was sufficient to do the damage caused. He examined Lipski's coat and concluded that the acid had spilled from inside the pocket:

I am of opinion that the burn in the left flap pocket was with great probability made by the acid liquid being poured or spilt inside the pocket or on the upper part. The spilling of the acid whilst a two ounce uncorked phial was being carried in the pocket would entirely account for the burns in this part of the coat. I am of opinion that the spilling of the acid on the outside of the pocket would not entirely account for the burns in the pocket.

Moreover, Stevenson examined Rosenbloom's clothes, which had recently been washed: 'Washing,' he wrote, 'would not entirely remove nitric acid stains or those produced by a mixture of sulphuric acid and nitric acids. I can detect no acid stains on the garments of Rosenbloom.' Stevenson and the Home Office assumed, of course, that these were the clothes worn by Rosenbloom on the day of the murder. Further, Stevenson found a number of acid stains near the bed, but found 'the half of the room nearest the entrance door was free from acid stains'. There is nothing in the files concerning a possible search for acid stains on the landing where Lipski says he was attacked. Nevertheless, Stevenson's evidence was clearly unfavourable to Lipski.

The bottle was the subject of new evidence by Rabbi A. E. Gordon, the minister of the Hambro Synagogue. He stated that he had called on Harris Dywein, who, it will be recalled, had said that he had found the bottle on the bed. Rabbi Gordon wrote to the Home Office that Dywein told him that 'when he entered the murdered woman's bedroom he found the empty poison bottle on the table and being afraid that blame might be attached to the husband of the murdered woman, he put the bottle into his pocket. On the discovery of Lipski under the bed, he took the bottle from his pocket and placed it underneath the feather bed.' Gordon later told the Treasury solicitor: 'Other people have told me that they have heard the same from Harris [Dywein] that I have.' Hayward took the point one step further. He wrote to the Home Secretary that he had heard that Dywein had 'in the first place found the phial somewhere outside Mrs Angel's room', but then added: 'I have not yet been able to get evidence of this.' The *Pall Mall Gazette* commented: 'It would not be fair to other parties to draw any inferences from all this; but it is at least indisputable that this fresh evidence also gives a new aspect to one of the crucial points of the case.'[17]

What the inference is that could possibly be drawn is not

151

clear. Was it simply that Schmuss or Rosenbloom put the bottle on the table? Or was it that Mrs Angel's husband was somehow responsible for the murder?

Dywein denied the conversation: 'I did not tell Mr Gordon that I took up the bottle and put it in my pocket. I did not tell him I saw it on the table... What I told Mr Gordon was, "It is a good thing that the man was found, otherwise they would have accused the husband of it".' The Treasury solicitor who examined Dywein and Gordon was not impressed by Gordon's evidence, particularly as Gordon had been assisting Hayward (by translating for him when Hayward visited Lipski in jail):

> The Home Secretary must form his opinion – but mine is that Mr Gordon has somehow or other persuaded himself that the statements respecting the bottle were made to him by Dywein, whereas in fact no such statements were ever made to him by Dywein or anything to the like effect.

Lushington agreed, noting on the file that the proof 'that it was found on the table seems to me altogether to fail.' In any event, said Lushington, 'the bottle having been found on the table is perfectly compatible with Lipski having committed the murder.'

The oddest letter in the Home Office files was in French from a Dr Apatowski, addressed to the Home Secretary and dated Monday, 15 August, the day first set for Lipski to be hanged. The translation of the full text of the letter is as follows:

> Your Excellency:
>
> I wish to address these few confidential words under the seal of your Excellency. The Polish Jews living in London have put into play all sorts of means to save their Lipski, despite the fact that they are themselves convinced that Lipski has committed this atrocious crime, accompanied by aggravating circumstance, revolting and rare in the annals of crime. But for these enraged fanatics, to see hanged one of their Jews by Christian hands is not only dishonourable for them, but also profaning to the highest degree the Mosaic religion, and especially the Rabbinical doctrines. And they are able to perjure themselves by the thousands to prevent one of theirs being hanged by Christians, were he the biggest and most atrocious criminal in the world. The Rabbinical laws permit perjury in such cases. Yes, Russia and Germany have given England a lovely present, in chasing these furious and outraged fanatics, a leprous and consuming vermin, from a civilised and admired society.
>
> I learned this morning the cause of this atrocious crime, and nothing in the world can make me doubt that Lipski is behind it. If Your Excellency wishes to know what I have learned today, I ask him to charge one of his

public servants (not from the police) to write to me and I will come to see him to make this communication.

> With the greatest respect.
> Dr Apatowski, former Chief Surgeon

P.S. I am an Israelite myself and quite well-versed in the Bible, Talmud, Rabbinical codes and in the cabbalistic or mystical doctrines, but I have nothing in common with these detestable fanatics. At the same time, not wishing to portray myself as Christian – I concern myself with only positive sciences, the celestial sciences are not my business.

Lushington noted on the file: 'Ask the Treasury solicitor to see this man.' The solicitor took the following equally bizarre statement from Apatowski later that week:

> Last Monday morning, a Jewess told me: 'perhaps Lipski is no more.' He was to have been hanged at eight thirty last Monday – and she didn't know that he had been reprieved. She added: 'I have not slept one wink all night because one of our nation has been hanged.'
> I asked her why he had done it.
> She answered me 'The woman he has murdered was his country woman and she was betrothed to him abroad in Poland, in his country, then they came to London, and she married another man, and had deserted him – and he wanted her to be his mistress, and she refused.'
> I cannot tell you the name of this woman – my life would not be safe.
> If the Government will make me safe – give me say twenty pounds so that I may go from this quarter of London to another, I will tell you the name of this woman.

The Treasury solicitor reported to the Home Office: 'In my judgement he knows nothing and his information is worth nothing.' Whether or not the information was worth nothing, it should be noted that the Home Office had earlier tried to ascertain whether Lipski and Mrs Angel knew each other in Poland. A question concerning this matter had been raised by one of the jurors at the coroner's inquest. In July, the Foreign Office asked the British Consul in Warsaw 'to make inquiries as to the antecedents of the deceased and of the prisoner with a view to ascertain if they were acquainted with one another in Poland.' A reply came back in early August, after the trial, saying that the Russian authorities in Warsaw were having no success in following any of the leads offered by the British police, but that 'researches continue with the view of proving the identity of the prisoner Lipski'. Nothing further was heard from the Russian authorities.

There were, of course, follow-up investigations of Rosenbloom and Schmuss by the Home Office and the defence. A number of witnesses came forward with further incriminating statements allegedly made by Schmuss. Nothing incriminating against Rosenbloom was uncovered. Indeed, witnesses gave him good character references. His landlord stated: 'Rosenbloom has lodged with me ever since he came to this country except the first week or two. He has been here I think about ten months. He is a very quiet steady young man, sober and inoffensive.' Of perhaps greater significance was the evidence of Sarah Katz, the sister of Lipski's fiancée and the wife of Mark Katz, the employer of Lipski and Rosenbloom:

> Rosenbloom has worked for us for the past twelve months or thereabouts. Almost ever since he has been in this country . . . He worked for us on the day before the murder and we took him back again the week after. We have always found him regular in his habits, quiet, honest and sober, and have no complaint to make respecting him.

The fact that the Katzes would re-employ Rosenbloom, knowing that Lipski was accusing him of murdering Mrs Angel and attempting to murder him, certainly suggests that they disbelieved Lipski's story. On the other hand, Mark Katz publicly expressed the view that Lipski was innocent, stating:

> He was a very good workman. He always gave me plenty of work for my money, and that is more than a good many do. He never got drunk, and always came to his time. I should be very glad to take him into my employ again, as I do not believe he ever did it.[18]

The evidence about Schmuss raised a number of unanswered questions. Why did he not stay to work at Lipski's? What did he do after he left Batty Street? Where did he get the money to go to Birmingham? Did he later make statements inconsistent with the story he told the police?

Schmidt, the hardware dealer next to the shop where Lipski is said to have bought the acid, supplemented his earlier testimony by describing Schmuss as 'a very quiet and inoffensive man [who] never mixed with any other person and always likes to be by himself'. During the seven or eight months Schmuss had been in England he worked occasionally for Schmidt. The only other job he had recently had was for part of a week for an engineer, Mr Lieber. Schmuss was obviously very poor. His landlord, Nathan Rabbinowitz, with whom Schmuss had lived for about a month and who had known him in Russia, described him as 'a quiet, industrious civil man' who 'shared a bed with a boy named Lewis.' If Schmuss needed work, why did he not stay for more than ten or fifteen minutes at Lipski's, where there was obviously work to be had? He had nothing better to do. Did he, in fact, go back to his house in Stepney for breakfast, about a twenty-minute walk away, remaining there for two or three hours, sitting with Rabbinowitz, his wife and the boy, Lewis, as he said later? Rabbinowitz later said he 'could not remember having seen Schmuss on that morning'; and the police interviewer added to the file 'neither could any other person in the house except the young man Samuel Robinski.' Godfrey Lushington noted in the margin of the file that 'there was nothing to make them remember the circumstances with accuracy.' Is this so? Lipski's statement accusing Schmuss was in the papers shortly after the murder. Surely Rabbinowitz and others would have then made a mental note of whether or not they had seen Schmuss that morning? The only person who claimed to have seen Schmuss back at his house was Schmuss's friend, Samuel Robinski (Schmuss and he had been apprenticed to the same master in Odessa), who had left for America on the very day Lipski was to be hanged and so was no longer available for questioning.

About a week after the murder, Schmuss went to Birmingham. His landlord had given him the name of a person who would be likely to find him work, which he did find as a slipper maker. Schmuss, when later questioned by the Home Office, said that he had earned the nine shillings and seven pence that it had cost to go to Birmingham by working at Mr Lieber's. But, as previously pointed out, Schmuss had only been employed by Mr Lieber for part of a week. Did he earn the money from this source, or was the train fare paid for from the sovereign that Lipski said he had given Rosenbloom? If the sovereign was not used for this purpose, where was the twenty-five shillings that Lipski had borrowed from his future mother-in-law the day before the murder?

The police investigated the places where Schmuss stayed and worked in Birmingham, in part because a rabbi in Birmingham was suspicious when Schmuss was reported to have said, in respect to the Lipski case: 'I shall never have any peace, life has gone for me.' Schmuss's Birmingham landlord described him as 'a very quiet young man' and had 'never noticed anything strange in his manner and behaviour.' The people at the place where he worked all stated that Schmuss 'had never said anything to make anyone believe there was anything against him.'

A number of witnesses came forward to say that Totakoski said that he, Totakoski, had lied at the trial. Totakoski, one of the four Russian locksmiths, it will be recalled, was supposed to have met Schmuss the morning of the murder, but Schmuss did not show up until about noon. These new witnesses, who lived in the same boarding house as Totakoski, said they heard him say more than once: 'If I had stated the truth at the police court two people would be locked up and Lipski would get off free.' He was also heard to say that 'he could open the door of the room in which the murder took place when the key was inside, shut, and fasten it again.' Moreover, a second-hand report was sent to the Home Office of a statement by Totakoski that he, along with Schmuss and Rosenbloom, 'had connection with the deceased woman on the morning of the murder.'

Totakoski, who was to be sent to Nottingham that very week by the Jewish Board of Guardians, gave a statement to the police:

> I have never said the words they accuse me of saying. I do not know where Lipski lived . . . I did not speak particularly of the door of Lipski's room. I spoke of the locks of doors generally . . . It is not true that I ever had connection with the deceased woman. I never knew her . . . I saw Schmuss about eleven o'clock the same morning when he told me he had been to Lipski's early that morning and said he should not like to work there.

Note that Totakoski now places Schmuss in the neighbourhood of the murder at eleven o'clock and not at twelve o'clock as Schmuss claimed.

The second-hand report about Totakoski came from an important new witness, Emil Barsook, who had just come out of prison where he had served some time for petty theft. It will be recalled that Barsook was one of the four Russian locksmiths identified at the trial as having been at Schmidt's shop the day before the murder. (Schmuss, Totakoski, and, most likely, Robinski were the others.) Barsook informed the Home Office that Schmuss told him a far different story than Schmuss told at the trial:

> A day or two after the murder Schmuss told me that when he went to Lipski's place on the morning of the murder, Lipski told him to wait in his workroom. This was about seven in the morning. He waited between ten minutes and a quarter of an hour. While waiting he heard a struggle in the deceased woman's room. Then he tried to look into the room; he opened

156

the door and looked in. He saw Lipski there with a man named Simon
Rosenbloom. As Schmuss opened the door Lipski came to it and said to
Schmuss 'Go, go, I will follow you.' Schmuss then went back into Lipski's
workshop and after waiting some time, not seeing Lipski, he went away.

Schmuss has told me that on the morning of the murder he had a
woman. I asked him what sort of a woman it was. He said 'You don't want
to know all about that, she is gone.'

The Home Office arranged to have Schmuss and Barsook
confront each other in the presence of the Home Secretary and
Mr Justice Stephen. Matthews acted as the interpreter.[19]
Whether his fluency in German enabled him fully to com-
prehend the witnesses' Yiddish is another matter, a point made
by a number of persons with respect to Mr Karamelli's
translation at the trial.

Schmuss was first questioned alone. He denied Barsook's
story: 'I never spoke to Barsook about the murder.' Barsook
was then brought in. Schmuss was examined further:

I know him [Barsook] by sight. I have seen him at Schmidt's.
I never told Barsook anything of what I had seen at Lipski's.
I did not speak to him about it.

Barsook repeated his allegation, stating that Schmuss told
him he 'had had a woman' and that when Barsook asked who it
was, Schmuss said: 'Why do you want to know; you won't get
her.' Schmuss protested: 'I can swear I did not tell Barsook I
had had a woman.' Barsook appears to have believed that
Lipski was innocent, stating, 'when I heard that Lipski said two
greeners had killed the woman, I believed Schmuss and Simon
had done it.'

Barsook was about to leave for America that very week.
Inspector Final reported to the Home Office that Barsook told
him that Hayward had paid for the passage and that Hayward
had the ticket in his possession, the clear implication being that
Hayward was purchasing Barsook's testimony. Barsook later
denied this, however, saying that his brother in New York paid
for the passage; Hayward, he said, had the ticket in order to
change the sailing date and had paid only his travelling
expenses in England.

Hayward complained publicly about the way the defence had
been conducted. He told the *Evening News*: 'The whole case was
in the brief, but not a point was put by the counsel for the
defence. I could not get the facts brought out which I wanted

brought out. It was scandalous, and I don't care who knows it.'[20] The *Evening News* later said that Hayward 'went farther than that; but, on the advice of his clerk, he considerably modified his words to what our representative reported as above.'[21] The paper, a rival of the *Pall Mall Gazette*, sent a reporter to see the two defence counsel, but they declined to say very much. Geoghegan wisely said that he 'made it a rule never to make any statements to anyone about any case he was concerned in.' McIntyre said a little more. He was asked about Geoghegan:

> I can only say this: He gave me every assistance. I know him very well. He is a very good [counsel] indeed, and always works his cases up thoroughly well. I am quite sure he did his very best.
> *Then, at any rate, you think Mr Hayward had not just cause for finding fault with him?*
> I would rather not make any statement about Mr Hayward, but I can say Mr Geoghegan gave me every satisfaction.
> *Don't you think Mr Hayward is a bit of a fanatic?*
> I will not say that. Every one takes a different view of every case. He was very clear in his brief and thoroughly believed in his client, which, it seems to me, is what a solicitor ought to do.
> *And you will not answer his accusation against you?*
> No. I would rather not. He can say what he likes, but I must say this, and I am at liberty to say it. He was most industrious, most persevering, and most energetic in getting up the evidence in the case. I can only say I did my best, and I am quite sure Mr Geoghegan did his – the result is what you know.[22]

The Home Office followed up Hayward's concerns about the performance of counsel by examining McIntyre shortly after the respite was granted. A number of alleged omissions were put to him by Matthews. The notes on the file indicate that he did raise some of the points (e.g. Lipski's insensibility) and that he refrained from putting others because they did not seem important (e.g. Angel's coat on Lipski's, the abrasions on Lipski's elbows).

McIntrye was also questioned about the failure of the prisoner to make an unsworn statement from the dock and said that the 'prisoner declined to make a statement although invited to do so' by him. Mr Justice Stephen confirmed in his later report to the Home Office that he told McIntyre that Lipski had the right to make an unsworn statement:

> I informed Mr McIntyre that it was my practice as it is that of Mr Justice Hawkins, Mr Justice Cave and I believe other judges, to allow every prisoner to make a statement to the jury before his counsel's address, but

after the conclusion of the evidence, but that this would entitle the counsel for the Crown to a reply. I added that I did not think he ought to be prejudiced by refusing my offer. After some consideration of the matter Mr McIntyre said that Lipski could only repeat what he had said before, and that he accordingly declined my suggestion: all therefore that the prisoner lost was the benefit of the manner which impressed Mr Hayward. This is a doubtful loss as people are in such cases very differently impressed by the same manner.

McIntyre did, however, support Hayward in one respect, by expressing concern over the judge's charge to the jury. Matthews' notes of the interview state:

McIntyre dissatisfied with the summing up. Stephen did not put the prisoner's points and showed his mind to be made up. A strong summing-up against the prisoner put forward the lust theory which the prosecution practically abandoned for the theory that he wanted Angel's new clothes to pawn having failed to get five shillings from the landlady.

Newgate Prison and the Old Bailey

Chapter Eight

Approaching the End

THE WEEK'S RESPITE was nearing an end. The Home
Secretary was to make his decision on Saturday, and if his
decision was, and remained, negative, Lipski was to hang on
Monday morning, 22 August, 1887.

Throughout the week a petition, or memorial, had been
circulated to Members of Parliament, not for a full pardon, but,
rather, to commute the sentence to life imprisonment: 'the case,
as presented by the prosecution,' the petition read, 'is not such
as to exclude all reasonable doubt, and that to enforce the last
penalty of the law would be to run a dangerous risk of an
irremediable mistake.'[1] By Wednesday, seventy-eight members had signed. The petition had been organised by R. B.
Cunninghame Graham, the radical MP, who has been called
by recent biographers 'a mixture of Hamlet and Don Quixote'[2]
and who was used by Shaw as a larger-than-life character in
several of his plays, including Sergius Saranoff in *Arms and the
Man*.[3] Cunninghame Graham, who strongly believed in
Lipski's cause ('Sir, this man is innocent,' he wrote to the *Jewish
World*[4]), pointed out to the Press that 'with barely two hundred
Members of Parliament in town, I have been able, in two days,
to get a petition signed by seventy-eight members, representing
all shades of political belief.'[5] By Friday evening, when it was
given to the Home Secretary, there were at least thirty-three
more signatures, making a total of over a hundred and ten
members, including such well-known names as R. B. Haldane
and the Irish leader Parnell. It should be noted, however, that
not one of the seven Jewish MPs signed the petition.

Matthews indicated in the House on Friday evening, in
answer to a question by Cunninghame Graham, that there was
no hope of a further respite: 'I am giving the most anxious care
and consideration to all the materials that have been laid before
me; and upon the materials that are before me at present I can
hold out no expectation of a further respite.'[6] The questioner
followed up by asking Matthews whether he was 'aware that a

petition, signed by one hundred Members of Parliament, is to be presented to him tomorrow in favour of the condemned man Lipski; and, whether, in view of that fact, he will reconsider his decision?' Matthews said he was aware of the petition, but again repeated the position he had earlier stated regarding questions relating to the exercise of his discretion: 'I must formally protest against interference with the ordinary course of the administration of justice by questions in the House.' *The Times* report noted that there were 'renewed loud cheers'.[7]

When the House met at noon on Saturday, Mr Cunninghame Graham presented 'a petition numerously signed by the inhabitants of Whitechapel and surrounding districts ... praying for the further respite of the condemned man Lipski.'[8] Matthews was not in the House, but the Leader of the House, W. H. Smith, protested 'in the strongest manner against any attempt being made to bring Parliamentary pressure to bear on the Secretary of State in the discharge of his solemn and responsible duty'; and the Speaker ruled that the petition was out of order because it was addressed to the Secretary of State.

The *Pall Mall Gazette* devoted almost four pages to Lipski in its Saturday edition. Other papers also supported Lipski's cause. *The Daily Telegraph*, for example, wanted the sentence commuted because 'what is patent to everybody is that the case is now involved in far too much uncertainty to make the execution of the prisoner at all safe.'[9] The *Methodist Times* stated that 'it is now morally impossible to hang Israel Lipski';[10] and the prestigious medical journal, *The Lancet*, analysed the evidence and concluded that 'after careful and anxious inquiry, and after balancing the evidence, we unhesitatingly avow that Lipski's guilt has not been proved beyond reasonable doubt.'[11]

All the Jewish papers supported Lipski, ranging from the committed Yiddish journal *Die Tsukunft* (as we have already noted), to the establishment English-language weekly, the *Jewish Chronicle*, which was more hesitant in its support:

Circumstantial evidence is rarely completely satisfactory, and in the present instance the case against the prisoner was by no means overwhelming. According to Jewish law it would have been impossible to convict Lipski on such evidence. The attitude of the community towards such cases is a very difficult one. To defend a criminal merely because he is a Jew is impossible, yet it seems only right that we should aid those who are nearest to us. Especially is this our duty where there is a possibility of

162

injustice being done owing to want of means. This certainly applies to Lipski as his position has now been placed before us.[12]

Between these two positions was the *Jewish World* which hoped 'that mercy will temper the Home Secretary's decision, and that he may be brought to see that . . . he may send a man to the gallows who one of these days may be known, above all question, to be entirely innocent.'[13]

Most of the Press reports were, however, opposed to a commutation, although some, such as *The Times*, took no position on the question. Some, like Henry Labouchere's *Truth*, were not concerned that Lipski might turn out to be innocent: 'To say that Lipski ought not to be hanged if a doubt as to his guilt exists,' wrote Labouchere, 'is practically to say that no one ought to be hanged upon circumstantial evidence.'[14] Much of the Press comment centred on Stead and the *Pall Mall Gazette* as much as on Lipski. 'We have been exposing the miserable tactics of that organ in the Lipski case,' wrote the *Gazette*'s competitor, the *Evening News*, 'and have proved that the means adopted to make capital out of the wretched convict have been as contemptible as the conclusions have been false.'[15] A Sunday journal, *Lloyd's Weekly*, whose masthead claimed that it had the 'largest circulation in the world', wrote of the 'screechings of one particular journal, which has mistaken violent declamation and heated abuse for evidence.'[16] The *Glasgow Herald*, referring to the earlier respite, said that 'it was the *Pall Mall Gazette* that frightened the Home Secretary, and . . . another step in the direction of government by journalism has been taken'[17]; and the *Birmingham Post*, from Matthews' own constituency, wrote of Matthews' 'latest exhibition of pliancy and vacillation' and the danger that 'trial by jury is to give place to trial by journalism.'[18]

Did the sensationalism of the *Gazette*, and the reaction against it by much of the establishment, influence the Home Office? While there is nothing in the surviving Home Office files to indicate that the Home Secretary, the permanent officials or the judge were influenced by these considerations, it would be surprising if they were not.

Stephen spent three days analysing the case, had two long consultations with Matthews, and completed his thirty-page report for the Home Secretary on Thursday. He concluded his report by stating that he now had 'no doubt of Lipski's guilt.' 'You are in substance asked,' he wrote, 'to reverse the decision of the jury upon a case fairly and fully tried before them and at which every opportunity was given for urging upon the jury all the matters now pressed upon you.' Stephen seems to have suppressed his earlier concern, confided to his wife, that Lipski's defence was nót adequate and that his own charge to the jury was not fair to the accused. ('The man was not quite properly defended,' he had written a week after the trial, 'and I myself did not exactly hit the right point in summing up.') Note, however, that his report again brings forward the lust theory which he had adopted in his summing up:

> No motive except lust or robbery can be suggested. There are several indications that lust rather than robbery was the motive. I refer in particular to the evidence of Piper and Dr Kay as to the position of the body and the dress. No doubt the matter in the vagina did not contain semen or at least spermatazoa, but the position of the body and of the dress is to say the least very remarkable.

The judge wished to uphold the sanctity of verdicts by juries and to discourage similar appeals to the Home Secretary. The Lipski case was 'an attempt to appeal from the decision of the jury on matters specially suited for their consideration to the Secretary of State. I believe that it is, and I am sure it ought to be, the practice of the Home Office to discourage such attempts. If it were not so, the functioning of juries would be seriously interfered with.' Stephen tested the new evidence, using the test of whether it could have been produced at the trial: 'Substantially the whole of it, and in particular the observations on Lipski's coat, in the markings on the elbows, on the lock, and on the prisoner's statement are observations which Mr McIntyre had every opportunity of making at the trial . . . The strong probability is that he deliberately acted as he did from a conviction that he was taking the best course for his client's interests.' The new evidence produced by Hayward, which showed that a door could easily be locked from the outside by a knowledgeable person, was dismissed by Stephen by stating that 'Hayward has suggested nothing about the lock which was not or might not have been submitted to the jury.' Stephen's approach is one that an appeal court would take today, but it is surely not the proper view when deciding whether to hang a person.

Godfrey Lushington, the Permanent Under-Secretary, refrained from expressing a conclusion in his twenty-six-page analysis, but there is no doubt that he was against a commutation. Lushington viewed the issue in the case not as whether there was a reasonable doubt, but rather as a 'choice ... between the two stories: was the murder committed by Lipski or by Rosenbloom and Schmuss?' His theory was, therefore, as unfair as Stephen's. But even if he had looked only for a reasonable doubt, he would not have found it. The only point which he conceded was possibly in Lipski's favour was the fact that there was no blood on Lipski: 'Mr Hayward is entitled to the benefit of this argument so far as it goes,' he wrote, but added that the circumstances of the murder were not known and so 'it would be perfectly possible that the blood which Mrs Angel threw up should have fallen on the coverlet alone.' He made no such concession, for example, on the possibility that the door was not locked from the inside, stating with respect to Hayward's theories that 'there is not a particle of evidence to support any one of these improbable sugges-tions.' Moreover, he took the preposterous position that it should be held against Lipski that he had not laid charges against Schmuss and Rosenbloom: 'more than six weeks have gone by and neither he nor his solicitor has made the slightest attempt to bring either of these people to justice, who according to his own view had not only robbed and ill-used him, but were causing him to be tried for his life.'

Lushington thought it was more likely that Lipski entered the room intending to steal rather than to rape 'because it is free from the difficulty which attaches to that of lust, *viz.* that Lipski must have known that if he ravished Mrs Angel, he could not escape detection.' But he wove in the lust theory by speculating that having killed her when she awoke, 'he now hoped to be undisturbed until the husband of the woman came back for dinner. He then either ravished the body or prepared to do so' when he was interrupted. Once again, Lushington put forward the possibility of necrophilia.

Stephen continued to advise the Home Office. On Friday, 19 August, he wrote to his wife:

> Just after I had settled everything nicely, came a letter from Matthews, or rather from G. Lushington, like the blind fury, with the abhorred shears, to say I must stay Lipski-ing till Monday. A whole mass of papers is coming to me tomorrow, on which I must give my opinion. Having a

willing horse at his service, I think Matthews is quite right to ride him. A regular ass is being made of him by all sorts of blackguards, parliamentary and otherwise, and I must do my best to help him, poor man . . . I am quite well and happy, and not too hard worked, though this affair is most anxious and worrying.

And on Saturday he wrote:

This certainly has been, and still is, a most painful time. I stayed because Matthews said he wanted me to advise on all the new representations and statements he had received, and I must pass today in doing so, and go down to the H of C tonight to give him my final report. It is distressing to the last degree, but is a satisfaction that I feel no shadow of regret for anything I have done.

Stephen wrote to the Home Secretary that the new papers that he looked at did not 'affect the opinion already expressed.'

Once again, Matthews, after a lengthy meeting with Stephen and Lushington, penned the crucial words on Stephen's note, 'Upon this, Nil. H.M.', which meant that he would not recommend any interference with the sentence. Matthews' rough notes in the file show that he was, perhaps, not quite as convinced as Stephen: 'Judge satisfied with verdict. I see no cause for being dissatisfied.' This reversed the position of the week before, when it was Stephen who had said to the Home Secretary: 'I did not . . . feel so clear and strong in my opinion as you did.'[19] Matthews was obviously impressed with Stephen's argument that the Home Secretary should not consider material which could have been introduced at the trial. The year after the Lipski case, and with specific reference to Lipski, Matthews told the House how he dealt with 'new facts' in such cases: 'the principle upon which he had gone,' Matthews stated, 'had been not to listen, but to refuse to listen, to allegations which were contradicted by sworn testimony at the trial, and to listen with great reluctance, and an unwilling mind to any statements of fact that might have been proved at the trial, but were not, and only to lend a willing ear to matters that had *bona fide* come to light since the trial.'[20]

On Saturday evening, Lushington forwarded the news by special messenger to Hayward:

Whitehall, August 20, 1887.

Sir

With reference to the case of Israel Lipski, I am directed to acquaint you that, after full consideration of the circumstances, and of all the representations made by yourself and others on behalf of the prisoner, the

166

Secretary of State sees no reason for advising any interference with the due course of the law.

I am, Sir, your obedient servant,

Godfrey Lushington[21]

Hayward then left to rejoin his family at Eastbourne, telling the Press: 'I have done my best for the poor fellow, and I feel sick at heart when I think that in a few hours he will be no more. I shall still hope that something may yet arise to prove that the life of an innocent man has been taken away.'[22]

The next morning, Sunday, Hayward sent a telegram from Eastbourne to the Queen, who was still at Osborne, urging, on behalf of a juror, that Lipski's life be saved because there was no premeditation. Three other jurors had sent a telegram to the Queen the previous evening, praying for mercy: 'To Queen Victoria. We, jurors on the trial of Lipski, pray your Majesty mercifully to commute the sentence into penal servitude.'[23] Shortly after noon on Sunday, the Queen's private secretary, Sir Henry Ponsonby, sent Matthews a telegram stating that the Queen had received the above telegram from Hayward. 'Have answered him,' wired Ponsonby, 'that it has been referred to you.' A telegram was sent by Matthews in reply to Ponsonby stating that 'no further respite could be granted, and that the only option was between carrying out the capital sentence or commutation to penal servitude.'

Matthews and Stephen met throughout the day to reconsider whether the law should, in fact, take its course. Stephen wrote to his wife in the late afternoon: 'I have had a very bad day, in and out of the Home Office. We cannot justify a commutation to ourselves though most anxious to do so ... I hope and believe I have kept the straight path, but it has been a dreadful affair.'

They met again at five o'clock at the Home Office. I will let an unnamed former official of the Home Office tell this part of the story, as he recollected it in 1921 when he was asked by a newspaperman to describe 'the most dramatic' episode he could remember. 'I need not pause to answer that question,' he replied, and described the late afternoon meeting between Matthews and Stephen:

I was then on the Home Office staff, and it was my duty to be in attendance while this critical conference was in progress. Time passed without a sound or sign coming from the room where the argument of life or death was proceeding. In the quiet of the late Sunday afternoon the chimes of Big Ben sounded the quarters from the Clock Tower. Six o'clock struck. I was tired of sitting alone, and opening the door of the Secretary's room quietly I entered and took a seat in the shadow.

It was a strange scene that I had broken in on. Absolute silence prevailed; but both men were so engrossed in thought that my entrance passed quite unnoticed. Matthews was seated in his chair, his elbows on his knees, his head buried in his hands. Stephen, his eyes fixed on the carpet before him, strode to and fro across the room.

I sat and waited. Outside, the church bells had begun ringing for the evening service, and their music alone broke the heavy silence of the room. Then Matthews spoke briefly, raising a point that had been hammered to weariness before. There was a brief answer from Stephen, and the silence was resumed, Matthews with his head still resting in his hands, Stephen still pacing the floor. Time passed. The bells ceased ringing, seven o'clock struck, and we passed into a soundless quiet. Now and then a question was put and an answer given, but there was no discussion. It seemed that the strange scene might continue until the hangman slipped his bolt next morning. I counted the quarters – one – two – three – eight o'clock. Three hours had gone by and no light had broken on the silent struggle.

I had ceased to expect any change in this drama of indecision, and resigned myself to an all-night vigil. Presently my ears caught the sound of a step in the corridor without. It paused at the door. A sudden thought flashed in my mind as I waited for what should follow. There came a low tap at the door, and I hastily opened it. As I did so a messenger handed me a letter. I took it eagerly, raised the flap sufficiently to catch the words 'I, Lipski, hereby confess . . .' and passed it to Matthews. As he read it he leapt to his feet with a cry as of one who had himself escaped from a sentence of death, and for a moment the load lifted from the two men made them almost beside themselves with joy. Then Matthews remembered the circumstances and turned grave.[24]

Lipski had signed a full confession. Rabbi Simeon Singer, who had been seeing Lipski almost daily for over a week, arrived at Newgate from his summer residence on the south coast on Sunday afternoon. He translated for Lipski Lushington's dispatch, which had stated that the Home Secretary was not going to interfere with the sentence – the first information that Lipski had of the decision. 'All hope of a reprieve was abandoned by the prisoner,' Singer later wrote,[25] and after a two-hour discussion Singer wrote, in English, Lipski's confession:

I, Israel Lipski, before I appear before God in judgement, desire to speak the whole truth concerning the crime of which I am accused. I will not die with a lie on my lips. I will not let others suffer, even in suspicion, for my sin. I alone was guilty of the murder of Miriam Angel. I thought the woman had money in her room. So I entered, the door being unlocked, and the woman asleep. I had no thought of violating her, and I swear I

168

never approached her with that object, nor did I wrong her in this way. Miriam Angel awoke before I could search about for money and cried out, but very softly. Thereupon I struck her on the head, and seized her by the neck and closed her mouth with my hand, so that she should not arouse the attention of those who were about the house. I had long been tired of my life, and had bought a pennyworth of aqua fortis that morning for the purpose of putting an end to myself. Suddenly I thought of the bottle I had in my pocket, and drew it out, and poured some of the contents down her throat. She fainted, and, recognising my desperate condition, I took the rest. The bottle was an old one which I had formerly used, and was the same as that which I had taken with me to the oil-shop. The quantity of aqua fortis I took had no effect on me. Hearing the voices of people coming up stairs, I crawled under the bed. The woman seemed already dead. There was only a very short time from the moment of my entering the room until I was taken away. In the agitation I also fainted. I do not know how it was that my arms became abraded. I did not feel it and was not aware of it. As to the door being locked from the inside, I myself did this immediately after I entered the room, wishing not to be interrupted. I solemnly declare that Rosenbloom and Schmuss knew nothing whatever of the crime of which I have been guilty, and I alone. I implore them to pardon me for having in my despair tried to cast the blame upon them. I also beseech the forgiveness of the bereaved husband.

I admit that I have had a fair trial, and acknowledge the justice of the sentence that has been passed upon me. I desire to thank Mr Hayward for his efforts on my behalf, as well as all those who have interested themselves in me during this unhappy time.

This confession is made of my own free will and is written down by Mr Singer at my request.

May God comfort my loving father and mother, and may He accept my repentance and my death as an atonement for all my sins!

Sunday 21st August 1887

Israel Lipski

The confession was signed by Lipski and witnessed by Rabbi Singer and the governor of Newgate. Singer later wrote that Lipski 'left it to my discretion to make whatever use I thought right of the document, and it was accordingly handed over to the governor to be at once made public with Lipski's knowledge and approval.'[26] The governor immediately released the document to the Press, explaining in his letter to the Home Office that he 'thought it well to forward a copy of the confession to the Press Association for publication in the morning's papers before the execution,' a procedure which was later strongly criticised by Lushington as 'contrary to the rule by which any such confession should be sent immediately to the Secretary of State, who then decides whether or not it ought to be published and in what form.' The governor apologised for an 'error of judgment', stating that he thought it 'improbable that my messenger would find the Right Honourable Secretary of State at the Home Office, and ... I thought I should be anticipating his wishes by securing its publication in the morning papers to relieve the public mind before the execution.'

A number of questions require consideration. Why would Rabbi Singer have authorised the release of the confession prior to Lipski's execution? What prompted Lipski to confess? And was the confession, in fact, true?

Releasing the confession virtually sealed Lipski's fate – he would now almost certainly be hanged. Why, then, did Rabbi Singer approve this step? Perhaps the simple explanation is that Singer believed that there was now, indeed, no chance of a reprieve, although we know from the Home Office records that this was a mistaken belief. Even the governor of the prison did not know that Matthews was still considering the question. Moreover, Singer might well have wanted, as much as the Governor, 'to relieve the public mind before the execution.' He would have been aware of the danger of violent clashes between Jews and non-Jews the next morning at Newgate and in the East End where, the night before, 'some hundreds of persons in Backchurch Lane, Whitechapel ... were in a state of great excitement concerning Lipski' and Jews were taunted by non-Jews, requiring intervention by the police.[27]

The confession that Lipski made was the least damaging to the Jewish community, involving a single person, rather than several, in a killing which arose from theft, rather than rape. Moreover, a confession would end the attack being made on the administration of justice in the name of Lipski. (Note that Lipski admitted that he had had a 'fair trial', which was clearly not so, and acknowledged 'the justice of the sentence'.)

Singer was painfully aware of the growing anti-Semitism in England which concentrated on the poor Jews arriving from Eastern Europe, with the danger, as he later said, of 'a possible Judenhetze in England.'[28] Throughout the 1880s and the 1890s Singer took a strong interest in the refugees. He resisted attempts to curtail the then unrestricted immigration of poor refugees, pointing out that 'there is a rising tide of public opinion against them – a tide that is not likely to nicely discriminate among those whom it may sweep away.'[29] He

170

helped to found a society to protect Jewish girls from involvement in the 'White Slave Trade';[30] spent considerable time as a 'visitor' in the East End; and assisted in organising a bureau to encourage individual contact with needy Jewish immigrants.[31] Several months earlier, he, along with the Chief Rabbi, had publicly refuted in the *Pall Mall Gazette* a 'foul libel on the Jewish community', respecting Jewish 'fallen women', contained in the *Gazette*;[32] and the previous year, in another letter to the *Gazette*, as we have previously seen, he refuted a correspondent who claimed that Jewish refugees 'are becoming a pest and a menace to the poor native-born East-ender.'[33] No doubt Singer found it ironic that it was the *Pall Mall Gazette* that was now championing a poor Jew.

The Lipski case was being used to put pressure on the Government to stop the immigration of 'pauper foreigners'. It is not entirely coincidental that on the first day a question was asked in the House of Commons about Lipski, there was also a question about destitute aliens.[34] One of the leading propagandists against the Jews at the time was Arnold White,[35] who wrote a letter to *The Times*[36] in July, published after Lipski had been committed for trial, under the heading *England For The English*, stating that if the Government lets the question of the pauper foreigner 'drift until the chapel bell is set a-ringing [that is, the chapel bell at Newgate after a hanging] by a few Jews being done to death in Whitechapel or Mile End, then there is a reasonable probability of the Home Secretary having to deal with an explosion of public opinion even more memorable than that he has lately experienced' [referring, presumably, to the Cass case].

A confession by Lipski, Singer may have thought, would end the controversy surrounding the trial, and might help calm the troubled waters and prevent the 'explosion' predicted by White.

We do not know what Singer and Lipski talked about in their meetings in the preceding weeks. We do not know whether Singer and Lipski talked about the harm that the case was doing to their fellow-Jews in England and the possibility that it would be used to assist in curtailing immigration from Eastern Europe to England, perhaps the principal escape route from the East. We do know, however, that they were both devout Jews, and death would not seem as final to them as it does to

171

many today. Singer's views on the afterlife and the possibility of salvation are contained in a scholarly essay he published several years before, entitled *Is Salvation Possible After Death?*[37] It was necessary to discuss salvation *after* death because, as the *Jewish Chronicle* had stated earlier that month with reference to the Lipski case: 'Unlike other religions ours does not hold out hopes in such cases that a mere deathbed repentance will be efficacious in appeasing the offended dignity of Heaven.'[38] Singer's answer was a clear 'Yes' to the possibility of salvation after death: 'the absolute reprobation of the worst sinner, his condemnation, that is, to undergo a penalty that shall have no end, is excluded by every notion we can form of the justice of God.' 'Salvation after death is rendered possible,' he wrote, 'by the sufferings of the sinner on earth, his death, and . . . the soul's unexhausted faculty of repentence . . . Death provided an atonement for sin.' The Jewish prayer for the dying, as found in *The Authorized Daily Prayer Book*, edited and translated in 1890 by Rabbi Singer, and still used throughout the English-speaking world, includes the words: 'O may my death be an atonement for all the sins, iniquities and transgressions of which I have been guilty against Thee.'[39] So, according to Singer, salvation was possible after death, but first the guilty person must acknowledge his guilt to God. Singer held the traditional view that 'there can be no remission of sin without consciousness and confession of sin. That is the first and indispensable condition . . . There can be no repentance without confession.'[40] If Lipski was guilty, Singer's view of God, confession and salvation may have been a strong factor in bringing about Lipski's confession and his willingness to face death.

We also know Singer's views on martyrdom, about which he wrote in the very month that Miriam Angel was murdered. He explained the 'glory' of martyrdom, referring to the Jews who had committed suicide during the crusades.[41] The sermon ended with the words:

> We are the heirs of that treasure. Times indeed have changed since the days we have been recalling. Martyrdom is not within our reach, even if any wished for it. But the spirit that gave an almost superhuman strength to our fathers, ought not to have perished. There is abundant need for it still. It is the spirit of rectitude which knows the right and wills it. It is the spirit of the Fear of God, which banishes from the heart all other fear. It is the spirit of sacrifice, that purifies and hallows every life, as nought else can do.

Is it possible that Lipski, whether guilty or innocent, sacrificed the possibility of a reprieve as an act of martyrdom to end the controversy and the consequent harm to the Jewish community that the case had brought about? There was now no possibility of a free pardon; the most that he could look forward to was life imprisonment, and, as previously mentioned, he had said to Hayward earlier in the week that if that was the result he 'would rather die.'[42] Further, whether he was guilty or innocent, the confession permitted him to place on the record a strong denial that he had 'violated' Mrs Angel, in his mind, no doubt, and in the view of others, the most damaging allegation of all.

Was the confession true? No doubt, Rabbi Singer believed Lipski was guilty. There are aspects of the confession, however, that are disturbing. The murder, according to the confession, took place shortly before he was discovered. This is totally inconsistent with the doctor's evidence that Mrs Angel had been dead a number of hours when he examined her. Where was Lipski during the previous two to three hours? Why would he have entered her room to steal, knowing she was sleeping and could wake up at any time and recognise him? Why was she still in bed at eleven o'clock when she always went to her mother-in-law's for breakfast before nine o'clock? Why would Lipski lock the door immediately after he entered the room and thus risk waking her up, and moreover, making it more difficult for him to leave quickly?

Perhaps the oddest part of the confession was his statement: 'I had long been tired of my life, and had bought a pennyworth of aqua fortis that morning for the purpose of putting an end to myself.' Why would he have contemplated suicide on the very morning that he had started up a new business? An unnamed 'compatriot who laboured on his behalf' wrote the next day in the *Pall Mall Gazette*:[43]

> His statement that he had the acid to commit suicide with is utterly incredible. Lipski commit suicide! The man who was just fitting up a workshop – who was busy upon his first business order – who was young and apparently in excellent spirits. Why on earth he of all men should have wanted to commit suicide it is simply impossible to say.

Was the mention of suicide simply a way of signalling to his fiancée and supporters that his confession was itself an act of suicide? The day before he had maintained his innocence to his landlord, and the day before that, to his solicitor.

Lipski's last communication to his fiancée's family does not, understandably, indicate that the confession was untrue. Immediately after the confession, Rabbi Singer sent a note that Lipski dictated to him to Lipski's intended mother-in-law:[44]

Newgate, 21 August 1887.

Dear Mrs Lyons

I send you a last goodbye as well as to Katie. You will forgive me, I am sure, for the wrong I have done. God will help me, I pray, to bear my punishment. I thank you with all my heart for your kindness to me. I have left some things at Mrs Lipski's, and I wish them to be sold, and the money to be equally divided between you and Mrs Lipski. You are also to take the pawnticket of my gold stud. Mrs Lipski has the ticket. My kind love to you both.

Your sincere friend,

Israel Lipski

A letter in Yiddish was also sent to Lipski's parents in Poland, but there is no record of what that letter contained.

Shortly after the confession arrived at the Home Office, Stephen sent another note to his wife: 'Home Office. Lipski has made a full confession, and my mind is quite relieved, and I am at peace, and have the delight of thinking I did right all through.'

A telegram was immediately sent in cypher to the Queen, informing her that Lipski had confessed. Her personal reply, also sent in cypher, from Osborne at 8.25 pm and signed simply 'Queen', must necessarily have come as a surprise to the Home Office:

To Secretary of State
Home Office, London

Glad he confessed, but are there any extenuating circumstances which would justify a commutation to penal servitude for life?

Queen

For the next two and a half hours they again agonised over the case. The Queen was obviously suggesting that a commutation was in order. She had been following the course of the case. The previous week her journal entry states: 'After luncheon, saw Mr Ritchie, who is a very clever and intelligent man, and we talked over the state of affairs . . . Spoke of a

174

murderer, about whom I have had so many appeals for mercy.'[45]

Matthews and Stephen could not recommend a commutation. Matthews' telegram was sent, again in cypher, at 11.10 pm.

> To The Queen
>
> The matter was fully considered by the judge in consultation with me today. It was a most cruel murder committed in the prosecution of a felonious purpose, and without any extenuating circumstances. I fully concur with the judge that the law must take its course. I thank Your Majesty for your gracious suggestion.
>
> Henry Matthews

The telegram probably was not seen by the Queen before she retired for the evening. Her journal entry for the day does not indicate, however, that the question of a commutation was of great significance to her. The complete entry for Sunday, 21 August reads:

> A fine morning – breakfast under the cedar tree. Service at a quarter to eleven, performed by Mr Peile, who preached very well. Vicky and her girls came – saw Mr Muther while I sat out, who is going on leave. Many telegrams about a young Jew, Lipski, who has murdered a poor woman and a violent effort is being made to get him pardoned, or rather, his sentence commuted. However, I heard that he had confessed and admitted the justice of his sentence – out to tea with Irene and Alicky. A lovely evening, and drove later. Vicky, with young Vicky and Sophy, Ct Hatzfeldt, Cts Perfoucher, J. Ely, Col Byng and Major Bigge dined.

A telegram was also sent to the Prime Minister, Lord Salisbury, at his home, Hatfield House. Lord Salisbury had tried to stay out of the affair. The previous week he had been called upon at Hatfield House by Cunninghame Graham, the MP who had asked the questions in the Commons about Lipski, but had refused to see him, informing him that 'he intended to have no responsibility cast on his shoulders'.[46] A copy of Matthews' telegram is not in the Home Office files nor in the Salisbury papers, but a note from Matthews to Salisbury[47] sent late that Sunday evening indicates that Salisbury was annoyed at having received a cypher telegram:

> Dear Lord Salisbury
>
> I am sorry I have puzzled you with a cypher telegram. I do not think it worthwhile at this hour (10 pm) to send you another telegram. I thought it possible that you had been worried today – as I have been, and the Queen – with telegrams abusing me and praising Lipski; and therefore I

telegraphed to let you know that Lipski had made a full confession of his guilt: and I sent the telegram in cypher, lest the news should leak out.

Yours very truly
Henry Matthews

Why was the telegram sent in cypher? Matthews said 'lest the news should leak out'. He did not know at that time that the governor of the prison had already released the confession to the Press. It seems likely that the Home Office had decided not to disclose the confession until after Lipski had been hanged – when there would be no longer any possibility of Lipski denying it. To release it beforehand meant that it could be questioned and possibly recanted. Perhaps the Home Office did not have complete confidence in the validity of the confession?

Rabbi Singer left Newgate Prison early on Sunday evening and returned the next morning shortly after six. Lipski is reported to have slept fairly well, rising at five in the morning and 'sparingly'[48] eating his breakfast of coffee, eggs and toast. For almost two hours, Rabbi Singer and Lipski prayed together.

Meanwhile, a large crowd was starting to form outside Newgate. By eight o'clock there were, according to some estimates, between five and six thousand people congregated: 'the largest gathering ever known', said one paper, 'since capital punishment has been performed in private at Newgate.'[49] Public hangings had been abolished in 1868, partly due to the writings of Charles Dickens, although contrary to the strong advice given at the time by James Fitzjames Stephen to the Royal Commission investigating the issue.[50] In 1887, only the officials and representatives of the Press attended a hanging.

Many in the crowd, composed to a considerable extent of East End Jews, did not know until they arrived that Lipski had already confessed. The leaflets sold to the crowd were no doubt prepared before the confession. One leaflet contained the following verse:[51]

What would my poor old mother say and father could they see
Their son to die for murder upon that fatal tree?
Through circumstantial evidence I met a dreadful fate.
They may find out I am innocent, alas, when it's too late.

The scaffold, a permanent one, used until Newgate was torn down in 1902 to build the present Old Bailey, and thereafter used at Pentonville Prison, was in an open stone-paved quadrangle abutting the prison building, about twenty yards from Lipski's cell.[52] No other prisoner was then in Newgate, the prison, as already indicated, being used at that time only for those awaiting execution or during the Old Bailey sessions for those being tried.

Executions were arranged by the sheriff of the county. As if to highlight the marked contrast between East and West End Jewry, the senior sheriff of London was a Jew, Alderman Sir Henry Aaron Isaacs (later the Lord Mayor), head of a very successful fruit importing firm, who had that very month been awarded Queen Victoria's Jubilee Medal and been knighted.[53]

The hangman selected by Isaacs was James Berry, who between 1884 and his retirement in 1892 (when he joined a music hall circuit to argue against capital punishment) performed over two hundred executions.[54] Berry, a former police constable, who had been forced to resign from police work because of an injury and was later an unsuccessful shoe salesman, was paid ten guineas for each hanging and half that amount if there was a reprieve. He introduced some technical changes in the art of hanging, such as the railway lever used to open the trap door and the type of rope used (three-quarter inch Italian hemp), but he was mainly known for perfecting the controversial 'long drop'.

Hanging was controversial during the 1880s, not so much on the question of its abolition, but because of the techniques used. A House of Lords committee had been set up the previous year to look into the matter.[55] The 'long drop' had the advantage of breaking the neck (technically a 'fracture dislocation of cervical vertebrae with laceration or crushing of the cord'),[56] resulting in an almost instantaneous death, rather than the much slower death that often occurred through suffocation when a shorter drop was used. Unfortunately, the 'long drop' had the disadvantage of risking the decapitation of the person executed, which had occurred in some earlier cases, including at least one performed by Berry. Frenchmen, not Englishmen, decapitate. The subject was debated in *The Lancet*, *The British Medical Journal* and in the popular Press.[57] *The Lancet*, for example, wanted new techniques to be explored, such as electricity (then being examined by the State of New York, and introduced there in 1889), poison or lethal injections. In any event, *The Lancet* wanted to get rid of the practice whereby the public hangman

177

made the decision on what drop should be employed: it should be a medical, not a lay opinion. It was at that time Berry's decision, and over the years he had worked out a scale which depended on the convict's weight and physical features. He told the Press that he would use a drop of six feet in this case because he estimated that Lipski weighed nine stone.[58]

The resonant bells of St Sepulchre's Church opposite Newgate ('there are no more beautiful bells in London' stated one paper)[59] started ringing, as they always did before an execution, at a quarter to eight. They were joined by the discordant execution bell of the Newgate chapel at five minutes to eight.

Shortly before eight, the hangman, the prison governor, an interpreter, the warders and the sheriffs (dressed in their official robes) went to Lipski's cell. Lipski, dressed in the suit he wore at the trial and with a small blue skull-cap on his head, was asked through the interpreter whether he had any further statement he wished to make. He replied: 'No, I have nothing more to add to what I have already said; it is all true, and I am guilty.'[60] He then expressed his thanks to the officials for their kindness to him, adding in broken English that he had never been so well treated in his life as he had been in prison. Berry pinioned Lipski's arms and Lipski began the slow march, with, as *The Times* reported, 'a firm step',[61] to the scaffold, a warder on either side, Rabbi Singer in front and Berry, the executioner, behind.

Rabbi Singer chanted – joined by Lipski in 'a tremulous and scarcely audible tone'[62] but 'with wonderful composure'[63] – the ancient sacred Hebrew prayer *Adon Olom*, (*Lord of the World*) attributed to the eleventh century Spanish poet Solomon ibn Gabirol, but possibly much older, stemming from Babylonian times. It is known to all practising Jews, said in daily prayers, on the Sabbath, on the eve of the Day of Atonement – and on the death bed of the dying:

> *Adon olom asher molach, b'terem kol y'tseer niv'ro*
> *L'ays naa'so vheftso kol, azye melech sh'monikro*

There could surely be no more appropriate or powerful prayer for the occasion, one English translation of the first and last verse being:

> Lord of the world, the King supreme
> Ere aught was formed, He reigned alone.

178

When by His will all things were wrought,
Then was His sovereign name made known.

My soul I give unto His care,
Asleep, awake, for He is near,
And with my soul, my body, too;
God is with me, I have no fear.[64]

The procession was now at the scaffold. There were no steps to climb, the platform of the scaffold and the walkway to it being on the same level. Lipski was now under the gallows and repeated with Rabbi Singer the traditional chant said over the centuries by Jews as they are about to die. Three times they said in Hebrew:

The Lord reigneth; the Lord hath reigned; the Lord shall reign for ever and ever.

Berry fastened Lipski's legs together. Three times they said:

Blessed be His name, whose glorious kingdom is for ever and ever.

Berry placed the noose around his neck. Seven times they said:

The Lord He is God.

Berry adjusted the noose, placing the knot behind the left ear.

Sh'ma yisroayl, Adonoy elohaynu, Adonoy echod.
Hear, O Israel: the Lord our God, the Lord is one.

Berry placed a white hood over Lipski's face and pulled the lever. At precisely three minutes past eight the trap door opened, and Lipski plunged to his death.

Immediately after the trap door was sprung, the traditional black flag was raised above Newgate, indicating to the waiting crowd that Lipski had been hanged. To the surprise of the officials within, they heard three loud and prolonged cheers from the crowd outside.[65] Berry later said that 'if they had watched it, they would not be cheering but would be feeling sick in body and mind as [I] did.'[66] He had been greatly moved by the solemnity of death in the Jewish service, although, of course, he did not understand what was taking place. He swore that he would never hang another Jew.

The activities of the crowd were considered scandalous by many, resembling the public executions in the past in England

and in France at that time. The following week the Home Secretary was asked in the House whether 'the Government have power to enable the authorities at Newgate to dispense with the hoisting of the flag, and thus prevent these public demonstrations?'[67] Matthews replied that 'the question of dispensing with the hoisting of the black flag will be considered', but then added that 'some public intimation that an execution has taken place is, I think, desirable.' The black flag was not dispensed with, but remained part of hangings at Newgate until the prison was torn down.

Rabbi Singer remained on the scaffold and recited the Kaddish, the familiar prayer recited by mourners. He had earlier written that 'the prayers and pious works of survivors are capable of affording relief to the departed soul in its state of punishment.'[68] It may be that Singer continued to offer prayers for Lipski in future years. It may even be that he had undertaken to Lipski to do so.

Hidden below the scaffold, three doctors were testing Lipski's pulse. Even in a well-executed hanging the pulse can beat for as long as twenty minutes after the drop.[69] In this case, the pulse finally stopped after thirteen minutes, stopping once at the end of five minutes. It was initially a rate of 160 beats per minute, indicating, according to one of the doctors who had been present, immediate insensibility.[70] What was not revealed at the time, but came out the following year in the columns of *The Lancet* and *The British Medical Journal*, was that Lipski had a 'quite narrow escape' from decapitation.[71] One of the doctors attending the hanging revealed that the drop was not, in fact, six feet as reported in the Press, but eight feet.[72] Even in the act of hanging Lipski created controversy!

By law, the body had to remain on the scaffold for one hour. Shortly after nine the body was cut down and placed in a crude coffin. A fourteen-member coroner's jury at the Old Bailey held an inquest as they were required to do within twenty-four hours of the execution.[73] In spite of what we know about 'the narrow escape' from decapitation and the jury's expressed concern about 'a severe discolouration extending over the left side of the neck,' the governor of the prison, when asked if the execution was satisfactorily carried out, replied 'Perfectly' and the prison surgeon gave evidence that the execution was carried out satisfactorily 'in every way.'[74] The members of the jury then signed the inquisition certificate (a certificate which had originally had the date of 15 August, but was changed to the 22nd after the respite), which concluded by stating:

> The body of the said Israel Lipski now here lying dead, is the identical body of the said offender, who was so convicted and executed for the offence aforesaid. And that the said offender, at the time of his death was a male person, of the age of twenty-two years, and a Jew.

Israel Lipski was placed in the grave already dug in the row of graves between the Old Bailey and the prison. Quicklime was placed below and on top of the body to ensure its rapid decomposition.

FIFTH EDITION.

Israel Lipski from the *Evening News*, 22 August, 1887

Chapter Nine

Conclusion

STEAD'S PUBLIC REACTION to the confession and hanging was contained in a leading article on the day of the execution in the *Pall Mall Gazette* under the preposterous heading *All's Well That Ends Well*.[1] 'Lipski's confession,' he wrote, 'fortunately removes all doubt that he has been justly accused, justly convicted, and justly executed. He has been hanged, and few criminals ever went to the gallows who better deserved their fate.' Stead pointed out, however, that although 'the confession proves that they convicted the right man, it also proves that they convicted him on the wrong evidence.' Thus, his intervention was justified; 'it would have been unpardonable,' he argued, 'if we had remained apathetic in face of the uncertainty which existed as to the soundness of the case for the prosecution.'

His private reaction was one of humiliation. At the end of the week he wrote to his friend Mme Novikoff, the Russian apologist for the Tsar's policies, including the treatment of the Jews:[2] 'Lipski!!!! Alas could any human being not a Pole and also a Jew have played the *PMG* so scandalous a trick. It was a bad fall. The Respite brought me immense fame. The Confession dashed me to the ground again. And the baying of the hounds at my heels is something strange. How I am hated!' The letter indicated he was also having serious marital problems at the time, stating that 'it may be that I may have to live as a hermit cut off from even contact with a woman's hand.' Several weeks later Stead indicated in another letter to Mme Novikoff that his wife was concerned about his women friends: 'My wife . . . is very low in her mind and the worst of it all is that she attributes all her sufferings to you and Mrs Fredericks. She has just told me that she has never had a happy year since you saw me . . . She refuses any longer to be my wife unless all this ceases.'[3] He then said, 'Destroy this letter,' which, obviously, Mme Novikoff did not do.

The 'baying hounds' consisted of a large section of the daily,

183

weekly and periodical press. The attacks on Stead were vicious:

The Evening News: 'He has during the last few years done more to degrade the Press than any man living; but in his efforts over the Lipski case, he has surely touched low-water mark.'[4]

St James's Gazette: 'Perhaps the greatest disgrace that has ever happened to English journalism.'[5]

Lloyd's Weekly: 'It would be difficult to find a more flagrant instance of an attempt to tamper with justice than was shown in Lipski's case.'[6]

The Law Times: 'The ignominious collapse of trial by newspaper in the case of the wretched man Lipski is a matter for unmitigated satisfaction.'[7]

The Spectator: 'A deep disgrace to English journalism.'[8]

The Saturday Review: 'If the practice of endeavouring to re-try convicted criminals in the columns of newspapers never recovers from the crushing blow it received at the beginning of this week, the late Israel Lipski will not have sinned altogether in vain.'[9]

Even *The Lancet*, which had strongly supported Lipski, congratulated Matthews on 'not having made an ignoble surrender to the mob advocacy of Lipski with which he was beset.'[10]

The only paper, it seems, that continued to support Lipski was the socialist weekly *The Commonweal*. An editorial under the heading *Is Lipski's Confession Genuine?* and signed by the radical editors Belfort Bax and William Morris (also the famous designer) stated:

> So Lipski has confessed and all is right, 'he has been brought to a frame of mind that has enabled him to make the reparation,' says the *Daily News*. Bourgeois justice and the Home Secretary are triumphantly vindicated. Thus, doubtless, thought the 'respectable' world on Monday morning.
>
> There is nothing to be surprised at in Lipski's confession. Indeed, it was just what was to be expected; those who have never believed in his guilt have no need to do so now, the evidence is entirely against such an hypothesis; but that under the circumstances the world should be given to understand that he has confessed, and 'admitted the justice of his sentence,' was absolutely essential to the stability of the government, of the system of capital punishment, and to the credit of our judicial machinery generally. What goes on within the walls of a prison is known only to those in the swim of the bureaucratic trade, and we do not pretend to decide dogmatically with respect to the origin of the document. We need only call the reader's attention to the fact that the bureaucrat is by the necessities of his profession a liar, skilful or unskilful; the value of official disclaimers is proverbial.

Who knows what kind of cajolery or even threats might not have been employed, since the occasion was so urgent and so much was at stake?

In connection with this it is well to remember that the witches who were burnt in the seventeenth century almost always confessed their guilt, and 'admitted the justice of their sentence', or were said to have done so.[11]

Perhaps Stead regretted that he had capitulated so quickly; he included an article later in the week that asserted that the same opinion as expressed by *The Commonweal* 'is common among Lipski's own brethren . . . One and all agree that . . . "the Whitechapel mystery will remain a mystery".'[12]

'The practice of endeavouring to re-try convicted criminals in the columns of newspapers,' to use the words of the *Saturday Review*, never did recover 'from the crushing blow it received'. The Press thereafter became somewhat more cautious in attacking the administration of justice. In the notorious Maybrick case, two years later, *The Times* reflected the general view of the Press in stating that they 'are very sensible of the inadvisability of re-trying by the Press a case which has been decided, after much careful consideration, by a competent jury.' 'The warning given by Lipski's case,' *The Times* editorial stated, 'should never be forgotten.'[13]

Even Stead did not, it would seem, again champion a convicted murderer until he jumped into the Maybrick case five years after Lipski – and three years after Mrs Maybrick's conviction for murder and the subsequent commutation of her sentence to life imprisonment. 'In accordance with principles on which I had always acted, with one fatal exception,' he wrote in the *Review of Reviews* in 1892, explaining why he had not said anything about Mrs Maybrick earlier, 'the *Pall Mall Gazette* objected to any re-trial of the case by the Home Secretary in deference to clamour.'[14] (His reason for now taking on Mrs Maybrick's cause was because of evidence sent to him from South Africa of a death-bed confession by a man who claimed to have conspired with others to bring suspicion upon Mrs Maybrick.) His attack on the administration of justice in the Maybrick case did not have quite the flair of his earlier years, but he still could, for example, talk about 'senile malevolence on the Bench or in the Home Office', referring, of course, to Stephen and Matthews.[15]

Stead's attacks on Matthews, Stephen and the administration of justice did not, therefore, cease after Lipski. Indeed, in the very week of Lipski's hanging, Stead attacked the 'extraordinary severity' of a sentence of eight years' penal servitude imposed on a sixteen-year-old for the attempted murder of her child, suggesting that 'the time has come for the superannuation of Mr Justice Field', the judge who imposed the sentence.[16] And Stead raised questions about the propriety of Stephen's directed verdict of acquittal of the police officer charged with perjury arising out of the earlier Cass case (she had, it will be recalled, been 'wrongly' accused of being a prostitute),[17] a result which would obviously have pleased Matthews. 'We do not go so far' as to say it was a 'put-up job', Stead wrote, 'but on the face of it the facts are very strange.' Stead also attacked Matthews' handling of the Trafalgar Square riots later that autumn and the 'vindictive outbursts of temper' by 'Mr Injustice Stephen' in the trials following the riots.[18] So Stead did not completely change his ways.

Stead's stand on the Trafalgar Square riots and, no doubt, the humiliation over Lipski caused a drop in advertisements and circulation. His publisher was not happy with his editorship.[19] Stead quietly left the *Pall Mall Gazette* in 1890 to found the influential *Review of Reviews*, a weekly that was widely read both in England and America. The *Gazette* was sold in 1892 to the American Lord Astor[20] (as he later became), and was eventually absorbed by the *Evening Standard* in 1923. Stead himself remained active in editing and writing for the *Review of Reviews* until he died on the Titanic in 1912. 'When last seen by survivors,' the *Dictionary of National Biography* records, 'Stead was assisting women and children to make their escape from the vessel.' His death was as sensational as his life.

Hayward wrote to the Press on the day of the hanging that the confession was 'an immense relief' to him.[21] 'I was not alone,' he wrote, 'in my belief that he was not guilty of the crime for which he has just paid the penalty. The prisoner's demeanour carried a conviction of innocence to all with whom he came into contact, and he stoutly maintained his innocence to me last Friday, and the rabbi was also much impressed with the prisoner's apparent truthfulness.'

A fund was set up within the Jewish community to recognise by 'a fitting testimonial' the 'chivalrous conduct' of Hayward.[22] The *Jewish World* asked in early September[23] that contributions be sent to their office, but subsequent issues of the paper recorded only two contributions, one of three guineas and

186

another from 'An Admirer' of two shillings. It may be, however, that contributions were sent directly to the organisers of the fund. As previously pointed out, very little is known about Hayward's further career. He died in 1917, leaving a gross estate of one hundred and fifty-eight pounds, which was completely used up in settling debts and funeral expenses.

The Home Office officials were, of course, delighted with the result. Unfortunately, all but one of the seventeen sub-files made after the execution were later destroyed, so we cannot discover whether any subsequent misgivings were expressed. Perhaps not, because six months after the hanging Matthews publicly stated that 'he never had a shadow of a doubt' as to Lipski's guilt.[24]

It seems likely that Lipski's confession saved Matthews' political career. Press coverage was very favourable. *The Spectator*, for example, described his action as 'firm and independent throughout, and entirely worthy of an English Minister';[25] and *Lloyd's Weekly* said that 'the highest credit is due to Mr Matthews.'[26] A former Home Secretary, Sir William Harcourt, congratulated Matthews stating that 'it has been a knock-down blow for the outrageous injustice of the *P.M. Gazette*, and will not be forgotten.'[27] He remained as Home Secretary until 1892, was in opposition for the next three years, and when the Conservatives were returned to power in 1895 he was appointed to the House of Lords as Viscount Llandaff, thereafter taking little part in public life. He died in 1913, still a bachelor. A later Permanent Under-Secretary of State, Sir Edward Troup, certainly thought Lipski's confession saved Matthews. In his book on the Home Office, Troup stated: 'In the famous case of Lipski . . . a storm of protest was raised which would almost certainly have driven him from office had not Lipski on the eve of his execution confessed to the murder.'[28] Moreover, it is possible that if Matthews, the only Catholic in the Cabinet, had resigned, the Government would have fallen and Home Rule for Ireland would have been introduced. Incredible as it may seem, then, the confession of a poor immigrant Jew, who could not even speak English, may have been a factor in the future of the United Kingdom, having repercussions even today in the troubles of Northern Ireland.

Godfrey Lushington, the Permanent Under-Secretary, continued in that position until 1895. No subsequent comments he may have made on the Lipski case have been discovered. It seems unlikely that his strong feelings on the case were motivated by anti-Semitism, because he later played a key role in promoting Alfred Dreyfus's cause in England in the late 1890s by writing a series of very lengthy letters to *The Times*.[29] Similarly, I have seen no evidence of anti-Semitism on Matthews' part or on Stephen's.

We have already seen Stephen's expression of relief in his letter to his wife after Lipski confessed: 'my mind is quite relieved, and I am at peace.' The following month he wrote to an old family friend about 'a scoundrel called Lipski who was however happily hanged[30]; and he wrote to his friend Lord Lytton that he was 'very glad of your sympathy in respect of Stead's humiliation and Lipski's hanging,' but, he added in Greek, 'all things must come to an end.'[31]

Matthews and Stephen met again two years later, following Mrs Maybrick's conviction for murder. Again it was alleged that Stephen had forced a verdict of guilty by an overstrong charge in favour of the prosecution. And once again Dr Stevenson from Guy's Hospital was the principal expert for the Crown. This time, Matthews recommended – two years to the day after Lipski was hanged – that the sentence be commuted to life imprisonment. Maybrick, Stephen later wrote, was 'the only case in which there could be any doubt about the facts.'[32]

Stephen's judicial career ended soon after the Maybrick case. In the latter part of 1889, his health started to deteriorate further and in 1890 he was again ordered to rest for three months. He then returned to the Bench, but the Press, including *The Times*, commented on his inability to conduct judicial proceedings. He resigned in 1891 and died in 1894 in a home in Ipswich to which he had been moved the previous year. His brother, Leslie Stephen, wrote that in this last year 'his friends felt painfully that he was no longer quite with them in mind.'[33]

All things may have an end, as Stephen said, but it seems that this was not to be so in the Lipski case. After the confession, a new controversy arose. On the morning of the hanging, *The Daily Telegraph* contained the following report:[34]

> Extraordinary as it may appear, the fact that a confession of this character was probable was known to several people during the past few days, and it is stated that yesterday week the convict was engaged in putting it into writing when the respite of the Home Secretary arrived, to his great

surprise. The paper already filled was hurriedly torn up, and every care taken to prevent the publication of the circumstances, and it was believed that no clue was left to inform any person of what had actually happened.

Did the Home Office know about this earlier episode? The *Pall Mall Gazette* said that 'although the fact was not otherwise divulged, it is believed that the Home Office authorities were made acquainted with it.'[35] 'It is absurd to suppose,' wrote the *Westminster Review*, 'that nobody in the prison knew what Lipski was doing; and if anybody knew it, are we expected to believe that the knowledge was kept from the Home Secretary?'[36]

Rumours that the earlier confession was known to the Home Office circulated throughout the week. Early the following week, the papers carried a letter from Rabbi Singer, who was then in Zürich, explaining what had taken place on the Sunday the respite was granted:

> On Sunday afternoon, the 14th inst, the day before the date originally fixed for his execution, I had succeeded in so far impressing the convict with a sense of his position that he promised to tell the whole truth about the crime of which he was accused. I suggested that what he had to say should be taken down in writing, and pledged myself, at his request, that the contents of the document, whatever they might be, should not be divulged until after his death on the following morning. I then asked for pen, ink, and paper. Meanwhile a letter arrived from the Home Office, which proved to be a respite for another week. This induced the prisoner to withhold the communication he was, I presume, on the point of making. As a fact, no actual admission of his guilt had yet proceeded from him. Not a soul besides myself knew of what had been spoken in the condemned cell, and the limited confidence Lipski had up to that time reposed in me was shared, it need hardly be said, by no one. The authorities at the Home Office were in this respect no better informed than the outside public.[37]

Singer concluded by hoping that the whole matter might now be 'allowed to pass into oblivion'. Hayward, however, would not let it. The next day he wrote to the papers (the *East London Advertiser* asked: 'Are we never to hear the last of the wretched man, Lipski?'):[38]

> Mr Singer's letter . . . agrees substantially with the statement which had previously appeared in the newspapers: it is therefore clear this interrupted confession was known to the prison authorities; indeed, I myself have evidence of that. It was of course known to the Home Office also. It therefore becomes manifest that if this 'pen, ink, and paper' had been sent for a few hours earlier there would have been no respite, and if they had never been sent for at all there would have been no execution.[39]

Matthews was asked in the House about Hayward's letter

and replied:[40] 'My attention has been called to this letter. There is no truth whatever in the allegation referred to, either as regards the Home Office or the Governor of Newgate.' The matter was, however, kept alive by a letter to the Home Secretary, published in the *Pall Mall Gazette*, from Mr L. J. Greenberg, who had been assisting Mr Hayward:[41]

> On the 21st ult I was at Newgate Prison, together with a representative of Mr Hayward, and an official informed us that he knew Lipski had 'confessed' on the previous Sunday, and knew it when your respite arrived. He told us that so soon as your decision was received postponing execution for a week the 'confession' that had been written was destroyed . . . I have reason to believe that what the official told us was true, as on the 14th ult I saw him twice. On the first occasion, which was before Mr Singer had been to the prison, he spoke very positively of his belief in the prisoner's innocence. On the second occasion, which was late in the evening, I particularly noticed that he did not speak in the same confident strain.

Did the Home Office know? The Home Office files do not indicate that Lushington or Matthews did, in fact, know. Lushington asked for a full report from the Governor on the day the article appeared in *The Daily Telegraph* 'as to all the circumstances of the confession alleged to have been commenced by Lipski on Sunday the 14th instant – in what language was it written? To whom was it made? What persons were aware that it had been made? By whom was it destroyed?' The Governor replied that Singer 'did not give [him] the slightest hint that a confession of any kind had been commenced.' He noted, however, that Singer told him after the confession on the 21st that he, Singer, 'thought the prisoner was about to make some confession on the previous Sunday.' This certainly indicates that Singer knew that a confession was about to be made. As a Home Office official noted in the file in response to the Governor's reply, if Singer '*thought* the prisoner was about to make a statement, the prisoner must have said something to give him that thought.' So, even though the Home Office and the Governor may not have known about the earlier confession, Singer and the prison officials who were involved in getting the 'pen, ink, and paper' would, as Hayward and Greenberg said, have known. Matthews was careful to limit his Parliamentary denial to the Home Office and the Governor of Newgate.

There is nothing to indicate whether Stephen knew of the earlier confession. But if the prison officials knew, it is not

190

unlikely that some of the lawyers who practised at the Old Bailey would also have known. There is a brief account of the case written much later which suggests that at least one lawyer, who had arranged to be present at the execution, knew about the earlier confession.[42] If lawyers knew about it, then perhaps Stephen, who was at that time the Treasurer of his Inn of Court, would have been told about the rumour. There is no mention of the confession in Stephen's letters to his wife, but these are only edited excerpts made by his wife from the originals, which were destroyed. It seems to have been well known during the final week that Stephen was going to conclude that Lipski was guilty. Arthur Balfour, later the Prime Minister, but then a member of the cabinet, wrote to Stead in the middle of the week (17 August) saying: 'I am sure that the judge entertains no doubt about his guilt.' (The letter goes on to say that 'in any case, things will be arranged as you wish', which seems to indicate that at least some members of the Government were expecting that Lipski would not hang.)[43] Stephen's knowledge of the earlier 'confession' could account for his firmness in resolving the earlier doubts he had about Lipski's guilt.

A further issue raised by *The Daily Telegraph* was, assuming there had been an earlier confession, 'how far any minister of religion is justified in withholding knowledge so obtained from the authorities.'[44] Lushington considered the question in a note to Matthews, stating:

A Protestant minister would I think feel it his duty to make known to the authorities any such confession received by him. A Catholic priest I presume would not make it known himself but would press upon the convict his obligation to make it known. What might be the view of a Jewish minister is more than I can say.

Lushington concluded by stating that 'on the whole I think the matter had better be left alone.'

The courts had to deal with a number of repercussions of the Lipski case. There were prosecutions of those causing a disturbance on the streets near Batty Street. There was also a rather bizarre proceeding brought by the landlady, Mrs Lipski, against Isaac Angel, the husband of the murdered woman. Some time on Tuesday, the day after the hanging, Mrs Lipski went to the magistrate's court and complained that on the day of the hanging Mr Angel came to her house with his brothers and sisters, damaged her door and windows, and also kicked her.[45] She lodged another complaint on Wednesday saying that on Tuesday, the day after the hanging, Angel came 'accompanied by a mob' and threatened to kill her.[46] She also said that on the previous Saturday (before the execution), Angel had come to her house with his two brothers, knocked her down, kicked her in the stomach and said: 'I will not rest till I have killed you . . . I will do for you as you have done for my wife.'[47] Angel was arrested and tried the next day. The magistrate had no doubt there was 'a squabble between the prisoner and the woman.' 'Everyone,' he added, 'had great sympathy with the prisoner for having his wife murdered, but the unhappy man who committed the murder had been hanged. Because Mrs Lipski bore the same name as the man who was hanged there was no reason why she should be assaulted. The prisoner would be bound over to keep the peace, but if he or his friends again molested Mrs Lipski they would be severely dealt with.'[48]

What is the meaning of these episodes? Surely Mr Angel was not assaulting Mrs Lipski, a mother of seven children, only because she bore the same name as Israel Lipski, nor because the murder took place in her house? Perhaps Mr Angel felt that the landlady was lying to save Lipski's life by, for example, making up stories about the box being broken into. Or, perhaps there is more to the entire Lipski story that never came out at the trial or in the Press reports.

What is to be made of another incident brought to light after the execution, in which Mark Schmidt, the dealer who gave evidence at the trial, brought a complaint that a man named Grant, who had been assisting Hayward, 'burst open his [Schmidt's] door' on the Saturday night before the hanging 'in order to get a man named Schmuss away'? The complainant said that his 'daughter had been much frightened, and was seized with a fit. In consequence she had to be removed to the London Hospital.' The magistrate said that as there had been 'no further annoyance . . . he saw no reason to interfere in the matter.'[49] Why was Grant looking for Schmuss? Why was Schmuss staying with Schmidt? The episode again suggests that there may be more to the story than we are aware of.

The magistrate (another Mr Lushington), who heard the case against Mr Angel, also dealt with an application that same day by Mrs Lyons, the mother of Lipski's fiancée. She wanted to get the property that Lipski had left to her in the note he sent her on the day of his confession. The police inspector would not give anything to her. The magistrate said he had 'no power whatever to make any order about the things. If Lipski's things were not forfeited and he had left no will, they would go to his next-of-kin.'[50]

The magistrate was, of course, legally correct: the letter to Mrs Lyons was not signed by two witnesses, as English wills have to be. It does seem harsh, however, that there were two witnesses to the confession, but that no one told Lipski that two witnesses were required for his will. The absurdity of the situation must have been apparent to others because the following week the Jewish prison visitor, Mr Emanuel, wrote to the magistrate saying that arrangements had been made to follow Lipski's wishes and that Mrs Lyons would receive two pounds, Mrs Lipski two pounds, and the lad, Pitman, ten shillings – a total estate of under five pounds.[51]

There may well have been other legal proceedings, not reported in the Press, arising out of the case. There is no mention of any libel suit by Schmuss or Rosenbloom against the *Pall Mall Gazette*, although such a lawsuit was urged by some. The *Evening News*, for example, wrote that 'Justice has been done upon Lipski, but it still remains for justice to be done upon others [referring, of course, to Stead]. If no one else moves in this direction Messrs Rosenbloom and Schmuss ought to do so. They have been most foully libelled, not only by the dead convict, but by his living champion, and we are certain that an English jury would give them the redress they deserve.'[52] But there is no evidence of a lawsuit or a settlement because of the threat of a lawsuit.

Almost all *causes célèbres* seem to have some impact on law reform. The Lipski case was no exception. The impact, however, was a negative one. It slowed down the growing movement for the establishment of a Court of Criminal Appeal. At that time, with some very limited exceptions, appeals were not permitted in criminal cases.[53] But many influential persons had been advocating an appeal court to replace the discretion of the Home Secretary. Indeed, Stephen himself had taken this position, and so had the Criminal Code Commissioners, of which Stephen was a member, in their report of 1879.[54] A number of Bills were introduced in the intervening years, and it seemed likely that legislation would soon be enacted. During the Lipski agitation many newspapers supported the establishment of an appeal tribunal.

Lipski's confession, however, made some important former advocates of an appeal court change their minds. In particular, Stephen no longer supported a Court of Criminal Appeal. In the second edition of his *General View of the Criminal Law of England*, published in 1890, Stephen, after referring to the case of Mrs Maybrick, whose sentence was commuted to life imprisonment, and to Lipski, wrote:[55]

> Upon the question whether there ought to be an appeal in criminal cases there has been much discussion. I was at one time in favour of such an appeal. The Report of the Criminal Code Commission, of which I was a member, contained a recommendation of a scheme for such a court, which I concurred in. Subsequent experience, however, has led me entirely to change my opinion, and to think that substantially the existing system cannot be improved, and that such defects as exist in it are inevitable consequences of the nature of trial by jury, or are easily removable . . . My belief, from personal experience during ten years, is, that any change which could be made would necessarily be for the worse.

While the Maybrick case was being considered by the Home Secretary, a Bill to establish a Court of Criminal Appeal was introduced in the House of Lords, but was not proceeded with because, as the Lord Chancellor, Lord Halsbury, observed, 'such questions as these are not appropriately discussed at times of public excitement about them.'[56] In the course of the debate, however, Lord Denman, the brother of Mr Justice Denman, supported the existing system, stating: 'I have witnessed the struggles of the present Home Secretary in the case of an unfortunate Jew, who afterwards confessed that he was guilty. The pressure that was put upon the Home Secretary was something extraordinary; and I am quite certain that until we can see clearly a much better system than the present, we had much better not cast a slur upon the existing authority.'[57]

Mrs Maybrick's commutation again took away the pressure for change. As a later Permanent Under-Secretary in the Home Office wrote, 'the subject did not excite much interest so long as it was felt that practical justice was being done.'[58] A Court of Criminal Appeal was not introduced until the clear miscarriage of justice in the Adolph Beck case brought about its passage in 1907. Had Lipski not confessed and been hanged, it is likely that the Court of Criminal Appeal would have been introduced in England at a far earlier date.

The Lipski case was also used as an argument to prevent any change in the exercise of the power of commutation. After Queen Victoria died, the new monarch, Edward VII, wanted to be more involved in the exercise of the prerogative of mercy. The then Home Secretary, Akers-Douglas, argued that 'it is most important that the practice of the last eighty years . . . not be departed from.'[59] He pointed out to the King that 'the power of reprieve involves the power, and duty to refuse to reprieve,' and referring to the Lipski case in which 'public opinion is lashed up by an unscrupulous partisan press,' he concluded that 'it would be intolerable that Your Majesty's name should be dragged into the mire to serve the temporary purposes of some wretched newspaper.' As a result, the prerogative of mercy remained in the hands of the Home Secretary.

The one significant policy that did emerge was the rule established in the Lipski case, and followed for the next eighty years until capital punishment was abolished, that Parliamentary questions should not be asked about the exercise of the prerogative while the Home Secretary was considering the matter.

Those who favoured controls on Jewish immigration made much of the Lipski case, although it is possible that they might have made even more capital out of an acquittal or a pardon, as it would then have placed the blame on two other immigrant Jews. 'The low class of Polish Jews which Lipski belonged to,' wrote the *Evening News*, adopting a Press service report, 'are the pariahs of modern European life . . . In the districts blighted by their presence the standard of living and morality alike is lowered . . . For the man one may feel sorrow, but one cannot look with equanimity on this social cancer which is spreading in our midst, and is so baneful to all human progress.'[60] The *Daily News*, in a less virulent attack, wrote that 'the fate of Lipski calls attention once more to the misery endured by the hordes of Polish and Russian Jews in the East End of London . . . The Jewish Board of Guardians have done their best to stop the influx of these needy refugees into England . . . The Board have often told the story of London misery to their co-religionists abroad; this terrible case may help them to point the moral.'[61]

The Times did not comment directly on this aspect of the case, but on the day of Lipski's execution it printed a report from St Petersburg under the title *Jews in Russia*, stating: 'There are symptoms of a revival of the Jewish question, or rather of the persecution of the Jews, in several parts of the Empire . . . A project is on foot, if it has not been actually adopted, to prevent all Jews in the provinces of Poland from residing outside of the towns or settlements among the peasants, and to restrict their acquisition and possession of property in the rural districts of the . . . provinces.'[62]

The West End Jewish community was worried. 'There is, unfortunately, but too much truth in [the observations of the *Daily News*],' wrote the *Jewish Chronicle*; 'Happily, the tide of immigration into England has sensibly diminished through the energetic action of the Board of Guardians. But if the threatened restrictions on the Jews in Poland should come into force, it will require all the power of that Board to prevent emigration on a large scale from that country into our own.'[63]

For some time the Jewish Board of Guardians, which provided social services to English Jews,[64] had been active in discouraging immigration to England. At the annual meeting of the Board in March, 1887, the chairman of the meeting reported that 'there have been inserted advertisements in Hebrew newspapers in Russia, Poland, and elsewhere, warning intending emigrants of the futility of coming here in the hope of getting employment.'[65] And, he pointed out, they were becoming 'more severe in imposing the rule of the Board which requires that persons should have been six months in this country before any relief will be given to them.' There was, however, an exception to the six-month rule: the Board would pay to have immigrants return to Eastern Europe – and more were assisted to return to Europe than were assisted to go to America or the colonies. This, the chairman said, 'will have a great effect in preventing others similarly situated from coming over here.' No evidence has been seen to indicate that the Lipski case was specifically used by the Board in its advertisements, but there is no doubt that those who returned to Eastern Europe would have told of one of their numbers who was hanged.

The question of 'restricting the immigration of foreign paupers', as the issue·was called, had been under the consideration of the Government for several months. The Lipski case dramatically drew attention to it. Parliamentary questions were asked in both July and August, and the Government said that the matter was 'under their careful

196

consideration'.[66] It will be recalled that Arnold White had written to *The Times* in July (before he had left for South Africa) urging the Government to appoint a Parliamentary Committee and warning them not to let the matter 'drift until the chapel bell is set a-ringing by a few Jews being done to death in Whitechapel,' with the resulting 'explosion of public opinion'.[67] He had earlier written about the possibility of 'a Judenhetze in the heart of London.'[68] White returned from South Africa in late November and again wrote to *The Times*: 'The time for inquiry is over. The hour for action has arrived'; the question, he stated, was whether 'our own kith shall be sacrificed to an obsolete shibboleth and the bloodthirsty operation of an artificial competition.'[69] That same month, Charles Ritchie, the cabinet minister who represented St George's-in-the-East, wrote to the Prime Minister, warning him that immigration was a question that the Government would 'have to face the moment Parliament meets'.[70]

As a result of such pressure – including a visit to the Prime Minister by White, accompanied by a former Lord Chancellor,[71] Lord Herschell, whose father was born a Jew but had converted – two Parliamentary Committees were established in 1888, a House of Lords Committee on the Sweating System and a Commons Committee on Immigration. Arnold White, the erratic and increasingly open anti-Semite (in the 1890s he suggested that it was 'high time for other nations to smite the Chosen People hip and thigh and to join Holy Russia in her artless effort to revenge the tragedy at Calvary'),[72] was active in presenting evidence before both committees – in some cases clearly tainted and bought evidence.[73] He was supported by the *Pall Mall Gazette*, which stated that 'Mr White's evidence will confirm all that we have urged as to the wisdom of not allowing this country to become the rubbish-bin of European labourers.'[74] A few days earlier, in a leading article under the heading *The Invasion of England*, Stead quoted with approval the Frenchman, General Georges Boulanger, who was supposed to have said: 'Above all we must get rid of the Jews.' 'It is by no means improbable,' wrote Stead, 'that a crusade against the foreign paupers in our midst will rapidly come within the range of practical politics. The invasion of England is unquestionably a matter for grave alarm. It has gone on until the enemy is already in possession of the capital . . . We shall be surprised if the combined result of the Sweating and the Immigration

Committees is not to place some check upon the invasion of England . . .'[75] Stead's championing of Lipski may not have been quite so altruistic as it might at first appear.

Neither Committee, however, recommended a curtailment of immigration. The Lords' Committee on Sweating, which reported in 1889, found that 'Undue stress has been laid on the injurious effect on wages caused by foreign immigration, inasmuch as we found that the evils complained of obtain in trades which do not appear to be affected by foreign immigration.'[76] The Commons Immigration Committee reported in the same year that 'while they are not prepared to recommend such legislation at present, they contemplate the possibility of such legislation becoming necessary in the future, in view of the crowded conditions of our great towns, the extreme pressure for existence among the poorer part of the population, and the tendency of destitute foreigners to reduce still lower the social and material condition of our own poor.[77] The resistance to controls was due in part to the resistance of the Jewish members of the Committee (Baron Henry de Worms, Lord Rothschild and Samuel Montagu), in part to the historical tradition of allowing the persecuted (for example, the Huguenots) to settle in England and, in part, to the acceptance of the economic principle of free trade, whether in goods or paupers. After all, it was argued, if one prevents paupers from coming and producing low-priced goods in England, one should also prevent the importation of low-priced goods produced abroad.[78]

Lionel Alexander, the Honorary Secretary of the Jewish Board of Guardians, gave evidence to the Commons Committee in 1888, referring to the *exodus* – a remarkably inappropriate word – back to Poland and Russia:[79]

> The registered arrivals in 1887 were two hundred and ninety-seven cases, whereas my Board returned home during that year three hundred and five cases; there was therefore in this form shown to be a balance actually of eight cases migrating from west to east over and above those from east to west. And my Board has now for several years past assisted back to the Continent each year a larger number of cases than have in each of such years applied as newcomers for relief. The operations, therefore, of the Board have removed from London probably more poverty-stricken cases of Jews than have come here.

He went on to say that 'neither trouble nor expense is permitted to interfere against the free operations of this

198

department of the work of my Board, for it is found that the sending back of persons who have wandered hither, and who have suffered whilst here, acts automatically as a warning to others not to come.'[80] The official historian of the Board, writing in 1959, estimated that between 1880 and 1914 the Board sent back 'altogether some fifty thousand individuals' and concluded that in spite of the fact that the Board was 'undoubtedly dominated by the underlying motive of preventing statutory restriction of immigration, the "repatriation" . . . leaves one with the tragic thought that some at least of those thus returned must have become victims of persecution once they were back . . . It would have been far better had it been possible for them to emigrate to the United States or to the Colonies.'[81]

This is not the place to outline the history of Jewish immigration to England. Suffice it to say that restrictive legislation was finally passed in 1905.[82] The reader will see from the little that has been written here that the established English Jewry were receptive to alternatives to widespread Jewish immigration to England. There was, of course, a range of Jewish opinion, from the restrictive view of one leading Jew who wrote that ' "Our people" are the English, and the English only',[83] to the more liberal view of the Jewish MP for Whitechapel, Samuel Montagu, who said 'we must either contentedly maintain the foreign poor in our country or help to place them where they can best maintain themselves.'[84]

Views on the place where 'they can best maintain themselves' varied. Arnold White was active in the search for alternatives. In the early 1890s, acting as the agent of the Austrian, Baron de Hirsch, White paid several visits to Russia to persuade the Tsar's Government to permit the establishment of a colony in Argentina for poor Russian Jews.[85] White's later solution was for Jews to go to Turkish Armenia, between the Tigris and Euphrates, the 'cradle of the race', depopulated by Turkish massacres.[86] Another solution, offered by Joseph Chamberlain, was for Jews to settle under the British flag in Uganda.[87] The plan was seriously considered by the Zionist movement, represented in the negotiations by the journalist L. J. Greenberg, who sixteen years earlier had assisted Hayward in the Lipski case.

When Theodore Herzl came to England in the mid-1890s, there was, therefore, a willingness to consider Zionism, i.e., to

199

establish a Jewish homeland in Israel. It was, in fact, Rabbi Singer who convened the first meeting in England at which Herzl met the leaders of the Jewish community.[88] Herzl recorded in his diary in November 1895 that Singer was his 'chief representative in London. He seems to be very devoted to the cause.'[89] As it turned out, many of these leaders, including Rabbi Singer, did not support political Zionism,[90] but the movement flourished among English Jewry, particularly outside London, leading eventually to the Balfour Declaration of 2 November 1917, in which the British Cabinet viewed 'with favour the establishment in Palestine of a national home for the Jewish people, and will use their best endeavours to facilitate the achievement of this object'.[91] The Lipski case, by focusing public attention on conditions in the East End, on the plight of the Jews in Eastern Europe and on unrestricted immigration, in its own way played a minor part in the long series of events leading to this momentous declaration.

The Jack the Ripper murders in Whitechapel in 1888, the year after Lipski was hanged, also created hysteria against the Jewish community in the East End. Indeed, the more one studies the unsolved murders of the five prostitutes who were brutally killed and had various organs removed from their bodies in the ten-week period from 31 August to 9 November 1888,[92] the more one must agree with the *Jewish Chronicle* that 'there are not wanting signs of a deliberate attempt to connect the Jews with the Whitechapel murders.'[93]

On the day of the second murder, 8 September 1888, the *Pall Mall Gazette*, which, it should be noted, was the first paper with a journalist at the scene, fanned the flames of hysteria by reporting that no one looking at the corpse 'could think otherwise than that the murder had been committed by a maniac or wretch of the lowest type of humanity.' The *Gazette* went on to recirculate rumours that had been current in Whitechapel for a week or more, and printed in other papers, that the murders were committed by a 'mysterious being bearing the name of "Leather Apron"':

He is five feet four or five inches in height, and wears a dark close-fitting cap . . . His expression is sinister, and seems to be full of terror for the women who describe it. His eyes are small and glittering. His lips are usually parted in a grin which is not only not reassuring, but excessively repellent. He is a slipper-maker by trade, but does not work . . . His name nobody knows, but all are united in the belief that he is a Jew or of Jewish parentage, his face being of a marked Hebrew type.

One can understand the claim by a writer who carefully studied the voluminous Ripper literature that 'any prize for wringing copy out of the situation would probably go to the *Pall Mall Gazette*.'[94] That evening, crowds assembled in the East End and, in the words of the *East London Observer*, 'began to assume a very threatening attitude towards the Hebrew population of the district'. 'It was repeatedly asserted,' the paper wrote, 'that no Englishman could have perpetrated such a horrible crime, and that it must have been done by a Jew – and forthwith the crowds proceeded to threaten and abuse such of the unfortunate Hebrews as they found in the streets.'[95] On Monday morning, Detective Sergeant Thick, who was in charge of the investigation – and had earlier, with Inspector Final, been in charge of the Lipski case – arrested another Polish Jew, John Pizer, a thirty-three-year-old shoemaker, but he was released the following day after he produced an unshakeable alibi.[96] The East End crowds were not the only persons to display hostility; the day after Pizer was released, a magistrate, in an unrelated case, said:[97] 'The Pole has no business in this country. He is taking the bread out of the mouths of Englishmen.'

The third and fourth murders took place very early on Sunday morning, 30 September 1888. They appear to have been carefully planned to throw as much suspicion as possible on the Jewish community. The earlier of the two murders took place in Berner Street, one street away from Batty Street, in front of the radical Jewish Workingmen's Club, which had just finished hearing a lecture on *Judaism and Socialism*.[98] A witness to the murder said that he saw two men in the street, one of whom approached a prostitute and shouted 'Lipski' to the other man across the road, while striking her down. The witness then ran away. Was this a clumsy attempt to link the crime to Jews, or was the word 'Lipski', which had become a term of abuse, simply used, as the police believed, to frighten the witness away?[99] A police inspector reported to the Home Office that 'since a Jew named Lipski was hanged for the murder of a Jewess in 1887 the name has very frequently been used by persons as a mere ejaculation by way of endeavouring to insult the Jew to whom it has been addressed.' The police, it was

201

much later reported, found a shirt saturated with blood at 22 Batty Street, a house beside a lane leading to Berner Street.[100]

The shouting of 'Lipski' and the placing of a blood-stained shirt in Batty Street may well have been contrived to cause the public and the authorities to believe that it was a Polish Jew who was the Ripper, possibly, as the *Pall Mall Gazette* included in a list of speculations, for the purpose of 'avenging Lipski'.[101] Indeed, Godfrey Lushington, the Permanent Under-Secretary in the Home Office, noted on the file[102] that 'the use of "Lipski" increases my belief that the murderer was a Jew'. As an aside, it should be noted that the police, at Henry Matthews' request, made inquiries in the neighbourhood about a 'Lipski', but 'no person named Lipski could be found.'[103] So the landlord of 16 Batty Street had either moved from the neighbourhood or he had changed his name.

The later murder that morning, which was reported to the mass circulation *Lloyd's Weekly* within minutes of its commission, was an even more blatant attempt to throw suspicion on the Jews. A message was written in chalk, apparently by the murderer, close to the murder scene and near the spot where a blood-stained piece of cloth was left, stating: 'The Juwes are the men that will not be blamed for nothing.'[104] Sir Charles Warren, the Commissioner of the Metropolitan Police, ordered the writing to be rubbed out, fearing that it would lead to 'an onslaught upon the Jews' if it remained on the wall. He reported later to the Home Office that it was 'evidently written with the intention of inflaming the public mind against the Jews';[105] and he ordered fifty additional constables to be stationed on the evening after the murder at each of the chief police stations in the East End. Chief Rabbi Adler personally thanked Sir Charles for his 'humane and vigilant actions during this critical time.'[106]

Of course, when the *Pall Mall Gazette* learned of the words on the wall almost two weeks later, they drew the intended inference, observing: 'The language of the Jews in the East End is a hybrid dialect, known as Yiddish, and their mode of spelling the word Jews would be "Juwes". This the police consider a strong indication that the crime was committed by one of the numerous foreigners by whom the East End is infested.'[107] The Chief Rabbi pointed out to the Commissioner of the Metropolitan Police that the Yiddish word for Jews is 'Yidden' and not 'Juwes'; and Samuel Montagu, the Jewish

MP for Whitechapel, wrote in a letter to the *Gazette* that 'if the "handwriting on the wall" was done by the monster himself, can there be any doubt of his intention to throw the pursuers on a wrong track, while showing hostility to the Jews in the vicinity?'[108] The situation was not helped by a news report in *The Times*, just after the double murder, from its Vienna correspondent that the Talmud says that a Jew who is intimate with a Christian must slay and mutilate her. The Chief Rabbi wrote immediately to *The Times* that he could 'assert, without hesitation, that in no Jewish book is such a barbarity even hinted at.' And the Chief Rabbi of the Sephardic Congregations wrote to *The Times*: 'Baseless and without foundation as those legends are, they are dangerous even in normal times: how much more in abnormal? Who can foresee to what terrible consequences such a superstition might lead, when the people frantic with rage and terror, get hold of it and wreak their vengeance on innocent men?'[109]

Many persons have been suspected of being Jack the Ripper, including Queen Victoria's grandson, the Duke of Clarence; James Fitzjames Stephen's son, J. K. Stephen; Druitt, a barrister who later committed suicide; a group of masonic conspirators that included a leading doctor; and even Detective Sergeant Thick. I cannot, unfortunately, offer a solution. It is clear, however, that most of the voluminous Ripper literature has neglected to place the murders in the context of the then-growing anti-Semitism in England and the possibility that someone was trying to place the responsibility for the murders on the Jews, possibly to curtail further immigration to England.

Lipski found a place in Madame Tussaud's Chamber of Horrors, his figure being placed beside a reconstruction of the condemned cell at Newgate. His portrait figure had been modelled 'with power and resemblance' (according to one contemporary newspaper report) by Joseph Tussaud, the grandson of Madame Tussaud, who had attended the trial with his notebook and sketch-pad. Like all aspects of the Lipski case, there was even controversy over the placing of his figure in Madame Tussaud's. Some papers protested that the figure was said to be going into the Chamber of Horrors while the reprieve was still under consideration, but, in fact, the first report of the figure actually being on show was on 28 August, after the hanging. The catalogue stated that the crime was 'remarkable for the apparently weak motive for the atrocious deed.' Lipski's figure remained in the Chamber of Horrors until 1899.[110]

This story has placed one trial in the context of the social, political and economic conditions of the time. A trial may in theory be an objective pursuit of truth, but in practice there are many subjective factors which influence the course of events. Justice may in theory be blind, but in practice she has altogether too human a perspective. The Lipski story is, no doubt, more dramatic, and the wealth of material richer, than in most cases; yet, by looking at this extreme example one can better understand some of the factors that may influence any criminal trial: the personality of the judge; the adequacy of counsel; the reaction of the press; the cry of popular opinion; the vulnerability of the Government, and many more. The case shows the inherent fallibility of the trial process and the constant danger of error. Society should think twice before shifting the balance too far in favour of the prosecution. Further, the case strengthens the arguments against capital punishment.

A number of questions have been raised in this study. Was Lipski properly convicted? I believe that he was not. The judge's charge was grossly unfair in stressing the 'lust' theory and effectively took the case out of the hands of the jury. An appeal court today would, I think, quash the conviction. Moreover, Lipski's defence counsel, perhaps through drunkenness in one case and inexperience in criminal matters coupled with unpreparedness in the other, did not adequately present Lipski's defence. If the trial had been properly conducted, the jury might well have found reasonable doubt about his guilt.

Did the Home Office act properly in considering the case for a commutation? The Home Secretary and the permanent officials certainly gave the matter a surprising amount of attention. No one can accuse them of a cursory treatment of the matter. The same is true of the judge's time and effort. But one has the feeling that they were all judges in their own cause. The crucial decision not to give the chemist's report to Hayward was inexcusable, causing Hayward to pursue a dead-end, one the Home Office knew to be exactly that.

Other questions can be asked, although not easily answered. What effect did Stead's reporting in the *Pall Mall Gazette* have upon the judgement of Matthews, Lushington and Stephen? Did Rabbi Singer because of his own theological views, put any pressure on Lipski to confess? Should Rabbi Singer have authorised the release of Lipski's confession to the Press? Did the Home Office know about the confession that Lipski had been about to make the previous week? If the Home Office did not know about it, did Stephen know, and could this knowledge account for his change in attitude? Would Lipski have been hanged if he had not confessed?

The final question is whether Lipski was, in fact, guilty. I will not claim that Lipski was innocent, but there is at least a reasonable doubt about the truth of the confession and about his guilt. It must be remembered that his fiancée and his intended father-in-law believed in his innocence, as did his landlord and landlady, and, of course, his solicitor. Lipski may have confessed to a murder he did not commit rather than face a lifetime in prison. After all, when his counsel told him the previous week that this might be the result, he replied: 'Oh, I would rather die.' Moreover, a confession would permit him to place on record a view of the facts far less serious than a murder committed out of lust.

But even if Lipski was guilty, the offence may not have been committed in the way he says in his confession. The confession raises too many unanswered questions. Why is there such a glaring inconsistency between Lipski's statement that Mrs Angel was killed just before she was discovered and the doctor's evidence that death took place two or three hours earlier? Why would Lipski have bought acid to commit suicide? Was this part of his confession a signal that he was, in effect, committing suicide through his confession? Was his confession an act of martyrdom to calm the waters? We will never know the true story. Nor will we know why Mr Angel kicked the landlady, or why a person helping Hayward tried to get at Schmuss just before the execution. Nor will we know whether Lipski and Mrs Angel were, in fact, strangers to each other. The fifteen Home Office sub-files on the case prepared after the execution were destroyed many years ago, and thus we will never know if the Home Office ever had doubts about Lipski's guilt. Unlike a fictional mystery novel, there will be no 'solution' to the case offered here. As the unnamed 'compatriot who laboured on his behalf' wrote in the *Pall Mall Gazette* after the hanging: 'The Whitechapel mystery will remain a mystery.'

Notes on Sources

Specific references to the voluminous Home Office files on the case have not been included in these notes. The original files are contained in the Public Record Office H.O. 144/202.

Chapter One *Introduction*

1   20 June 1887
2   10 June 1887
3   25 June 1886
4   The *Jewish Chronicle*, 24 June 1887. The word rabbi has been used in the text, even though Rabbi Singer would, in fact, have been referred to as Reverend Singer or Mr Singer
5   The *Jewish Chronicle*, 10 December 1886
6   *See* Paul Thompson *Socialists, Liberals and Labour: The Struggle for London 1885–1914* (University of Toronto Press, 1967) p. 12
7   W. W. Rostow *British Economy of the Nineteenth Century* (Clarendon Press, Oxford, 1948) p. 49
8   *See* G. S. Jones *Outcast London* (Clarendon Press, Oxford, 1971) pp. 291–2. *See also* Bailey *The Metropolitan Police, the Home Office and the Threat of Outcast London* in V. Bailey (ed.) *Policing and Punishment in Nineteenth Century Britain* (Croom Helm, London, 1981) p. 94
9   3 May 1884. *See also* A. S. Wohl *The Eternal Slum: Housing and Social Policy in Victorian London* (Edward Arnold, London, 1977) p. 46 et seq
10 *See* Booth *Life and Labour of the People in London* (Third Series, vol. 2) (Macmillan, London, 1902), Chapter 1. I am grateful to Mrs. A. Abeles for investigating for me parts of the Booth Notebooks concerning 16 Batty Street kept at the London School of Economics and Political Science
11 *See* G. S. Jones *Outcast London*, p. 109
12 *See* W. J. Fishman *Jewish Radicals: From Czarist Stetl to London Ghetto* (Pantheon Books, New York, 1974) p. 27
13 *See* Milton Meltzer *World of Our Fathers: The Jews of Eastern Europe* (Farrar, Straus and Giroux, New York, 1974) pp. 190, 202
14 *See* W. J. Fishman p. 70; J. A. Garrard *The English and Immigration 1880–1910* (Oxford University Press, London, 1971) p. 25 et seq.; B. Gainer *The Alien Invasion: The Origins of the Aliens Act of 1905* (Heinemann, London, 1972) p. 166. et seq
15 *See* Colin Holmes *Anti-semitism in British Society 1876–1939* (Edward Arnold, London, 1979) p. 49 et seq.; Holmes *The Ritual Murder Accusation in Britain* (1981) 4 Ethnic and Racial Studies 265; the *Jewish Chronicle*, 16 July and 23 July 1886. Holmes has also provided an analysis of crime in the East

End, including a discussion of the Lipski case, in *East End Crime and the Jewish Community, 1887–1911* in *The Jewish East End 1840–1939* (Jewish Historical Society, London, 1981) p. 109

16 *Pall Mall Gazette*, 18 February 1886. *See* Rabbi Singer's reply in the *Gazette*, 23 February 1886

17 *See East London Advertiser*, 27 August 1887

18 *See* Booth *Life and Labour of the People in London* (Williams and Norgate, London, 1891), appendix to vol. II

19 Information for 1871 was supplied by D. T. Elliott, Chief Librarian, Tower Hamlets Library, London

20 The material in this section has, for the most part, been drawn from an article *A Life of Lipski* by *One Who Knows Him, Pall Mall Gazette*, 20 August 1887. A fourpenny Yiddish pamphlet on Lipski, written and published by Issac Stone, a radical tailor and journalist, in September, 1887 has, unfortunately, not been found, but would probably shed further light on Lipski's background. Stone is discussed in L. P. Gartner *The Jewish Immigrant in England 1870–1914* (Wayne State University Press, Detroit, 1960) pp. 108–9; and W. J. Fishman *Jewish Radicals*, passim

21 *See* Jósef Lipski *Diplomat in Berlin 1933–1939* (Columbia University Press, New York, 1968)

22 *See* Booth *Life and Labour of the People in London* (First Series: Poverty, vol. 4) (Macmillan, London, 1902) p. 268 et seq

23 *East London Observer*, 2 July 1887

24 The *Evening News*, 30 June 1887

25 *See* D. Rumbelow *The Complete Jack the Ripper* (W. H. Allen, London, 1975) p. 84

26 The best description of the inquest is in the *East London Observer*, 2 July 1887, et seq. The depositions of the witnesses are contained in an official printed document, *Inquest on the Body of Miriam Angel*

27 The *Illustrated Police News*, 9 July 1887

28 *See* the Criminal Law Act 1977, s. 56

29 9 July 1887

30 *East London Observer*, 9 July 1887. The Treasury Solicitor, Sir A. K. Stephenson, was both the Treasury Solicitor and the Director of Public Prosecutions; Treasury counsel would later prosecute at the Old Bailey. Because it was a poisoning case the Attorney-General could have led for the Crown, but he did not do so in this case. *See generally* J. Ll. J. Edwards *The Law Officers of the Crown* (Sweet and Maxwell, London, 1964)

31 *See Pall Mall Gazette*, 8 April 1886, referring to conditions of those at Clerkenwell awaiting trial at the Old Bailey

32 19 August 1887

33 E. B. Bowen-Rowlands *In the Light of the Law* (Grant Richards, London, 1931) p. 113

34 C. Biron *Without Prejudice* (Faber and Faber, London, 1936) p. 125

35 F. W. Ashley *My Sixty Years in the Law* (John Lane, London, 1936) p. 84

36 E. Abinger *Forty Years at the Bar* (Hutchinson, London, 1930) p. 21

37 T. E. Crispe *Reminiscences of a K.C.* (Methuen, London, 1909) p. 135

38 E. Marjoribanks *For the Defence: the Life of Sir Edward Marshall Hall* (Macmillan, New York, 1929) pp. 33 and 37

39 30 July 1887

40 *See generally* A. Babington *The English Bastille: A History of Newgate Gaol and Prison Conditions in Britain 1188–1902* (Macdonald, London, 1971)
41 Administration of Justice (Miscellaneous Provisions) Act 1933, s.1
42 *See* J. F. S. Stephen and H. Stephen *A Digest of the Law of Criminal Procedure in Indictable Offences* (Macmillan, London, 1883) p. 119 et seq: technically, not less than twelve nor more than twenty three
43 The *Daily Telegraph*, 26 July 1887
44 *The Lancet*, 3 November 1888
45 *Pall Mall Gazette*, 24 August, 1887
46 *The Times*, 1 January 1887 et seq
47 *East London Observer*, 30 July 1887

Chapter Two   *The Trial: The First Morning*

1 Contemporary descriptions can be found in F. W. Ashley *My Sixty Years in the Law*, p. 76 et seq; E. Abinger *Forty Years at the Bar*, p. 19 et seq
2 *See generally* L. Radzinowicz *Selden Society Lecture, Sir James Fitzjames Stephen* (Bernard Quaritch, London, 1957); Leslie Stephen's biography of his brother *The Life of James Fitzjames Stephen* (Smith Elder, London, 1895)
3 *See* Friedland *R. S. Wright's Model Criminal Code: A Forgotten Chapter in the History of the Criminal Law* (1981) 1 *Oxford J. of Legal Studies* 307
4 Stephen papers, Cambridge University Library, Add. MSS 7349
5 *See generally* N. G. Annan *Leslie Stephen* (MacGibbon & Kee, London, 1951)
6 2nd ed., 1874, reproduced with an introduction and notes by R. J. White (Cambridge University Press, 1967)
7 Cambridge University Library, Add. MSS 7349; see also his views after he retired from the Bench set out in *The Opium 'Resolution'* (1891) 29 *The Nineteenth Century* 851
8 *See generally* V. Berridge and G. Edwards *Opium and the People* (Allen Lane, London, 1981)
9 *See* T. L. Christie *Etched in Arsenic* (Lippincott, Philadelphia, 1968); H. B. Irving (ed.) *Trial of Mrs Maybrick, Notable British Trials* (Hodge and Co., London, 1912)
10 *Clarence: The Life of the Duke of Clarence and Avondale* (W. H. Allen, London, 1972)
11 *See generally* E. B. Bowen-Rowlands *Seventy-Two Years at the Bar* (Macmillan, London, 1924), a biography of Poland; *D.N.B.* 1922–1930; *The Times*, 5 March 1928
12 *Pall Mall Gazette*, 17 December 1888
13 *D.N.B.* 1922–1930
14 21 December 1888
15 E. Abinger *Forty Years at the Bar*, pp. 22 and 212
16 31 March 1887
17 *Huddersfield Daily Examiner*, 20 September 1889
18 20 September 1889
19 *The Times* 1 July 1887
20 *The Times*, 28 July 1887
21 F. W. Ashley *My Sixty Years in the Law* p. 86

22 E. B. Bowen-Rowlands *In the Light of the Law*, p. 113
23 T. E. Crispe *Reminiscences of a K.C.*, p. 135
24 Central Criminal Court Sessions Paper, Tenth Session, cases 795 and 802
25 The Law of Libel Amendment Act, 1888, gave newspapers an absolute privilege to report court proceedings, rather than the qualified privilege they formerly had
26 30 July 1887
27 Minor changes in the punctuation have occasionally been made to assist the reader
28 *The Lancet*, 12 March 1887, claimed that these cells were 2'6" × 3'
29 *See* F. W. Ashley *My Sixty Years in the Law*, p. 80
30 E. Abinger *Forty Years at the Bar*, p. 21

Chapter Three *The Trial: Afternoon*

1 *See* F. A. Jaffe *A guide to Pathological Evidence* (Carswell, Toronto, 1976). I am grateful to Dr Jaffe, the former Medical Director, Centre of Forensic Sciences, Province of Ontario, for his assistance with the scientific evidence
2 The *Evening News*, 30 July 1887

Chapter Four *The Trial: The Second Day*

1 *Die Tsukunft*, 5 August 1887; *East London Observer*, 6 August 1887; the *Evening News*, 30 July 1887; *The Daily Telegraph*, 1 August 1887
2 Criminal Evidence Act, 1898, ch. 36
3 *Regina v. Masters* (1886) 50 J.P. 104; *Regina v. Reiglehutt* (1886) 103 Central Criminal Court Sessions Paper 464 (a murder case defended by Geoghegan)
4 *See* infra, ch. 7
5 Ibid
6 1 August 1887, supplemented by material from the *Daily News*, 1 August, 1887
7 5 August 1887
8 1 August 1887
9 J. F. Stephen *Prisoners as Witnesses* (1886) 20 *The Nineteenth Century* 453, p. 468
10 1 August 1887
11 *The Daily Telegraph*, 1 August 1887
12 *The Times*, 1 August 1887

Chapter Five *The Fight for a Reprieve: The First Two Weeks*

1 Cambridge University Library, Add. MSS 7349. The originals of these letters were destroyed. These are excerpts, copied out, and possibly edited by Stephen's wife
2 *See* A. Babington *The English Bastille: A History of Newgate Gaol and Prison Conditions in Britain 1188–1902*, p. 227

3   6 August 1887
4   *See* F. Bressler *Reprieve* (Harrap, London, 1965); A. H. Manchester *A Modern Legal History of England and Wales 1750–1950* (Butterworths, London, 1980)
5   Vol. II (Macmillan, London, 1883) p. 88
6   Criminal Appeal Act 1907, ch. 23
7   *See* F. Bressler *Reprieve*, pp. 63–4
8   *The Times*, 14 March 1890
9   *See generally D.N.B.* 1912–1921; *The Times*, 4 April 1913; A.P.S., *Lord Llandaff at the Home Office* (1914) 63 *The National Review* 631; S. Leslie *Henry Matthews: Lord Llandaff* (1921) 168 *The Dublin Review* 1; S. Leslie *Sir Evelyn Ruggles-Brise* (John Murray, London, 1938); and a very good unpublished M.A. thesis from Vanderbilt University, J. C. Kelly *Henry Matthews at the Home Office* (1972). Unfortunately, Matthews' papers have not survived: see D. C. Richter *Riotous Victorians* (Ohio University Press, 1981) p. xi.
10 *See* S. Leslie *Sir Evelyn Ruggles-Brise*, p. 48
11 Ibid pp. 58–9
12 *See* R. F. V. Heuston *Lives of the Lord Chancellors 1885–1940* (Clarendon Press, Oxford, 1964) p. 34
13 *See* A. W. Fox *The Earl of Halsbury, Lord High Chancellor* (Chapman and Hall, London, 1929) p. 130
14 10 September 1887, p. 167
15 G. E. Buckle (ed.) *The Letters of Queen Victoria*, vol. 2 (John Murray, London, 1931) pp. 6–7
16 E. B. Bowen-Rowlands *Seventy Two Years at the Bar*, p. 206. On the other hand, Stead had an extensive and warm correspondence with Catholic prelates and did not appear to be biased against Catholics in general. *See generally*, W. L. Arnstein *Protestant versus Catholic in Mid-Victorian England* (University of Missouri Press, 1982)
17 J. Pellew *The Home Office 1848–1914: from Clerks to Bureaucrats* (Heinemann Educational Books, London, 1982) pp. 19–20, 187; *The Times*, 6 February, 1907; A.P.S., *Lord Llandaff at the Home Office* (1914) 63 *The National Review* 631, p. 634
18 Algernon West *Contemporary Portraits* (T. Fisher Unwin, London, 1920) p. 151
19 5 August 1887
20 J. Hayward *The Case of Israel Lipski now lying under Sentence of Death for the Murder of Miriam Angel* (London, 1887)
21 *Pall Mall Gazette*, 13 August 1887
22 Ibid
23 Taylor *Principles and Practice of Medical Jurisprudence*, 12th ed., K. Simpson (ed.) (Churchill Ltd., London, 1965)
24 Hansard, 12 August vol. 319, col. 253 (Cunninghame Graham, Lanark N.W.)
25 Ibid
26 *Hansard*, 16 February 1961, vol. 634, col. 1795
27 12 August 1887
28 *See* T. M. Endelman *The Jews of Georgian England 1714–1830* (Jewish Publication Society of America, Philadelphia, 1979) p. 198 et seq and p. 297 et seq

211

29   19 August 1887
30   *Pall Mall Gazette*, 13 August 1887

Chapter Six   *A Fight for Time*

1   *Pall Mall Gazette*, 13 August 1887
2   Ibid
3   E. Clarke *The Story of My Life* (John Murray, London, 1918) p. 261
4   *Hansard*, vol. 319, col. 364. *See* the excellent biography, C. Watts and L. Davies *Cunninghame Graham: A Critical Biography* (Cambridge University Press, 1979)
5   18 August 1887
6   20 August 1887
7   23 March 1886
8   13 August 1887
9   Ibid
10   The *Evening News*, 16 August 1887
11   *Pall Mall Gazette*, 18 January 1887
12   *See generally* S. Koss *The Rise and Fall of the Political Press in Britain*, vol. 1, (Hamish Hamilton, London, 1981) passim
13   *See D.N.B.* 1912–1921; E. W. Stead *My Father: Personal and Spiritual Reminiscences* (Heinemann, London, 1913); F. Whyte *The Life of W. T. Stead* (Cape, London, 1925); J. W. Robertson Scott *The Story of the Pall Mall Gazette* (Oxford University Press, 1950); J. W. Robertson Scott *The Life and Death of a Newspaper* (Methuen, London, 1952); R. L. Schults *Crusader in Babylon: W. T. Stead and the Pall Mall Gazette* (University of Nebraska Press, 1972), a fine book with an extended discussion of the Lipski case based on newspaper reports; J. O. Baylen *The 'New Journalism' in Late Victorian Britain* (1972) 18 *Australian Journal of Politics and History* 367. Professor Baylen, Regents' Professor of History, Georgia State University, who is in the process of publishing a book on Stead, has provided the author with a number of helpful references.
14   Cited in J. W. Robertson Scott *The Story of the Pall Mall Gazette*, p. 7
15   A. Mearns *The Bitter Cry of Outcast London* edited with an introduction by A. S. Wohl (Humanities Press, New York, 1970)
16   *Pall Mall Gazette*, 16 October 1883. The equally well-known book, *In Darkest England*, claimed to have been written in 1890 by the founder of the Salvation Army, William Booth, but actually written by Stead, used Stead's material, including the above newspaper article: *see* A. S. Wohl's introduction to A. Mearns *The Bitter Cry of Outcast London*, p. 23
17   *Government by Journalism* (1886) 49 *The Contemporary Review* 653, p. 669
18   *Up to Easter* (1887) *The Nineteenth Century* 629, p. 638
19   *See* S. Koss *The Rise and Fall of the Political Press in Britain*, vol. 1
20   (1886) 49 *The Contemporary Review* 653
21   *Pall Mall Gazette*, 15 and 17 August 1887
22   *Correspondence between Frederick Engels and Paul and Laura Lafargue*, vol. 2, (Foreign Languages Publishing House, Moscow, 1960) p. 82
23   10 May 1887
24   *See* R. L. Schults *Crusader in Babylon*; A. Plowden *The Case of Eliza Armstrong* (BBC, London, 1974); A. Robson *The Significance of 'The Maiden Tribute of Modern Babylon'* (1978) 11 *Victorian Periodicals Newsletter* 51

25 *The Times*, 13 November 1885
26 13 November 1885
27 13 November 1885
28 *See* E. W. Stead *My Father*, p. 130
29 *The Times*, 9 November 1885
30 J. W. Robertson Scott *The Life and Death of a Newspaper*, p. 144
31 Letter from Havelock Ellis to F. Whyte, *The Life of W. T. Stead*, pp. 341–2
32 20 January 1889, J. W. Robertson Scott *The Life and Death of a Newspaper*, p. 244
33 *See* W. J. Fishman *Jewish Radicals*, p. 69
34 18 February 1886
35 23 February 1886
36 9 March 1887
37 (Cassell & Co., London, 1888) pp. 305–6
38 *Hansard*, 13 August, vol. 319, col. 448–9
39 *See Encyclopaedia Judaica* (Keter Publishing Ltd., Jerusalem, 1971); *Jewish Chronicle*, 20 November 1931
40 *See D.N.B.*
41 *The Times*, 15 August 1887
42 Royal Archives, Windsor: RA B39/31, reproduced here with the gracious permission of Her Majesty The Queen. I am indebted to Mrs G. de Bellaigue, Assistant Registrar, for her kind assistance
43 *See* W. H. Dunn *James Anthony Froude, A Biography (1857–1894)* (Clarendon Press, Oxford, 1963) p. 472
44 *See* F. Whyte *The Life of W. T. Stead*, p. 48

Chapter Seven *A Further Week*

1 *Encyclopaedia Judaica*; *The Times*, 22 August 1916
2 *Die Tsukunft*, 19 August 1887. The case is reported in *The Times*, 24 November, 14 December, 15 December, 1876, and 3 January 1877
3 The *Jewish World*, 19 August 1887
4 *Die Tsukunft*, 19 August 1887
5 *Pall Mall Gazette*, 19 August 1887; *see also* the *Jewish World*, 19 August 1887
6 *Pall Mall Gazette*, 17 August 1887
7 *The Daily Telegraph*, 20 August 1887
8 *The Daily Telegraph*, 17 August 1887
9 *The Daily Telegraph*, 19 August 1887
10 Ibid
11 *The Daily Telegraph*, 18 August 1887
12 *The Daily Telegraph*, 22 August 1887
13 16 August 1887
14 16 and 20 August 1887
15 *See* H. S. Santesson *The Locked Room Reader: Stories of Impossible Crimes and Escapes* (Random House, New York, 1968); R. Adey *Locked Room Murders and Other Impossible Crimes* (Ferret, London, 1979). I am indebted to D. B. Stirling for his knowledgeable assistance with this issue
16 *Pall Mall Gazette*, 20 August 1887
17 20 August 1887

18 *Pall Mall Gazette*, 18 August 1887
19 *See* Shane Leslie *Sir Evelyn Ruggles-Brise* (John Murray, London, 1938) p. 59
20 17 August 1887
21 19 August 1887
22 Ibid

Chapter Eight *Approaching the End*

1 *Pall Mall Gazette*, 17 August 1887
2 C. Watts and L. Davies *Cunninghame Graham: A Critical Biography* (Cambridge University Press, 1979) p. xiii, 181 et seq
3 Ibid p. 126 et seq; also, Hector Hushabye in *Heartbreak House* and Dick Dudgeon in *The Devil's Disciple*
4 19 August 1887
5 The *Jewish World*, 19 August 1887
6 *Hansard*, 19 August 1887, vol. 319, col. 1103
7 20 August 1887
8 *Hansard*, 20 August 1887, vol. 319, col. 1255
9 19 August 1887
10 Cited in the *Jewish World*, 19 August 1887
11 20 August 1887
12 19 August 1887
13 19 August 1887
14 Cited in the *Pall Mall Gazette*, 17 August 1887
15 20 August 1887
16 21 August 1887
17 Cited in the *Pall Mall Gazette*, 17 August 1887
18 Ibid
19 *Hansard*, 13 August 1887, vol. 319, col. 449
20 *Hansard*, 6 April 1888, vol. 324, col. 680
21 The *Evening News*, 22 August 1887
22 Ibid
23 The *Evening News*, 22 August 1887
24 The *Star*, 18 November 1921. The official was clearly Evelyn Ruggles-Brise, then Matthews' Principal Secretary, later the prison reformer: *see* Shane Leslie *Sir Evelyn Ruggles-Brise* (John Murray, London, 1938) pp. 61–3
25 *The Times*, 30 August 1887
26 Ibid
27 The *Daily News*, 22 August 1887
28 The *Jewish Chronicle*, 9 December 1887
29 The *Jewish Chronicle*, 9 December 1887
30 *See generally* E. J. Bristow *Prostitution and Prejudice: The Jewish Fight against White Slavery 1870–1939* (Oxford University Press, 1982)
31 The *Jewish Chronicle*, 3 February 1893; C. Battersea *Reminiscences* (Macmillan, London, 1923) pp. 420 et seq; V. D. Lipman *A Century of Social Service 1859–1959: The Jewish Board of Guardians* (Routledge and Kegan Paul, London, 1959) p. 248
32 10 March 1887; *see* the *Jewish Chronicle*, 11 March 1887

33 *Pall Mall Gazette*, 18 February 1886 and 23 February 1886

34 *The Times*, 13 August 1887

35 For biographical information *see The Times*, 14 February 1925; the introduction by G. R. Searle to A. White *Efficiency and Empire* (The Harvester Press, Brighton, 1973). *See* White *The Invasion of Pauper Foreigners* (1888) 26 *The Nineteenth Century* 414; White *The Truth about the Russian Jew* (1892) 61 *Contemporary Review* 695; White *The Modern Jew* (Heinemann, London, 1899)

36 23 July 1887, written 14 July 1887

37 *Homiletical Magazine*, May 1885, reprinted in I. Abrahams, (ed.) *The Literary Remains of the Rev. Simeon Singer: Lectures and Addresses* (Routledge, London, 1908) p. 55

38 5 August 1887

39 American edition (Hebrew Publishing Co., New York, 1924) p. 317

40 *Confession*, a sermon delivered in September, 1898, reprinted in I. Abrahams *The Literary Remains of the Rev. Simeon Singer: Sermons* (Routledge, London, 1908) p. 69

41 The *Jewish Chronicle*, 3 June 1887

42 *The Daily Telegraph*, 20 August 1887

43 22 August 1887

44 The *Evening News*, 23 August 1887

45 RA B39/31

46 *East London Observer*, 20 August 1887; the *Jewish World*, 19 August 1887

47 Hatfield House mss. 3M/Class E, 23 August 1887, reproduced with the kind permission of the Marquess of Salisbury

48 The *Evening News*, 22 August 1887

49 Ibid

50 Royal Commission on Capital Punishment, 1866, resulting in the Capital Punishment Amendment Act, 1868; D. D. Cooper *The Lesson of the Scaffold: The Public Execution Controversy in Victorian England* (Ohio University Press, 1974)

51 *Pall Mall Gazette*, 26 August 1887

52 *See The Daily Telegraph*, 23 August 1887; J. Lawrence *A History of Capital Punishment with Special Reference to Capital Punishment in Great Britain* (Kennikat Press, Port Washington, New York, 1932) p. 53

53 *See The Times*, 5 August 1909; the *Jewish World*, 12 August 1887

54 *See generally*, J. Berry *My Experiences as an Executioner* (David and Charles Reprints, Devon, 1972), J. Lawrence *A History of Capital Punishment*

55 *See The British Medical Journal*, 6 October 1888, p. 779. No report by the Committee was ever made public

56 *Report of the Royal Commission on Capital Punishment 1949–1953*, 1953, Cmd. 8932, p. 250

57 *See*, e.g., the following discussions in *The Lancet*: 5 January, 1884; 6 June, 11 July, 12 December 1885; 22 May 1886; 6 August 1887; 28 July, 11 August 1888

58 *See* the *Daily Telegraph*, 23 August 1887

59 The *Evening News*, 15 August 1887

60 The *Daily News*, 23 August 1887

61 23 August 1887

62 The *Evening News*, 22 August 1887

63 The *Daily Chronicle*, 23 August 1887

64 *Sabbath and Festival Prayer Book* (Rabbinical Assembly of America, 1946)
65 The *Daily Chronicle*, 23 August 1887
66 J. Atholl *The Reluctant Hangman: The Story of James Berry, Executioner 1884–1892* (John Long Co., London, 1956) p. 159
67 *Hansard*, 1 September 1887, vol. 320, col. 718–19
68 *Is Salvation Possible After Death?*, *Homiletical Magazine*, May 1885, p. 69
69 *The Report of the Royal Commission on Capital Punishment 1949–1953*, 1953, CMD. 8932, p. 250
70 *See The British Medical Journal*, 28 July 1888 (a letter from one of the attending doctors)
71 Ibid; *The Lancet*, 28 July 1888
72 Ibid
73 Capital Punishment Amendment Act, 1868
74 The *Daily Chronicle*, 23 August 1887

Chapter Nine *Conclusion*

1 22 August 1887
2 27 August 1887. Mme Olga Novikoff Collection, Bodleian Library, Oxford, MSS. Eng. Misc. d.182. *See* Stead's two volumes on *Mme Novikoff, the MP for Russia: Reminiscences and Correspondence of Madame Olga Novikoff* (Andrew Melrose, London, 1909)
3 12 September 1887. Ibid
4 22 August 1887
5 22 August 1887
6 28 August 1887
7 27 August 1887
8 27 August 1887
9 27 August 1887
10 27 August 1887
11 22 August 1887
12 24 August 1887
13 8 August 1889
14 1892, p. 390
15 Ibid p. 392
16 *Pall Mall Gazette*, 1 September 1887
17 2 November 1887. The case is mentioned in Chapter 5
18 21 December 1887
19 J. W. Robertson Scott *The Life and Death of a Newspaper*, p. 149 et seq
20 *See* S. Koss *The Rise and Fall of the Political Press in Britain*, p. 316 et seq
21 The *Daily Chronicle*, 23 August 1887
22 The *Jewish World*, 26 August 1887
23 9 September 1887
24 *The Times*, 26 January 1888
25 27 August 1887
26 28 August 1887
27 S. Leslie *Sir Evelyn Ruggles-Brise* (John Murray, London, 1938) p. 68
28 E. Troup *The Home Office* (G. P. Putnam, London, 1925) p. 59; *see also* S. Leslie *Sir Evelyn Ruggles-Brise*, p. 51

29   13 October 1898; 31 January 1899; 13 March 1899; 30 August 1899
30   23 September 1887, to Mr Venables, Cambridge University Library, Add. MSS 7349
31   25 September 1887, ibid
32   J. F. Stephen *A General View of the Criminal Law of England*, 2nd ed., (Macmillan, London, 1890) p. 174
33   L. Stephen *The Life of Sir James Fitzjames Stephen*, p. 479
34   22 August 1887
35   22 August 1887
36   (1887) 128 *Westminster Review* 792
37   *The Times*, 30 August 1887
38   10 September 1887
39   *Pall Mall Gazette*, 1 September 1887
40   *Hansard*, 3 September 1887, vol. 320, col. 1072
41   5 September 1887
42   E. Bowen-Rowlands *In The Light of the Law*, p. 66
43   *Arthur J. Balfour Papers*, British Library Add. MSS. 49872. I am grateful to Professor Joseph Baylen for this reference
44   23 August 1887
45   *The Times*, 24 August 1887
46   *The Times*, 25 August 1887
47   Ibid
48   The *Daily Chronicle*, 26 August 1887
49   The *Evening News*, 29 August 1887
50   The *Daily News*, 26 August 1887
51   The *Evening News*, 31 August 1887
52   22 August 1887
53   *See* M. L. Friedland *Double Jeopardy* (Clarendon Press, Oxford, 1969), Chapter 9
54   Report of the Royal Commission appointed to consider the law Relating to Indictable Offences, 1879, c.2345
55   At pp. 172 and 177. Stephen's son, Herbert, took the same view, stating that a court of criminal appeal 'will be productive of no good result, and will do a great deal of mischief': *Appeal in Criminal Cases* (1895) 12 *The New Review* 434. Harry Poland was also against such appeals: *see* the *Pall Mall Gazette*, 29 November 1887
56   *Hansard*, 15 August 1889, vol. 339, col. 1304
57   Ibid, col. 1310
58   E. Troup *The Home Office* (G. P. Putnam, London, 1925) p. 59
59   E. Alexander *Chief Whip* (University of Toronto Press, 1962) p. 310
60   24 August 1887
61   23 August 1887
62   22 August 1887
63   26 August 1887
64   *See* V. D. Lipman *A Century of Social Service 1859–1959: The Jewish Board of Guardians*
65   The *Jewish Chronicle*, 25 March 1887
66   *Hansard*, 12 July 1887, vol. 317, col. 520–1; 12 August 1887, vol. 319, col. 256–7
67   *The Times*, 23 July 1887

68   A. White *The Problems of a Great City* (Remington, London, 1887) p. 143
69   30 November 1887
70   B. Gainer *The Alien Invasion,* p. 167
71   Ibid
72   A. White *The Modern Jew* (Heinemann, London, 1899) p. 13; see also *The Truth About the Russian Jew* (1892) 61 *The Contemporary Review* 695 p. 696
73   *See generally,* B. Gainer *The Alien Invasion;* J. A. Garrard *The English and Immigration 1880–1910*
74   *Pall Mall Gazette,* 9 May 1888
75   *Pall Mall Gazette,* 7 May 1888
76   Report of the House of Lords Select Committee on the Sweating System, S.P. 1888, xx, xxi; 1889, xiii, xiv; 1890, xvii, p. 257, cited in V. D. Lipman *A Century of Social Service,* p. 90.
77   Report of the House of Commons Select Committee on Emigration and Immigration (Foreigners), S.P. 1888, xi, p. 419; 1889, x, p. 265, cited in J. A. Garrard *The English and Immigration 1880–1910,* p. 28
78   *See* B. Gainer *The Alien Invasion,* p. 132 et seq; J. E. Tyler *The Struggle for Imperial Unity* (Longman, London, 1938)
79   House of Commons Select Committee, Minutes of Evidence, p. 167
80   Ibid p. 168
81   V. D. Lipman *A Century of Social Service,* pp. 94 and 96
82   *See generally* B. Gainer *The Alien Invasion;* J. A. Garrard *The English and Immigration 1880–1910;* L. P. Gartner *The Jewish Immigrant in England 1870–1914*
83   Letter from Claude Montefiore to the *Jewish Chronicle,* 10 December 1886
84   Ibid
85   *See* G. R. Searle's introduction to A. White *Efficiency and Empire,* p. ix; B. Gainer *The Alien Invasion,* pp. 125–6
86   *See* A. White *The Modern Jew,* pp. 274–5
87   *See* B. Gainer *The Alien Invasion,* p. 117
88   *Encyclopaedia Judaica*
89   M. Lowenthal ed. *The Diaries of Theodor Herzl* (Dial Press, New York, 1956) pp. 84–5, diary entry dated 28 November 1895
90   *See* S. A. Cohen *British Zionists and British Jews: the Communal Politics of Anglo-Jewry, 1895–1920* (Princeton University Press, 1982) pp. 33–4, 188–9
91   *See generally,* L. Stein *The Balfour Declaration* (Vallentine, Mitchell, London, 1961)
92   *See* A. Kelly *Jack the Ripper: A Bibliography and Review of the Literature,* with an introduction by Colin Wilson (Association of Assistant Librarians, S.E.D., London, 1973)
93   12 October 1888
94   A. Kelly *Jack the Ripper,* p. 21
95   15 September 1888, cited in C. Bermant *London's East End: Point of Arrival* (Macmillan, New York, 1976) p. 112
96   T. Cullen *Autumn of Terror* (The Bodley Head, London, 1965) p. 61 et seq
97   The *Jewish Chronicle,* 14 September 1888
98   *Pall Mall Gazette,* 1 October 1888
99   *See* S. Knight *Jack the Ripper: The Final Solution* (Harrap, London, 1976) pp. 238–9. *See* P.R.O. records on the Stride case: MEPO 3/140, XC/A02835; *see also* HO 144/221/A49301, letter from Commissioner Warren dated 6 November 1888

100   *Pall Mall Gazette*, 17 October 1888
101   *Pall Mall Gazette*, 2 October 1888
102   HO 144/221/A49301. *See also* R. Anderson *The Lighter Side of My Official Life* (Hodder & Stoughton, London, 1910) pp. 137–9
103   MEPO 3/140, XC/A02835; report to the Home Office from Inspector F. G. Abberline, 1 November 1888; *see also* HO 1441/221/A49301
104   S. Knight *Jack the Ripper*, pp. 178–9
105   PRO records HO 144/221/A49301, letter to Lushington dated 6 November 1888
106   Letter dated 13 October 1888, cited in C. Bermant *London's East End*, p. 117
107   12 October 1888
108   15 October 1888
109   The *Jewish Chronicle*, 5 October 1888
110   I am grateful to Lady Chapman, the Archivist of Madame Tussaud's, for this information